Strategic Leadership in the Business School

Business schools have come under fire in recent years, with criticisms centring on their academic rigour and the relevance of business education to the 'real' world of management. Alongside this ongoing debate, increasing international competition and media rankings have led to a fierce struggle between business schools for positioning and differentiation. These are among the challenges that are faced by the dean of the modern-day business school. In this book, Fernando Fragueiro and Howard Thomas show how deans of business schools can meet such challenges in terms of strategic direction setting and the execution of their leadership role. Drawing on their invaluable experience as deans of highly successful business schools, they present a series of case studies to show how leaders of five major business schools (IMD, LBS, INSEAD, IAE and Warwick) have built effective strategies in the context of internal and external political pressures.

FERNANDO FRAGUEIRO is Professor of General Management and Director of ENOVA Thinking, a centre for developing corporate leadership in emerging markets, at IAE Business School in Buenos Aires. He served previously as Dean of IAE Business School (1995–2008) and as Vice-President of Austral University (1995–2007).

HOWARD THOMAS is Dean and LKCSB Chair in Strategic Management at the Lee Kong Chian School of Business, Singapore Management University. Until recently he was Dean of Warwick Business School (2000–2010), and, prior to this, he was Dean of the College of Commerce and Business Administration at the University of Illinois at Urbana–Champaign (1991–2000).

Strategic Leadership in the Business School

Keeping One Step Ahead

FERNANDO FRAGUEIRO
and
HOWARD THOMAS

CAMBRIDGE
UNIVERSITY PRESS

CAMBRIDGE UNIVERSITY PRESS
Cambridge, New York, Melbourne, Madrid, Cape Town,
Singapore, São Paulo, Delhi, Tokyo, Mexico City

Cambridge University Press
The Edinburgh Building, Cambridge CB2 8RU, UK

Published in the United States of America by Cambridge University Press,
New York

www.cambridge.org
Information on this title: www.cambridge.org/9780521116121

First published 2011

Printed in the United Kingdom at the University Press, Cambridge

A catalogue record for this publication is available from the British Library

Library of Congress Cataloguing in Publication data
Fragueiro, Fernando.
  Strategic leadership in the business school : keeping one step ahead / Fernando
  Fragueiro, Howard Thomas.
    p.   cm.
  ISBN 978-0-521-11612-1 (hardback)
  1. Business schools–United States–Management.   2. Management–United
  States.   I. Thomas, Howard, 1943–   II. Title.
  HF1111.F724   2011
  650.071'173–dc22
  2010051861

ISBN 978-0-521-11612-1 Hardback

To Lynne and the Thomas family, who are Howard's foundation and who light up Howard's life.

To Carlos Cavallé of IESE, the dean of deans, who has been an indispensable mentor to Fernando and a long-standing friend to both of us.

Contents

Figures

Tables

Preface

This book is grounded in the research and writing of the two authors: on one side, the work Howard Thomas has undertaken over the past decade at Warwick Business School (WBS), the Association of Business Schools (ABS), the Association to Advance Collegiate Schools of Business (AACSB) International, the Global Foundation for Management Education (GFME) and on business schools and their strategic leadership; on the other, Fernando Fragueiro's five years of research on 'strategic leadership as processes in a specific organizational context from a political perspective' at three world-class European institutions: IMD, INSEAD and London Business School (LBS), as well as his own experience as dean of IAE Business School, from 1995 to 2008.

The logic of this book, which examines business school strategic leadership processes in practice, is explained in the following flow diagram (suggested by Alex Wilson, research fellow in strategic management at WBS).

Overall, the diagram tries to throw light on the critical role of strategic leadership in business schools. Deans have been variously described as 'jugglers', 'jacks of all trades, but masters of none', 'dictators', 'doves of peace' and 'dragons'. Taken together, these metaphors illustrate the multifaceted, important and often stressful role of leading a business school as a university discipline and department. Deans are faced with reconciling contested identities as CEO, entrepreneur and scholar. Some of the most successful, such as George Bain (at LBS and, earlier, WBS), demonstrate how a range of characteristics, including integrity, humour, confidence, resilience, determination and scholarship, define the personality of a leader in the political process of leadership, and enable the chosen path and strategic direction – e.g. to beat INSEAD – to be understood by the

The introduction, '**Global financial crisis: future challenges for strategic leadership, deans and business schools**', examines the impact of the global financial crisis and the opportunity it provides for deans and university leaders to create a new model for business schools and management education.

Link: given the current criticisms of business schools and their role, the introduction identifies potentially evolutionary patterns for business schools and leadership.

Chapter 1, '**The business school landscape: trends and dilemmas**', examines the contrast between European and US business schools; each is seen to be embedded in a different competitive context with different competitive advantages.

Link: between these US/EU business schools, there are similar organisational features: these position business schools as professional service firms or knowledge-intensive firms.

Chapter 2, '**Business schools as professional organisations (professional service firms)**', identifies the features of business schools as PSFs. There are clear similarities but the model is incomplete as the business school is neither a professional partnership (e.g. law firm) nor a consulting firm. Rather it is a hybrid form of the class P2 and MPB form seen in studies of PSFs.

However, these PSF characteristics present a particularly complex challenge to the leadership and strategic management of business schools.

Chapter 3, '**The leadership process in business schools**', examines the competitive dynamics and future challenges in management education (Chapter 1), which, combined with the organizational nuances of PSFs (Chapter 2), provides a unique challenge to business school deans. It argues for examining the strategic leadership process from a political process perspective using the authors' SLP model.

Link: leading business schools have set about becoming international (global) leaders (Chapter 1); what does the process of internationalisation look like in three of the leading European schools as they attack 'top ten' places in the rankings?

Chapter 4, '**Strategic leadership in practice: leading the strategic process in three top business schools**', examines the strategic processes of internationalisation at three top business schools: IMD (Lausanne), INSEAD (Fontainebleau) and LBS (London).

Link: given the unique and varied nature of business schools and their 'top ten' aspirations (Chapters 1 and 2) what is the role of the dean in the internationalisation of these three leading schools?

Chapter 5, '**Strategic leadership in practice: the role of the dean**', examines the specific cases of different deans at the three leading European business schools IMD, INSEAD and LBS.

Link: provides further insights into strategic leadership from the personal viewpoint of the authors' experiences as dean; WBS is a strong contrast to IAE as a publicly funded school.

Chapter 6, '**Learning from the trenches: personal reflections on deanship**', examines the deanship roles of Fernando Fragueiro's tenure as dean of IAE (a private school in Argentina) and Howard Thomas as dean at WBS (a leading publicly funded school in the United Kingdon).

school's multiple constituents (staff, students, alumni, business and government).

We hope that the insights developed from our strategic leadership process models and our case studies of strategic leadership in practice at IAE, IMD, INSEAD, LBS and WBS will provide useful material for debates and dialogue about future business school models, and, more importantly, stimulate further research in this area.

FERNANDO FRAGUEIRO

HOWARD THOMAS

Acknowledgements

This book would not have come into being without the collaboration of a number of people. Among key 'contributors', Andrew Pettigrew played an unparalleled role in the shaping of the particular approach to leadership presented here that of 'leadership as a process in a specific organisational context, from a political perspective'. His academic work on processual and contextual analysis in organisations has enlightened this research since its inception. The empirical research that has served as the basis for the core chapters of this work was made possible by the generosity and openness of nearly 100 people: deans, former deans, faculty, staff members and business leaders – at IMD, INSEAD and London Business School. Our special gratitude goes to Peter Lorange, Xavier Gilbert, Juan Rada and Jim Ellert at IMD; Gabriel Hawawini, Antonio Borges, Ludo Van der Heyden, Claude Rameau, Claude Janssen, Soumitra Dutta and Arnoud De Meyer at INSEAD; and George Bain, John Quelch, Laura Tyson, Michael Hay and Paul Marsh at LBS. We have also collaborated with, and learnt greatly from, a number of strategy fellows and doctoral students, including Don Antunes and Xiaoying Li (St Andrews), Amanda Goodall (WBS), Julie Davies (ABS and WBS) and Alex Wilson (WBS).

We would also like to thank our colleagues and researchers at IAE Business School and Warwick Business School for their support and understanding while we devoted the necessary time and effort to writing this book. Finally, our sincere appreciation goes to Claire New (Howard's PA at WBS) and Alex Wilson (WBS), with whom it has been our pleasure to work on this endeavour.

INTRODUCTION
Global financial crisis: future challenges for strategic leadership, deans and business schools

GLOBALISATION AND THE GLOBAL CRISIS

The world has been changing dramatically over the past two and a half decades, and this dynamic is only becoming more profound and faster. The global financial and economic crisis has marked the end of a stage in globalisation characterised by a thrust towards world-wide integration primarily on the basis of technical and scientific phenomena – breakthrough information and communication technologies as well as the emergence of biosciences, to name just a few. Part of the foundations for the 'global village' announced by pioneers in the 1980s has already been built. The current landscape is far from perfect, though, and we still have a long way to go if we want this to be a time of development and progress for all humankind.

The revolution in the twenty-first century hinges on essentially 'technical' drivers, and society has adjusted its organisation, customs and habits mostly in a reactive way, which has had the effect of bringing about – along with unimaginable advancement opportunities – significant social challenges and dilemmas. Only a handful of institutions have managed to redesign themselves, while not nearly enough new organisations have been created to address the issues stemming from this new scenario, with its local–global tensions in social life.

Economic activities in general and business companies in particular have been the first to plunge into globalisation. However, as

Some of the ideas in this chapter are heavily influenced by work with Julie Davies, a Warwick Ph.D. student; see Davies and Thomas (2009).

far as management is concerned, and as noted by Ghemawat (2007), among others, it may be more accurate to refer to this phenomenon as 'semi-globalisation' (Thomas, 2009). Although many business issues have become global, not all enterprise operations are handled globally. In general terms, it is safe to say that capital markets and labour-intensive product or service manufacturing centres have gone global – that is, they operate in a delocalised fashion, with globally oriented standardisation. However, there is still widespread evidence of how relevant 'local idiosyncrasies' are for consumer habits and behavioural patterns – not to mention other management issues closely associated with investment decisions and organisations' interactions with communities in the markets where they operate.

Amidst this semi-globalised setting of recent decades, management education and, in particular, business schools have come under strong pressure to adapt their knowledge creation and teaching practices to the new realities of business. Schools have responded proactively to these challenges – sometimes more effectively than others. It is crucial for these adjustments not only to be made swiftly but also to contribute academic rigour and relevant value to business executives.

However, although this significant effort has resulted in unquestionable progress, the economic crisis unleashed in 2008 – brought about mostly by key management actors, such as the financial and real estate sectors – has revealed that current business practices still fail to adequately address the dilemmas brought about by 'semi-globalisation'. In fact, this global crisis has built momentum for management education in general and business schools in particular to revisit and reshape key aspects of their core activities: research and teaching.

Indeed, it is important for management educators to realise that the nature of this crisis is unprecedented, and that it has very profound, deep and path-breaking implications (Bisoux, 2009). Consequently, the foundations of business practice are being questioned and re-examined very closely on several dimensions of global change, namely the relationship between government and business, the role of emerging markets in the global economy and the phenomenon of increasing ecological awareness in society. For example, the long-standing belief that open and deregulated markets know best has been discredited. A new era is emerging in which there will be closer collaboration between business and government and more heavily regulated markets at a national/global level. There will be a shift from the US/western European model of capitalism to a more enlightened, multicultural and responsible version. This new model will, necessarily, adapt to changes in the rules of the game because of the presence and increasing power of emerging economies (such as China, India and Brazil) and the critical need for beneficial global investment in sustainable technologies and ecological preservation.

In all its complexity, therefore, the current financial crisis requires a considered and carefully thought-through response, and it has also rekindled the debate on the mission of business schools. This could be an exceptional opportunity to reshape and improve the image and the core purpose of management education, reorienting it beyond the acquisition of indispensable knowledge and skills towards, for example, lifelong learning processes. Business schools should take a more committed look at providing programmes for alumni to periodically take time off in order to reassess their own professional goals and their contributions to the advancement of society as a whole.

Sadly, as the world was marching towards globalisation, the ambitions of new Master of Business Administration (M.B.A.) graduates seemed to zero in on salary and bonus rewards rather than on building long and reputable careers in management. With the current financial crisis shining an unforgiving light on managerial practices, M.B.A. programmes have come under heavy fire for their flawed contribution to business leaders' education. To turn this experience into a growth opportunity, business schools should concentrate on improving their academic offerings – particularly with respect to

M.B.A. and executive education programmes – so as to reinstate the value of management education as a lifelong endeavour.

With higher salaries as the dominant driver for the choice of an M.B.A. programme (and enshrined in the rankings methodologies used by, for example, *The Financial Times*) and almost 50 per cent of top schools' graduates taking jobs in the financial industry in order to enjoy its extremely generous bonuses, business schools seem to have turned a blind eye to signals warning of a disturbing imbalance between technical knowledge and personal judgement development in their overall value offerings. Over time, managers face ever more complex business responsibilities, and young executives grow older and wiser. As a result, M.B.A. and executive education programmes present a unique opportunity to embrace the notion of 'career management' as a 'lifelong learning journey', incorporating several stops along the way to reflect on achievements and failures, to learn about new challenges and to provide chances for renewed commitment to loftier aims.

'A diploma should expire every ten years,' said the dean of a top business school a while back. To have competent corporate leaders, and not short-sighted decision-makers who miss the higher purpose of management, business schools should teach students that business leadership roles require sound judgement based on a comprehensive, long-term perspective that complements knowledge and managerial skills.

At Harvard Business School's (HBS's) recent M.B.A. commencement ceremony, the dean, Jay Light, and James Dimon (HBS M.B.A. 1982), chairman and chief executive officer (CEO) of JP Morgan Chase, also focused on career management and lifelong learning as a cornerstone of professional growth, reminding future graduates of the importance of building a personal brand for hard work, integrity and trust. Similarly, at IESE Business School's M.B.A. commencement ceremony a year ago, Narayana Murthy, chairman of the board of Infosys Technologies, said: '[L]ive your life and lead your professional career in a way that makes a difference to your society. It is in such foundations that great business leaders and organisations flourish.'

Setting out to steer young professionals towards personal-value-driven lifelong careers does not exempt business schools from revising their programme curricula in the light of recent developments. In fact, many institutions are, rightly, reinforcing and updating their courses on ethics, business and society so that they emphasise the following values: long-term value creation, not short-termism; leadership and corporate responsibility; compensation systems and their impact on short- and long-term value creation; a broad and 'systemic' perspective on risk; corporate governance, board composition and responsibilities; and an awareness of shareholders' rights and obligations as ultimate company owners. Further, some have developed a critical course in the lessons of business, economic and financial history in order to understand past mistakes and answer the question of how, and why, basically good people did really bad things in the recent crisis.

Indeed, students have begun to recognise the need for a deeper purpose and set of values for their professional career. Rather than have an image as 'resilient wreckers' who wreaked such havoc in the economy over the past two years, M.B.A. students are jumping aboard a campaign led by Professors Nohria and Khurana at Harvard to turn management into a formal profession (Khurana and Nohria, 2008; *The Economist*, 2009b). Recently a large group of Harvard's second-year M.B.A. students promoted an oath before their graduation to 'serve the greater good', 'act with the utmost integrity' and guard against 'decisions that advance my own narrow ambitions, but harm the enterprise and the societies it services' (*The Economist*, 2009a: 70).

In short, globalisation has finally reached a stage at which it should address human reality in all its dimensions, setting boundaries for standardisation and rising to meet the challenges posed by diversity. There is no question about it: business schools should enlighten the path to globalisation with new knowledge, educating corporate leaders to work in a world that is essentially different from that of the late twentieth century.

CHANGING MODELS AND CONTINGENCIES

This is clearly the moment for business schools to do more, and undertake a major review of the future evolution of the business school and its curriculum. Perhaps a global commission, on the lines of the original Ford and Carnegie Reports of the 1960s but with a truly international set of business school leaders as authors, should be formed for this purpose.

Indeed, there is at present a wide-ranging debate in management education about how to move forward. For example, Carolyn Woo, dean at the Notre Dame Business School in the United States, stresses that 'this is definitely an opportunity for business schools to do more to make ethical thinking part of the fabric of their curriculum' (Adenekan, 2009). Antunes and Thomas (2007) observe that European business schools provide more heterogeneous offerings than the dominant US model, which has been widely adopted (see also Pfeffer and Fong, 2002). For Europe, Durand and Dameron (2008) challenge the current dominant model that has made North America the Mecca for management education by advocating the adoption of the 'catching up' mode with a 'differentiating' strategy. In the United Kingdom, Starkey has called for business schools to learn from the lessons of history in terms of past mistakes in business and leadership, and to create a model of the M.B.A. that goes beyond merely being a passport for careers in 'hedge funds, private equity, investment banking, venture capital and consulting' (Starkey, 2008). He argues that 'business schools will need to reflect on...how management education has contributed to the mindset that has led to the excesses of the last two decades... They will need to cultivate an appreciation of the role of the state and of collective action to counter the fixation on...greed and selfishness... *The Financial Times* also has a role to play [in changing values and attitudes]'. Its league tables (of full-time M.B.A. programmes) are heavily biased to the salary returns that accrue to M.B.As. who join these 'professions'. 'It is time to develop a more robust measure of what constitutes effective, sustainable management education,' he continues.

Starkey also (2009) believes that 'the economic sidelined the behavioural' and business schools must take greater account of ethics and aesthetics in the curriculum. Arnoud De Meyer, dean of Judge Business School, has added to the debate from a UK-based dean's viewpoint: 'We will have to rethink the basis of finance, we will need to understand how to adjust globalisation to a more regulated world. We need to give our students more insights into what the new role of business in society will be and how business has to take the rest of society more into account in its strategies' (Bradshaw, 2009a). Joel Podolny, a former dean of Yale School of Management, argues for US business schools to:

- integrate a range of academic disciplines to connect analysis with values;
- team-teach with hard and soft skills;
- promote qualitative research;
- abandon rankings based on graduates' salaries; and
- enforce a code of conduct.

He warns that, 'unless America's business schools make radical changes, society will become convinced that M.B.As. work to service only their own selfish interests' (Podolny, 2009). It is timely that Ferlie, McGivern and Moraes (2008) argue for a public interest business school model focused on social science and issues of 'major public importance'.

In the future the business school curriculum should offer students a value proposition beyond status and salary. It will have to set new goals and directions so as to ensure that it has a new, more exalted mission as a professional school (not as the football team of the university), acting as a conscience for business and focusing on how it can contribute to creating a better world by examining issues such as health, poverty, the problem of the growth of cities and sustainability. As Harney (2009) puts it, 'Business schools must develop a duty of care to those most valuable in the economy – workers – by teaching responsible business practices that help sustain and develop secure employment, that value other ways of life beyond the dragons. Only then will they be truly professional.'

LEADERSHIP CHALLENGES FOR DEANS

However, those of us who are part of the management education industry – all the more so if we have any experience in its governance and development – know that it is necessary to strengthen and professionalise the leadership in business schools so that they can respond swiftly and effectively to the new challenges of this century.

It is crucial for any organisation – and especially for those having a decisive impact on business management, such as business schools – to fully understand their specific leadership dynamics. Understanding the 'context' is easily recognised as a critical competence for deans, presidents and CEOs, as they are ultimately responsible for setting and executing strategic direction in their organisations. There is widespread consensus on the need for this expertise regarding the understanding of markets, consumers, competitors, etc. Nonetheless, the ability to understand specific idiosyncratic organisational traits, such as key people, developments, cultural aspects, systems and processes, seems to be less obvious and relevant. This view of leadership takes into account the determinant traits of each organisation – its internal context – as well as the salient and critical features of its external setting (competitors, customers, regulatory agencies, economic conditions, etc.). With this well-rounded outlook on the organisation, it is possible to link leadership and strategy, embodying strategy and providing leadership with an organisational context as well as a time frame.

The literature on academic deanship (not specific to business schools) presents some interesting insights. For example, Rosser, Johnsrud and Heck (2003: 2) have studied some of the metaphors applied to the multiple roles that deans perform: 'Deans have been variously described as "doves of peace" intervening among warring factions, "dragons" holding internal and external threats at bay, and "diplomats" guiding and encouraging people who live and work in the college' (see also Tucker and Bryan, 1991: ix). Gmelch (2004: 75) has extensively researched the changes happening to the role of deans in the United States and Australia, noting their Janus-like identity: 'They mediate the concerns of the university mission to faculty and at the same time try to champion the values of their faculty... [T]hey must learn to swivel without appearing dizzy, schizophrenic, or "two-faced".' Fagin (1997: 95) also sees the ambidextrous professional school dean 'as a person and position in the middle'. This suggests new forms of organising for the dean in 'hyper-turbulent' times to cope with managing at the 'edge of chaos' (Smith and Graetz, 2006).

More pragmatically, Starkey and Tiratsoo (2007: 55) portray the increasing complexity of the role of the business school dean over time: 'Forty years ago running a business school was something that a senior professor might well take as a matter of duty shortly before retirement. Nowadays deans almost constitute a profession in their own right, a cohort with unique and specialist skills... Deans may be likened to sports coaches, hired to improve performance, fired at will, but with one eye always on building their own careers... [T]he truth is that financial performance now largely makes or breaks a dean's reputation.' Symonds (2009) also highlights the dean's increasingly difficult position during a recession: 'There was a time when becoming the dean of a major business school was like winning the lottery. It meant a comfortable gig with good pay, prestige, the opportunity to mix with the great and good of business, politics and academia and, perhaps best of all, the kind of job security enjoyed now only by popes. In today's credit crunch world, however, things are very different.' On the other hand, successful schools tend to be led by first-rate academics. Indeed, Goodall (2007) finds that the leading business schools are led by top scholars who, through their background, signal their clear understanding of the culture of academia and their awareness of what it takes to be an intellectual leader and director of a business school.

In a recent business school research study, Davies and Thomas (2009) seek to answer the question 'What do business school deans do?'. It seems they perform a complex job as a buffer between the business school and the central university and the external world. They are delivering the bottom line for the vice chancellor, straddling academia and management professions, acting as a managing partner in a professional service firm (PSF) or knowledge-intensive firm (KIF), building a brand, raising their position in league tables, gaining business school accreditations. In addition, internally they have to build teams, consult, energise, create positivity, align staff around the strategy, recruit and nurture talent, communicate, make tough decisions, develop social and relational capital and make connections. They keep sane by being sufficiently disengaged to have their own identity and outside interests, not taking themselves too seriously.

However, frustrations expressed by deans included internal bureaucracy, not being able to hold individuals to account for performance in universities and the lack of big debates on new models of business schools because of a focus on compliance with accreditation bodies. Triple accreditations, relentless rankings (*Financial Times*, national student survey, Research Assessment Exercise (RAE), etc.) and the recession may move business schools away from innovation and distinctiveness towards mimetic institutional isomorphism (DiMaggio and Powell, 1983: 147) with 'processes that make organizations more similar without necessarily making them more efficient', and towards the rewarding of dysfunctional behaviour (Kerr, 1995). Devinney, Dowling and Perm-Ajchariyawong (2006) note in this respect how the annual *Financial Times* rankings define competition between business schools, which, in turn, may lead to dysfunctional strategies in pursuit of 'successful' rankings, as suggested by Khurana (2007) in his observation about the 'tyranny of rankings'. For example, schools may divert surplus resources (whether from endowment or elsewhere) to provide full scholarships for M.B.A. students who have GMAT (Graduate Management Admissions Test) scores in excess of 700 in order to optimise the student quality measure in the rankings survey. However, those resources could have been used to improve research or teaching excellence, or to reinforce important strategic objectives for improving business school performance.

Further, deans also face relentless pressures. This pressure may be considerably less than for a FTSE (Financial Times Stock Exchange) 100 CEO, but academic cultures require considerable shaping and influencing of leadership styles in a knowledge-intensive context. The role of ideology in academic cultures, pluralism and inherent conservatism enrich and complicate the dean's role (Clark, 2008). The university as a professional bureaucracy may engender high levels of trust and expertise amongst members of academic disciplines who collaborate on research but inflexible bureaucratic structures tend not to encourage the kind of enterprise and innovation necessary in a business school (Mintzberg, 1983).

It is interesting to note that the psychometric profile of the sample of deans in the Davies and Thomas (2009) study included extroversion, tough-mindedness, seeing patterns and making connections, strategic thinking and a tendency to bring issues to closure. However, few deans found themselves able to shift from what Collins (2001: 70) calls a level 4 leader ('effective and provides direction') to the humility required of a level 5 leader ('a paradoxical combination of personal humility plus professional will') – an attribute of great leaders who have lasting legacies. We can give more personal instances of high-quality leadership skills. For example, a few weeks ago we met a top executive from a multinational company that had been forced to review a major failure brought about by an associate he himself had recruited to manage the company's operations in one of the so-called BRIC (Brazil, Russia, India, China) nations. The executive indicated that his key lesson from the unsavoury experience had been the realisation that a CEO's competence set should include, in addition to analytical depth and communication skills, the courage to confront the status quo of the organisation (the internal context) and its value chain (the external context). The complexity of recognising and reconciling the internal and external contexts in the processes of strategic leadership, as outlined in Chapter 2, is much greater in organisations such as business schools than in the example above. In business school organisations, power is generally shared as a result of the distinctive set of external and internal characteristics and the strong need for autonomy and collegiality amongst business school professionals – i.e. academics.

Therefore, the political perspective, advocated in this book, helps to gain a better understanding of leadership issues and challenges, especially in organisations – business schools – in which collegiality tends to lead to power-sharing. This political approach to leadership should encompass two distinctive tasks – power mobilisation and issue legitimation – in order to promote any initiative effectively, as leadership must be construed as a social influence process.

1   The business school landscape: trends and dilemmas

1.1   INTRODUCTION

Never before has management education been the subject of such intense scrutiny and critical onslaught. Academics, the business press and the media all point out that business schools have failed to prepare students adequately in terms of the appropriate skills, and specifically in instilling ethical and leadership qualities (Cheit, 1985; Hayes and Abernathy, 1980). For example, Bennis and O'Toole (2005) ask why 'business schools have embraced the scientific model of physicists and economists rather than the professional model of doctors and lawyers'. They suggest that management professors favour the disciplinary prestige of high-ranking academic journals but note that few actually practise management, unlike professional counterparts such as surgeons in medical schools, who may still perform surgical operations. It is typically the case in business schools that tensions often exist between the pursuit of rigour and relevance in research and the need to focus on both academic and professional practice (Grey, 2002; Zell, 2005).

This re-evaluation of business schools has been prompted not only by their success but also by questions about the legitimacy of business and management as academic disciplines. Business schools have clearly been one of the major success stories and one of the fastest-growing areas in university education (Pfeffer and Fong, 2002). However, their image, identity and status, as both academic and professional schools, have come under critical scrutiny in recent years, particularly during the current financial crisis and in the

This chapter draws heavily on a number of articles written by one of the authors, but specifically Antunes and Thomas (2007) and Thomas (2007).

13

context of prior corporate scandals, such as Enron in the United States and Parmalat in Europe. They have been attacked for their perceived inability to promote satisfactory ethical and professional standards (see, for example, Hawawini, 2005; Ivory *et al.*, 2006; Lorange, 2005; Mintzberg, 2004; Mintzberg and Gosling, 2002; Pfeffer and Fong, 2004; Starkey, Hatchuel and Tempest, 2004).

This chapter presents the background to the evolution and current positioning of business schools. Particular attention is paid to the European schools, three of which – the Institut Européen d'Administration des Affaires (INSEAD), the Institute for Management Development (IMD) and London Business School (LBS) – are examined in detail in relation to strategic leadership processes (SLPs) in Chapters 3, 4 and 5.

We first review the literature on the history and development of business schools that will provide the context for the study. This analysis then leads to the development of a social construction model that explains the evolution of the modern business school. Evidence is drawn from a variety of secondary sources in order to arrive at an understanding of the institutional breadth of the competition in the business school landscape. This, in turn, leads to our examination of the strengths and characteristics of European business education relative to the US business school model, which is perceived to be dominant (Pfeffer and Fong, 2002). This close comparison highlights the main elements of differentiation between European and US business schools. The implications of these differences for strategic positioning and the development of future strategic pathways are then discussed. The trends, themes and challenges faced by deans in this evolution process are also pinpointed, so that the nature of the dean's role in strategising, energising and leading a major business school can be explored further.

We start with a brief review of the history of business schools.

1.2 CRITICAL BACKGROUND AND HISTORY

As already noted, business schools have gained strong international recognition over the last century or so. From their initial establishment in the nineteenth century in continental Europe and the United States, they became highly legitimised institutions in the United States from the early twentieth century onwards and expanded worldwide during the second half of that century, so that formidable competitors sensitive to local market needs now exist in Europe, Asia and Latin America.[1] The knowledge provided by business schools shapes the structure of management development activities via academic programmes, which, typically, include degrees at the undergraduate, masters and doctoral levels, as well as post-experience education through non-degree programmes such as company-sponsored executive courses. However, the question arises: who regulates this body of knowledge and which professional body determines whether management can be classified as a profession similar to the professions of law or medicine?

It is important to recognise that the impetus for the evaluation and development of business and management knowledge within higher education originally started in Europe, not in the United States. In fact, the idea that the knowledge of commerce should be institutionalised and taught began in continental Europe. In France, the Paris-based Ecole Supérieure de Commerce was founded by the Paris Chamber of Commerce as long ago as 1819, with the aim of complementing the quality of engineering education, and with the ambition of becoming a school offering a superior education to secondary technical education – an ambition not achieved until 1854. The middle of the nineteenth century also saw the foundation of a school of commerce in Anvers, Belgium – in 1852. In Italy, a school of commerce was founded in Venice in 1867. In the late nineteenth and early twentieth centuries similar schools appeared in Austria (Vienna, 1856), Germany (e.g. Aachen, 1898, Cologne, 1901,

---

[1] Political scientists argue that institutions designate the set of rules that evolve over time and shape organisational processes and outcomes. The variety of institutionalism we adopt is historical institutionalism. For an example of historical and institutional analysis of management education with particular reference to European countries and the United States, see Bourdieu (1996) and Kipping and Bjarnar (1998).

Frankfurt-am-Main, 1901, and Mannheim, 1907) and Switzerland (St Gallen, 1898) (see Engwall and Zamagni, 1998).

However, despite this initial burst of activity at the turn of the nineteenth century, business school education in Europe developed more slowly, and on a national rather than regional basis. In the United Kingdom, for example, there was little development after the foundation of schools of commerce at the universities of Birmingham (1902) and Manchester (1904). As Larson (2003) notes, 'The London School of Economics and the Universities of Birmingham and Manchester experimented with "business", "commerce" or "industrial administration" curricula throughout the first half of the twentieth century... There was no academic research to drive these courses and the lack of theoretical framework hurt their reputation.'

The post-World-War-II recommendation of the British Institute of Management, created in 1947, that business schools should be developed in the United Kingdom was not implemented. It was only in the 1960s, following the publication of what became known as the Franks Report, which had similar policy intent to the Ford and Carnegie Reports in the United States in 1959, that the business school model was accepted (see Franks, 1966; for the North American discussion, see Gordon and Howell, 1959, and Pierson, 1959). Franks' policy recommendations led to the birth of business schools to provide leaders and much-needed 'captains of industry', with the development of LBS and Manchester Business School (MBS) as providers of elite, full-time M.B.A. programmes designed around the two-year full-time US-based M.B.A. model.[2] Subsequently, newer business schools, such as Judge (Cambridge University), Cass (City), Cranfield, Henley, Lancaster University Management School (LUMS), Said (Oxford) and Warwick Business School (WBS), have

---

[2] For examples of contemporary policy reports commissioned by the British government and research agencies with the aim of evaluating and therefore shaping and institutionalising management thought and education, see Department for Education and Skills [DfES] (2002) and Ivory et al. (2006).

developed M.B.A. programmes of an increasingly diverse character, albeit primarily of a one-year, full-time duration.

The picture was rather different in the United States, though with extremely interesting linkages to developments in European management education. In the United States the development of business schools started taking shape just a little later than in Europe – that is, in the late nineteenth century – influenced heavily, as Spender (2007) notes, by the cameralist traditions of German universities such as Halle and Berlin (founded in 1906). This development was consolidated in the twentieth century (Bourdieu, 1996). The spread of this type of institution all over the United States was rapid, with the development of both independent and university-based business schools. By the early twentieth century brand names such as Wharton (formed by Edmund James after extensive study of economics in Germany), Chicago, Harvard (formed by Edwin Gay in 1904 after a doctoral study in economics at the German Cameralist School in Berlin), Columbia and Dartmouth had already started to gain recognition (Gay, 1927). The formalisation of degree-level business education progressed quickly. Wharton launched a bachelor's programme in business in 1881, Dartmouth offered the first Master's degree in business in 1900 and Harvard launched the Master of Business Administration (M.B.A. degree) in 1908. A number of business schools were created later, but they tended to rely upon the earlier European models. At the same time a group of leading US business schools set up the Association to Advance Collegiate Schools of Business (AACSB) in 1916 to bring scientific rigour to the study of business and to mandate the knowledge base required in business schools in order to establish and certify management as a legitimate profession.

The era of the development of business schools in the United States from the turn of the twentieth century until the late 1950s could be described as the 'trade school' era, which Simon (1967) describes as a 'wasteland of vocationalism'. These schools, typically, catered for undergraduate students (with some practically-based masters' programmes), did not undertake much research and taught from a 'descriptive' viewpoint. This 'trade school' orientation changed rapidly following influential reports on management education from the Ford and Carnegie Foundations in 1959 (a critical appreciation of the effects of these reports on business education is provided by Bennis and O'Toole, 2005). These reports formulated policy prescriptions that drove the development of business schools towards a research- and discipline-led focus with an emphasis on scientific method, investigation and knowledge creation and a strong focus on graduate education in business. Indeed, in the late 1950s and early 1960s the Ford Foundation spent nearly $40 million to promote business education and research in five business schools, namely Carnegie-Mellon, Chicago, Columbia, Harvard and Stanford. This also created a significant gap between the rigour of the scholarly, discipline-based, academic research tradition anchored firmly in the economic and social sciences and those who argued for a 'clinical' and 'practical experience' imperative that focused on the relevance of understanding and improving management practice for the management clients of business schools.

Despite the clear recognition of the importance of business schools in recent decades, there has been much critical discussion about their nature and value, particularly those that have adhered to the discipline-oriented prescriptions of the Ford, Carnegie and Franks Reports. For instance, some critics accuse business schools of a whole series of failings: carrying out irrelevant research; doing a poor job of preparing students; being too market-driven; pandering to the ratings; failing to ask important questions; and, in the process of responding to the demands from their environment, losing their claims to professionalism as they 'dumb down' the content of courses, inflate grades to keep students happy and pursue curricular fads. Others argue that contemporary management education does a disservice to the profession by standardising content, being too analytical and not action-oriented, focusing on business functions (instead of the process of managing) and training specialists (rather than general managers). They also criticise business schools for being too parochial and not global in their thinking and values, and for not fully integrating experience, theory and reflection into group (as opposed to individual) decision-making processes. Finally, these critics stress that business schools do not encourage managers to incorporate an integrative, team-based philosophy directly into the daily functioning of their workplaces and do not provide sufficient ethical and professional guidance (Ghoshal, 2005; Gosling and Mintzberg, 2004; Hawawini, 2005; Ivory *et al.*, 2006; Lorange, 2002; Mintzberg, 2004; Mintzberg and Gosling, 2002;Pfeffer and Fong, 2002, 2004).[3]

On the other hand, there are many advocates in favour of the importance of the business school as a research vehicle for new knowledge creation that produces the techniques, theories and approaches that enable businesses to succeed. To quote Thomas Cooley (2007; emphasis in original), the former dean of New York University's (NYU's) Stern School of Business, 'The research mindset brings a unique and powerful focus to business education. It is *forward looking* rather than *backward looking*. It moves education away from teaching students a collection of *facts* to teaching them how to *think*. It moves them from a stultifying 'best practice' mentality toward developing analytical ability.' Grey (2005), in contrast, notes that this analytic positivistic research tradition, particularly that found in US business schools, has created 'norms' of what 'good' research is and developed the bulk of textbook knowledge. All the same, according to him, much of the consensus that social science and business research can be thought of in that essentially positivistic way has been questioned, particularly by critical management theorists in European business schools.

This account of the evolution of business school models suggests that, given their original common European heritage but subsequent

---

[3] In contrast, a solid argument as to the positive influence of an M.B.A. education is given by Boyatzis, Stubbs and Taylor (2002).

different history and institutional shaping, European and US-based business schools have developed a range of different and quite distinctive approaches to management education (examples of such differences are provided by Amdam, 1997, Baden-Fuller and Ang, 2001, Kipping and Bjarnar, 1998, and Raimond and Halliburton, 1995). The key issue here is how these European business school models evolved and prospered: were they defined in local or regional terms, or by reference to international prototypes – e.g. the US model – or in terms of a mix of national role models and international prototypes (see Engwall, 2000)?

To develop this point further, we present a social constructionist model of the process of development of business schools. We then map the rich European landscape of management education and highlight the key drivers of European models in contrast to the US model.

1.3   BUSINESS SCHOOLS AND BUSINESS EDUCATION AS A SOCIAL CONSTRUCTION PROCESS

We use a social construction theoretical approach to understand and explore the creation and development of business schools and the business school 'industry' (Berger and Luckmann, 1966; Porac and Thomas, 2002; Weick, 1995). We argue that industries, such as the business school 'industry', are essentially 'cognitive communities' – that is, 'social constructions that emerge from the interplay of cognition and action over time' (Porac and Thomas, 2002). Over time, as social interactions occur within the business school cognitive community, a language and nomenclature evolve to capture the 'industry belief systems' (Weick, 1995; White, 1981, 1992) that consistently shape the strategies and actions of members of the community.

Key components in the creation of 'industry beliefs' are the different stories and 'models' of business education that become shared and interpreted through conversations between members of and participants in the community. Once they have been widely shared through public availability, a range of institutionalising processes – such as the imitation of other organisations, the search for legitimation and the powerful influence of legal and regulatory environments – reinforces the beliefs, which then become incorporated into the routines and operating strategies of members of the business school community (DiMaggio and Powell, 1983).

To explain the evolution of the business school, the social construction model consists of three elements. At the first level, there are beliefs about the boundaries of markets and competitive interactions. At this level, a range of very early commerce and business school models emerge with different frames of reference, such as 'We are a commerce school' or 'We are a trade school'. At the second level of evolution, 'industry recipes' or norms emerge (Spender, 1989), whereas, at the third level, reputational and status orderings of business schools develop as interorganisational performance differences manifest themselves. The 'three-level social construction model' views the process of development of business schools as a long-term social process, which builds up the reputation or 'social capital' of the institution.

Table 1.1 explains the model in greater detail and links it to the key drivers and characteristics that emerge at each level. The associated Figure 1.1 conceptualises the model, showing, at the top of the apex of the pyramid, the reputation or 'goodwill' that a school builds up as a consequence of the 'social capital' generated over time.

The *first level* – which covers the early twentieth century – is the period during which different business or commerce schools, typically in national contexts, began to create their unique product positions in order to achieve legitimation for management as a discipline. Through a process of developing and sharing their visions among each other, they defined frames of reference or boundary beliefs about the nature of such a school, usually with definitions such as 'We are a school of commerce' (UK schools). Each of the schools (such as the German Handelshochschulen) was also influenced by the set of cultural, legal and regulatory characteristics in

Table 1.1 *Business education and business schools as a social construction process*

Model	Time period	Behavioural characteristics and causes	Illustrative references
Level 1: • emergence of alternative business school models.	Nineteenth to early twentieth centuries.	Different knowledge structures, frames of reference and cognitive maps. Different beliefs about management education but mainly vocational trade-type models focusing on commercial and administrative practice to achieve status and legitimation for management.	Berger and Luckmann (1966); Eden (1988); Hodgkinson and Johnson (1994); Porac, Thomas and Baden-Fuller (1989).
Level 2: • clearly shaped national business schools.	Early twentieth century to 1970s.	Strategic reference points established in countries – US model is key reference point. Imitative behaviour at local/national levels. The image and identity of a business school becomes clear. Institutionalising and socialising processes.	Albert and Whetten, (1985); Engwall (2000); Fiegenbaum, Hart and Schendel (1996); DiMaggio and Powell (1991).
Level 3: • dominance of the US business school model. • Strength of national champions.	1970s to present.	Industry recipe is established – dominant design/role model is evident. Business schools as 'finishing' schools for power, prestige and status. Reputational structures and clear identities formed. Internationalising processes. Organisational adaptation and interpretation. Benchmarking processes.	Benjamin and Podolny (1999); Grey (2005); Porac *et al.* (1995); Spender (1989); White (1992).

Source: Modified from Antunes and Thomas (2007).

Consequences	Implications
Diagnosis of individual models of business education: • German Handelshoch- schulen (1900s), • French grandes écoles and écoles supérieures de commerce (1820 on), • UK commerce schools (1900s), • US schools (1880 on).	Beliefs about market boundaries vary between countries. Differential rates of growth and adoption across countries. Influence of culture, regulations, country characteristics and languages evident at local and national levels. Size of schools tends to be nationally determined.
Local/national role models and recipes become evident: • France – dominance of grandes écoles; • United Kingdom – establishment of London and Manchester Business Schools; • Scandinavia – Stockholm, Helsinki, Copenhagen, Bergen; • United States – Wharton, Harvard, etc.	The identification of national role models and a dominant industry recipe means that differences exist between the key drivers of: • governance; • funding and endowment; • international mindset; • innovation; • knowledge transmission; • corporate linkages.
• Dominance of US-style M.B.A. business school model, but distinctive national and European alternatives established. • Nature of players becomes clearer. • Rivalry, competition and economic language identifies a global business school. • Rankings and other reputational measures instituted. • Social capital is critical. • Choice of role models: US, European, etc. (late 1990s).	Issues of image and reputation become important. Social capital is built up in the long term. Rankings and league tables become indicators of success. International alliances form to enhance reputations and status of leading schools in the United States and Europe.

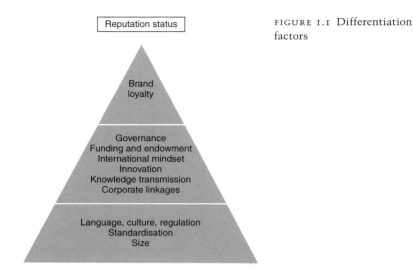

FIGURE 1.1 Differentiation factors

its home country, which also determined factors such as the rate of adoption and size of these schools.

Throughout the 'rump' of the twentieth century, and at the *second level* of our model, the different 'industry' logics and beliefs about business schools became much more widely shared. The rapid standardisation of the US-style business school model, focused around the M.B.A., established that model as a strategic reference point and, ultimately, as the dominant industry model or recipe (Spender, 1989), such that it became self-reinforcing and taken for granted. During this process, at the national level, locally defined schools tended to imitate each other and adapted to each other's norms and practices, then subsequently explored and embraced the promising practices from key reference points and countries, such as the US-style model (Engwall, 2000). Such institutionalising processes, involving the replication and legitimation of business schools, have occurred across the entire global business school domain, and argue that adaptation to consensual models or recipes is likely to occur. As a consequence, therefore, national – or, perhaps, key regional – players become the immediate role models, such as the grandes écoles in France, but with the elite US business schools (such as Wharton and Harvard) as the global role models or recipes.

As business schools evolved from the 1970s to the present day, the *third level* of our model – the powerful reputational elites and structures – became well developed, with clear identities as industry leaders, and national and regional champions becoming established. Harvard, Chicago, Stanford, the Massachusetts Insitute of Technology (MIT), etc. became the leaders in the United States, with IESE in Spain, Bocconi in Italy, etc. becoming established as the leading national schools in Europe. The pressures of consumerism – i.e. reputational and status rankings from *The Financial Times* (FT), *The Economist*, etc. – and accreditation processes such as AACSB (the Association to Advance Collegiate Schools of Business) International, EQUIS (European Quality Improvement System), etc. have also enhanced the reputations of national champions and the industry leaders through the regular publication of league tables and the strong social recognition of their values. In essence, the reputational rankings that emerge over time develop from the social codings and interpretations of business school differences in performance.

To summarise, the model suggests that first-level industry beliefs, second-level industry recipes and third-level reputational rankings together represent the cognitive foundation of the business school communities, leading to the present-day social construction of the business school 'industry'. The European schools of today, therefore, rely on insights drawn from a mix of national and European regional models as well as key reputationally strong US schools. To reinforce these points, we first review the current environmental landscape of management education. We then demonstrate, through a more detailed examination of the social construction model, how the differences between European- and US-style management education are formed.

I.4   THE MANAGEMENT EDUCATION ENVIRONMENT

The external context of strategic decision-making is very broad-ranging. It can include governments, competitors, technological and social change and the dynamics of buyer and supplier markets. One way for deans and senior managers to analyse their exposure to the set of potential contextual factors is through the application of a PEST (political, economic, sociological and technological) framework analysis (McGee, Thomas and Wilson, 2005). A PEST analysis of the business school education environment is provided in Table 1.2.

Among the key conclusions of the PEST analysis are the following.

- The funding of higher education is a critical issue throughout the world (highlighted, for example, by the introduction of so-called 'top-up' fees in UK higher education; see *Economist*, 2005). This has been exacerbated by the current global financial crisis, which is increasing the likelihood of severe spending and investment cutbacks across business and higher education. The consequences of continued underfunding of universities have been the increasing use of part-time faculty, the relative unattractiveness of academic careers and mounting evidence of financial failure. Further, pressure from governments and regulatory institutions, such as (in the United Kingdom) the Quality Assurance Agency (QAA), with its focus on teaching quality, and the Higher Education Funding Council for England's (HEFCE's) five-yearly Research Assessment Exercise, with an emphasis on research quality, will require business schools to reassess their business models and to balance high-quality education against the criteria of cost-efficiency and organisational effectiveness.
- Globalisation and the growth of the international economy create new opportunities and challenges for business schools, particularly in the developing world. In parallel with the rapid development of high-quality business schools in Europe and Asia (see, for example, the global M.B.A. programmes listing in *The Financial Times'* annual ranking of global business schools), successful competition and, in addition, cooperation through strategic alliances with foreign schools will require a balanced global view of business education and an increased awareness of the multinational dimension and ethnic diversity in teaching methods, teaching materials and case studies.
- Student demand patterns and the emergence of new learning technologies will require schools to pay increasing attention to flexible learning and

Table 1.2 *A PEST analysis of the business school environment*

Political	Economic
• Standardisation of business schools in Europe[a] (Bologna Accord: greater market, greater competition). • Regulatory pressures for programme and school accreditation[b] (EFMD, AMBA, AACSB). • Regulatory pressure for teaching and research quality (QAA, RAE) • Tighter visa regulations[c] for international students following 9/11 and terrorism. • Reduction of government[b] and public funding for higher education.	• Trend towards globalisation[bd] and free trade internationally (trading blocs: EU, NAFTA, WTO). • Rapid growth of Chinese[c] and Indian economies. • Increased competition[e] from consultants and private business schools (well-established business schools across Europe, America and Asia; emerging schools in Africa). • Mounting UK student debt[c] and student ability to fund education. • Global economic and financial crisis creates financial stresses and the likelihood of research and programme cuts.
Social	**Technological**

• Changing societal values:
  • ethical issues (e.g. Enron);
  • corporate social responsibility (e.g. Nike and use of child labour in Asia);
  • sustainable development and environmentally friendly considerations (e.g. alternative energy sources, global warming).
 • Demographic changes:[f]
  • age, lifestyle, cultural, ethnic influences.
	• Growth in e-learning[bd] and internet education.
	
	 • Blended learning.[bd]
	
	 • Technology and the classroom.
	
	 • Knowledge revolution[b] and knowledge information as assets for value creation in an organisation.
	
	 • Web-based dissemination of knowledge.[d]

Notes: EFMD = European Federation of Management Development, AMBA = Association of M.B.As., NAFTA = North American Free Trade Agreement, WTO = World Trade Organization.

Sources:

[a] Graduate Management Admission Council (GMAC) (2005).

[b] Hawawini (2005).

[c] Lorange (2005).

[d] Pfeffer and Fong (2002).

[e] Various recent issues of *The Financial Times, The Times, The Times Higher Education Supplement* and *The Economist*.

[f] Thomas (2007b).

the blend between face-to-face campus-style learning and interactive e-learning technologies.

- Social factors, including two-income families and increased life expectancy, will probably result in increased demand for innovative forms of lifelong learning. There will also be pressure for business schools to provide leadership in debates about ethics, corporate social responsibility and issues of sustainability and climate change.

As Lorange (2005) notes, '[A] new competitive landscape for today's business schools is emerging.' Idea innovation is clearly needed to overcome the strong and overly disciplinary focus of undergraduate business education and change M.B.A. offerings, in order to develop managers, not conventional M.B.As. (Mintzberg, 2004), perhaps with modified forms of project-based action learning. Executive and non-traditional forms of M.B.As. will grow in importance in a networked real world, often called a 'knowledge society', as flexible, 'on-the-job'-type training becomes the norm.

In summary, the implications of competition and competitive dynamics for management education include the following:

- a future shakedown of business school programmes;
- a consolidation of departments and programmes;
- a constant search for productivity improvements, because of competitive pricing and creative segmentation;
- continuing growth of alliance, inter-university consortia programmes;
- a renewed focus on business school core competences and viable niches – e.g. location, entrepreneurship;
- regular refocusing of the core disciplines; and
- a greater customer orientation.

1.5 THE EUROPEAN LANDSCAPE IN MANAGEMENT EDUCATION

Table 1.3 provides a partial 'map' of the management education landscape in Europe, which demonstrates the breadth of the marketplace. We comment briefly on some of the key areas of the European landscape below.

Table 1.3 *A partial 'map' of European management education*

Country	Representative schools
Austria	Wirtschaftsuniversität Wien (Vienna)
Belgium	Vlerick Leuven Gent Management School (Leuven, Ghent)
Czech Republic	CMC Postgraduate School (Prague)
Denmark	Copenhagen Business School
Finland	Helsinki School of Economics
France	INSEAD (Fontainebleau); HEC ESSEC, ESCP/EAP, EM Lyon, Sciences PO (Paris); Grenoble Ecole de Management; Audencia (Nantes); BEM (Bordeaux); ESCEM (Tours); ESC Toulouse
Germany	WHU (Koblenz); ESMT (Berlin); Munich Business School; Mannheim Business School; GISMA (Hanover); Handelshochschule Leipzig; Cologne Business School; Goethe Business School (Frankfurt)
Hungary	Central University Business School (Budapest)
Italy	SDA Bocconi (Milan)
Ireland	Smurfit/Quinn Schools, University College Dublin
Netherlands	TiasNimbas Business School (Tilburg, Utrecht), Rotterdam School of Management, Erasmus University; Nyenrode Business Universiteit (Breukelen)
Norway	BI Norwegian School of Management (Oslo)
Poland	University of Warsaw Postgraduate Management Centre; Koźmiński Academy of Entrepreneurship and Management (Warsaw)
Russia	Moscow State University
Slovenia	IEDC/Bled School of Management (Bled)
Spain	IESE Business School, University of Navarra (Barcelona, Madrid); ESADE, Ramon Llull University (Barcelona); Instituto de Empresa (Madrid); EADA (Madrid)
Sweden	Stockholm School of Economics
Switzerland	IMD (Lausanne); Hochschule St Gallen (St Gallen)
United Kingdom	LBS (London); WBS (Warwick); Said (Oxford); Judge (Cambridge); MBS (Manchester); LUMS (Lancaster); Imperial (London); Cass (London); Edinburgh; Cardiff; Henley; Cranfield; Ashridge

Sources: The Financial Times ('FT ratings'); *The Economist* ('Which M.B.A.?'); EFMD; AACSB; AMBA; Antunes and Thomas (2007: 389).

In France, for example, INSEAD, which is a private school based in Fontainebleau, is a European 'outlier', in that it competes strongly with the major US schools, whereas HEC, ESSEC, EM Lyon and ESCP/EAP are the so-called French grandes écoles, the French elite – i.e. the most prestigious and, perhaps, more theory-driven schools. BEM (Bordeaux), ESCEM (Tours), Grenoble Ecole de Management, Audencia (Nantes) and ESC Toulouse, on the other hand, are exemplars of the twenty-five Ecoles Supérieures de Commerce (essentially, more practice-oriented schools), all of which are linked institutionally with the training and education needs of local chambers of commerce and are anchored to their regions, whose companies provide significant financial support.

In Germany, business schools were 'slow off the mark' in adopting separate institutional forms, despite the long German heritage of education in management. This is largely because of the German traditions in education, with a five-year first degree course in business – the so-called Diploma-Kaufmann – as the dominant educational model. With the advent of the Bologna Accord in 1999, which sought to harmonise the framework of higher education degrees in forty European countries (a system whereby a bachelor's degree lasts three to four years at a maximum and a Master's course lasts one to two years), there has been a clear trend towards M.B.As. in Germany at schools such as Koblenz (a private school), Mannheim (a university-based school) and ESMT (the European School for Management and Technology – a prestige private school).

Spain, for a relatively small European economy, has three highly regarded business schools. IESE, supported by the Opus Dei (and developed with academic assistance from Wharton and Harvard) and ESADE, supported by the Jesuits, are both university-based schools, whereas Instituto de Empresa in Madrid is a 'stand-alone', perhaps more professionally oriented, business school.

In the United Kingdom, according to the Association of Business Schools (ABS) (2003), there are now over 100 M.B.A. programmes available from a wide range of schools. London Business

School (LBS), like INSEAD in France, follows a US-style business school model, and attempts to compete strongly with the major US schools. By contrast, Henley and Cranfield focus much more on M.B.A. and executive education programmes, whereas university-based business schools, such as Cass (City), Judge (Cambridge), LUMS (Lancaster), Said (Oxford) and WBS (Warwick), offer a wider range of programmes, from undergraduate to post-experience programmes.

Scandinavia and northern Europe have a widely regarded range of 'national champions' in management education in Stockholm, Oslo, Helsinki and Copenhagen, and a Scandinavian approach to management exemplified in such journals as the *Scandinavian Journal of Management* and the *Scandinavian Journal of Economics*. Switzerland, on the other hand, is home to a small but internationally prestigious school, IMD, and a 'national champion', St Gallen. Finally, eastern Europe has developed its own business schools during the last fifteen years, with schools such as University of Warsaw Postgraduate Management Centre at the University of Warsaw and the Koźmiński Academy of Entrepreneurship and Management in Poland and the Central University Business School, funded by George Soros, in Hungary leading the business school revolution in the transition economies.

The snapshot provided by Table 1.3 indicates the diversity, quality and range of cultural offerings provided by European business schools. For example, in the United Kingdom, there are clearly a range of different schools and models. LBS and, to some extent, Oxford model themselves very closely on the elite US models, such as Columbia, Harvard, Stanford, Wharton and Northwestern, based in Evanston, Illinois. Stand-alone schools, such as Ashridge and Henley, have a professional focus on practically oriented M.B.A., D.B.A. (doctor of business administration) and executive programmes, and do not emphasise basic research. Bath, Lancaster and Warwick, on the other hand, combine strong undergraduate and graduate programmes with an emphasis on social-science-based research. The Open University, Henley and Warwick have pioneered distance learning

M.B.As., whereas schools such as Leicester, with its focus on a critical school of management and a critical M.B.A., stress linkages between the humanities and social science research. The Imperial College Business School (formerly the Tanaka Business School) has adopted a technology and knowledge focus for its school, stressing research on finance and technology-based management. The Cass Business School (City) has an emphasis on economics, finance and insurance, given its close proximity to the City of London.

The evidence, therefore, suggests much greater diversity and niche behaviour in UK schools than the greater institutionalisation and model conformity that exists in the US market. As a result, the UK market demonstrates that a range of schools, namely quasi-US-model schools, professionally oriented schools, humanities-/social-science-based schools and specialist schools with specialisms such as finance or technology, can coexist in the marketplace. Similar clusters and patterns can be identified in other European countries, such as France, where INSEAD is seen as the 'US elite' model, the grandes écoles as the key social science schools and national elites, the écoles supérieures as the more professionally, practically oriented schools and Paris Dauphine as a specialist school. On the basis of these two examples, the other countries in the European 'map' should follow a similar pattern, of clusters involving internationally elite schools, national role model schools, practically focused schools and specialist schools.

Following this brief review of European business schools, we link the social constructionist perspective with the key differentiation elements or drivers that characterise the European business school model, and contrast it with the more common, and widely copied, US model.

1.6 DIFFERENCES BETWEEN EUROPEAN AND US BUSINESS SCHOOLS

Table 1.4 provides a 'map' of the key drivers of differentiation between US and European schools. It identifies three sources of difference, namely, *institutional differences*, which are associated with the first phase of our social construction model, in which different viewpoints and interpretations of business schools are debated and shared in a national context; *competitive differences*, which correspond to the second phase of the social construction model, in which markets and a dominant US recipe form, strong competition develops and the key drivers or differentiators between the US and Europe in management education become evident; and, finally, *social capital differences*, which reflect the processes of business school maturation and growth in the third phase of the social construction model, in which national and international brands and school images are formed. Here we examine output and reputation measures for US and European schools. Figure 1.1 also provides a conceptual framing of the differences model, showing the processes of business school evolution 'funnelling into' the mature, established rankings, status and reputation measures (examples of such differences are provided by Amdam, 1997, Baden-Fuller and Ang, 2001, Kipping and Bjarnar, 1998, and Raimond and Halliburton, 1995). Baden-Fuller and Ang (2001) note, in a constructionist vein, that '[s]tatus and reputation are close allies, and reputation is typically defined as the expectation of a high level of quality as perceived by an audience'.

Institutional differences

It is clear that, some thirty to forty years ago, it was important for aspiring European managers to travel to the United States and study at a leading business school there, since they were seen as the 'gold standard' at the time. At present, the situation in Europe (see Table 1.3) is such that there are a range of very good alternative indigenous schools, which focus on Europe's distinctive strengths. Such European models, therefore, have adapted to the institutional frameworks and the many different *languages, cultures* and *regulations* that exist across Europe.

It is also important to recognise that there is a new European order in management education, not only as a result of the Bologna

Table 1.4 *Broad differences between European and US business schools*

		Europe	United States
Institutional differences	Language/ culture/ regulation	Many languages. 27 nation states (European Union). Multicultural. Heavy regulation.	Single language. More homogeneous culture. Low level of regulation.
	Standardisation	Slower acceptance and institutionalisation of B schools.	Fast acceptance and institutionalisation of B schools.
	Size	Small to medium size (c.150 B schools)	Medium to large size (c.800 B schools)
Competitive differences	Governance/ values	Predominantly public funding. Strong public sector linkages.	Predominantly private funding. Weak public sector linkages.
	Funding and endowment	Small endowments. Weaker resource base.	Large endowments. Strong resource base.
	International mindset	International in outlook. Students/faculty more international.	Less international, more insular. Students/faculty less international.

	Innovation	Practical, problem-based learning. Critical, reflective thinking. Range of models: one-year M.B.A.; distance learning; action-oriented learning.	Two-year model for M.B.A. Discipline- and research-based.
	Knowledge transmission/ corporate links	Knowledge conveyed in books and practice-oriented journals. Greater reliance on executive education. Closer to business.	Knowledge conveyed in discipline- and research-based journals. Fewer schools promote executive education.
Social capital differences	Rankings	Lower overall rankings in league tables. Favoured for international outlook, career progress and value for money.	Higher overall rankings in league tables. Favoured for initial salary, salary progress, alumni and research quality.
	Reputation	Some strong brands but, generally, lower brand identity and reputation.	Many strong brands – particularly private schools. High brand identity and reputation.

Accord (signed in 1999) but also because of the influence of European accreditation agencies for degree endorsement. These may upset the balance of power in a significant way. In the case of the main accreditation agencies (AACSB International in the United States and EQUIS in Europe), which provide an attestation as to the quality of a school, there are clearly different criteria and philosophies involved in gaining the European accreditation (EQUIS) and the primarily North American accreditation (AACSB).[4] For EQUIS, there is a much broader focus, a clear examination of executive education and corporate linkages and a definite requirement to explain international linkages. On the other hand, AACSB does not require any discussion of international or corporate linkages, because it simply accredits the institutional range of degree and educational programmes and, mainly, the faculty inputs and curricula designs. As a consequence, EQUIS has a strong European flavour, which stresses the diversity and international linkage theme as an important element in the design of management education, and does not assume the primacy of a single unitary model – the US-based functional and discipline-oriented model – for management training.

As noted earlier, the focus in the United States, on a single, somewhat insular educational model, arose from a rapid institutional *standardisation* of business education. In the United States, the standardisation of business education started very early, and the founding of the AACSB in 1916 provided a significant building block for institutional development, since accreditation could improve the market recognition that various business schools needed.[5] This drove a process of convergence towards similarity and 'mass production'

---

[4] To see the criteria for accreditation, view either website, at www.efmd.org or www.aacsb.edu.

[5] To reflect its growing global role in business school accreditation, AACSB is now called AACSB International – that is, the Association to Advance Collegiate Schools of Business, International. Its website is www.aacsb.edu. An interesting report of contemporary issues facing business education is provided by AACSB (2002).

in business education (Hedmo, Sahlin-Andersson and Wedlin, 2006). The best example of such convergence and standardisation is the successful market acceptance of the M.B.A. title, which quickly established itself as the model for general management education worldwide, becoming both an effective licence to practice management and an attestation of a high standard of business analysis.

However, the standardisation of business education in Europe evolved at a much slower pace, reflecting the diverse influences and the importance of various national bodies and governmental policies. It was over eighty years after AACSB had created a US system of accreditation and audit of business schools that, in 1997, the European Foundation for Management Development developed the European Quality Improvement System. This international system of strategic audit and accreditation was designed by the Europeans for the assessment of their own business schools.[6] Five years earlier the Association of M.B.As. had created an accreditation scheme in the United Kingdom focusing specifically on the growing range of UK M.B.A.-awarding business schools, but this had a much less international focus. Thus, whereas the US-based business school environment achieved rapid standardisation, the European one was relatively slow to standardise; rather, there was a focus on 'national champions' that recognised the differential educational, cultural, legal and language requirements of each European country. In summary, the European model involves a range of 'national champions' as role models, whereas the US model has a much more homogeneous business school model.

The *size* of business schools differs significantly between those in the United States and those in Europe (Alsop, 2002). Size, as a strategic variable, indicates that the school has achieved significant growth and a sound resource base. Size enables business schools to

---

[6] In its first five years of existence EQUIS accredited some fifty institutions in fourteen European countries and another ten outside Europe, in countries such as Australia, Brazil, Canada, Hong Kong, Mexico, South Africa and the United States. Online information on the EFMD is found at www.efmd.be.

generate and exploit the potential of economies of scale and scope – e.g. a broader resource profile, a wider range of programmes and courses and the ability to attract and pay high-quality faculty in order to gain a sustainable, competitive advantage (see Porter, 1980, for a discussion of the role of size as a strategic variable). For example, as a consequence of standardisation and the early acceptance of the M.B.A. model, some of the largest American schools – e.g. Harvard, Kellogg (Northwestern) and Wharton – admit more than 500 M.B.A. students per year, given their much larger markets and global recognition, whereas most of the European programmes tend to be much smaller and focused on national or regional norms. However, it is important to note that, in the competitive marketplace, high-quality niche strategies and programmes offered by small business schools can be very successful. Such is the case, for instance, with IMD in Switzerland, which specialises in international management development for large corporations and offers a small but highly ranked one-year full-time M.B.A. programme. In general, US business schools tend to vary in size from medium-sized to very large (particularly in large state schools, such as Texas and Ohio State), whereas the European schools vary from small to medium-sized, reflecting the wide range of countries, resource bases and contexts in which they operate.

I.7   COMPETITIVE DIFFERENCES

The competitive differences in business school models reflect key drivers of management education and become evident as competitive recipes are shared and as imitative behaviour takes hold. The system of *governance* is a clear difference between the European and US-based business schools. We define governance as the type of financial and legal arrangements that structure the relationships of a school with governmental and private interests. These arrangements can be expressed along a continuum from a privately funded and owned institution to an institution almost entirely reliant on governmental and public funding. In general terms, the present pattern in the United States is one of a competitive abundance of private schools (which have a very significant resource base), alongside public or state schools, whereas in Europe it is one of a clear dominance of publicly funded schools (with more constrained resource bases). For instance, following a detailed analysis of the FT rankings data described earlier, we show in Table 1.5 that, out of the fourteen business schools (eleven from the United States and three from the European Union) that consistently appeared in the top twenty positions over seven years in the *Financial Times* M.B.A. rankings, virtually all of them are private. Thus, the private funding of business education common in the US model is a phenomenon rather uncommon to their European counterparts.

The *funding* and *endowment* of business schools also constitute a major difference between these two regions. Because of the speedy acceptance of the business school in the United States as an established institution and the recognition of the value of private education there – as we indicated above – the US business schools readily undertook fund-raising campaigns, and, as a result, generated financial resources from sponsors, corporations and loyal alumni. The success of this approach to business school development can be seen, for instance, in the case of Harvard Business School, the best endowed of all, which has amassed an endowment of more than $1 billion (Weisman, 2003). In comparison with the situation in the United States, European business schools either have very small endowments or none at all. This has made them much more reliant on annually acquired funds and budgets, and particularly the revenue stream from the M.B.A. programme, in order to manage and develop their resources (Barsoux, 2000). In Europe, typically, if the M.B.A. programme falters then so too does the revenue stream. Therefore, a business model dependent on cash flows – as is the case in most European business schools – is likely to be able to cover operating expenses and generate small surpluses but much less likely to provide significant cash flow to fund new business opportunities or facilities investments in the school. The existence

Table 1.5 Financial Times rankings of M.B.A. programmes, 1999–2005

Business school	Governance	1999	2000	2001	2002	2003	2004	2005	Average ranking
Harvard Business School (US)	Private	1	1	2	2	2	2	1	2
Pennsylvania/Wharton (US)	Private	4	2	1	1	1	1	1	2
Columbia Business School (US)	Private	2	5	5	3	3	3	3	3
Stanford Graduate School (US)	Private	3	3	3	4	4	7	4	4
Chicago GSB (US)	Private	6	6	4	5	5	4	6	5
INSEAD (EU)	Private	11	9	7	6	6	4	8	7
London Business School (EU)	Private/public	8	8	8	9	7	4	5	7
MIT/Sloan (US)	Private	5	4	6	7	10	9	13	8
Northwestern/Kellogg (US)	Private	7	7	9	10	9	11	11	9
NYU/Stern (US)	Private	17	13	10	8	8	8	9	10
Dartmouth/Amos Tuck (US)	Private	9	15	13	11	11	10	7	11
IMD (EU)	Private	13	11	11	14	13	12	13	12
Yale (US)	Private	20	18	20	12	12	13	9	15
Duke Fuqua (US)	Private	15	17	18	19	15	20	18	17

Notes: The following business schools appeared in the top twenty positions at least in one year of the period:
six times: UC Berkeley (Haas) and Virginia (Darden) [public schools];
five times: UCLA (Anderson) [public school];
four times: University of Michigan [public school];
three times: University of Western Ontario (Ivey) and University of North Carolina (Kenan–Flagler) [public schools]; and
two times: Emory and Cornell (Johnson) [private schools].

of private endowments clearly brings financial strength for a school, enabling it to weather the effects of M.B.A. programme downturns and to invest in future growth. This financial independence, autonomy and the capacity to deploy critical resources, in turn, reinforce and build upon a business school's image and strategic positioning.

Despite the relative lack of financial muscle in Europe, the European business schools and their leaders have always possessed a strong *international mindset* (Cabrera, 2003). This mindset means that the European openness to international business, languages, diversity and culture is a competitive advantage. Europeans have learnt how to deal with the complexities of international trade and, more importantly, have developed a strong motivation for success in international business and, with it, a distinctive approach to management education. It is also clear from a further detailed 'variance analysis' of the *Financial Times* rankings data that students attending European M.B.A. programmes will be taught by a more international faculty and meet a more diverse set of students than equivalent US students (see the analysis in Table 1.6). As a consequence, they should be able to develop language and cross-cultural skills and sensitivities during their business school experience that will help them to succeed in a world of international trade and globalisation.

Flexibility and *innovation* are also key competitive advantages of European schools. They have experimented with, and adopted, alternative delivery technologies much more speedily than their US counterparts. For example, Henley Management College, the Open University Business School and WBS in the United Kingdom are among the world leaders in distance learning forms of the M.B.A. Europeans have also innovated with a much more flexible one-year M.B.A. model (see Cass, Judge, Leicester and Warwick, for example) and have not slavishly followed the analytic, functional and discipline-oriented two-year US M.B.A. model. European schools have also focused on a learning style rather than a teaching style (defined by discipline-based knowledge and the faculty's way of knowing) of management education (Boyatzis, Cowen and Kolb,

Table 1.6 *Relative performance of US and EU business schools*

Criterion	Deviation of US business schools' average rating from top twenty average rating	Deviation of EU business schools' average rating from top twenty average rating	EU business schools' average rating performance relative to US business schools' average rating
Salary-weighted	−23	−42	−20
Salary increase	−14	−65	−51
Value for money	−6	10	15
Career progress	−16	6	21
Aims achieved	−3	−2	1
Placement success	−6	−34	−28
Employed at three months	−2	−3	−1
Alumni recommendation	−173	−651	−477
Women faculty	13	15	2
Women students	1	−3	−4
International faculty	−66	0	66
International students	−25	40	65
Faculty with doctorates	−2	−34	−32
FT doctoral rating	−5	−16	−11
FT research rating	−37	−296	−259

Notes: All figures are expressed as percentages. The criteria are those used in the FT rankings (see *The Financial Times*), which contains around 100 schools in its annual global ranking of M.B.A. programmes. The top twenty schools are similar to those in Table 1.5. The EU business schools are those in the FT rankings outside the top twenty, and their averages are compared to either the average of the top twenty schools or the average of US schools in the rankings outside the top twenty over the period 1999 to 2002. For example, in the case of the 'Alumni recommendation' criterion, the average US school ranking is 173 per cent below that of the average of the top twenty schools, while the average EU school rating is 651 per cent below that of the average of the top twenty schools. Further, the EU average performance is 477 per cent below that of the US schools on this criterion. Clearly, when positive signs occur in the percentages, EU schools score better than US or top twenty schools. This occurs across criteria such as 'Value for money', 'Career progress', 'Women faculty' and 'International students'.
Source: Antunes and Thomas (2007).

1994). They have adopted problem-centred, project-based learning, with field studies and consulting projects and an emphasis on practice and critical, reflective thinking – i.e. the aim is to understand the student's way of knowing and learning, and to pace the flow of understanding and logic with the student's manifest capabilities.

Europeans also tend to *transmit knowledge* through books, media articles and practice-based journals and often eschew the so-called 'top journals' in the field, which have a primarily academic, discipline-based orientation. For example, of the forty top journals in the ratings in the FT M.B.A. rankings, thirty-three are US-based with a focus on disciplines and cutting-edge research. Few European journals are listed; nevertheless, there is a strong knowledge development tradition in Europe, the Scandinavian approach, for instance, being codified in journals such as the *Scandinavian Journal of Economics and Management*. Moreover, the European Group of Organisational Studies (EGOS) has nearly 1,000 members at its annual conference, publishes the journal *Organisation Studies* and presents a critical and interpretative perspective on the field of organisation studies that is Europe-centred.

European schools have also been extremely successful in establishing *corporate linkages* and partnerships, and have managed to transfer that success to the classroom. With the absence of endowment funding in Europe, European schools have developed creative ways to develop research and learning programmes with corporations that are directly linked to corporate problems and issues. As a consequence, European schools have focused on solving relevant business (as opposed to academic) problems and have placed the solution of business problems and executive education as high priorities in their visions, missions and overarching strategic intent.

1.8   SOCIAL CAPITAL DIFFERENCES: REPUTATION EFFECTS AND BRAND LOYALTY

In aggregate, following the logic of the social construction model, the interactions of the institutionalising and market development processes over the longer term produce what are known as 'reputation effects'. Reputation effects can clearly influence the patterns of competition for resources in the business school market, since reputation hierarchies act as mobility barriers for the entry of new, upcoming schools into the elite, high-reputation category or strategic group (on competition for resources, see Podolny, 1993; on reputation hierarchies as mobility barriers, see Lippman and Rumelt, 1982, and McGee, Thomas and Wilson, 2005). Moreover, this elite category tends to form a 'closed system', which is difficult to penetrate. In the case of business schools, as D'Aveni (1996) argues, reputation across different audiences influences the ability to gather resources.

In parallel with these reputation effects, a high degree of brand loyalty also develops amongst a school's alumni. Those who invested their time and money in acquiring a degree or qualification from a high-quality school want the symbolic value of this degree to be recognised and enhanced over time. Since reputation has self-reinforcing dynamics, this loyalty reinforces the reputation of the business school itself, facilitates the acquisition of new students and resources and produces a virtuous circle. Baden-Fuller and Ang (2001) describe this process as 'building a "charmed-circle" of resources and benefits'.

We can further substantiate our argument for these reputation effects by re-examining the evolution of the rank performance of the top twenty business schools over the seven-year period of the full-time M.B.A. ranking of *The Financial Times*. Table 1.5, described earlier, shows that fourteen schools were present in this top twenty for the whole seven-year period, with little change in their average ranking. Out of these fourteen top business schools, only three were European (INSEAD, LBS and IMD – which are primarily private and tend to follow a US-style model), while eleven were from the United States. Table 1.5 shows the remarkable lack of mobility in the top schools' rankings, particularly when bearing in mind that the FT ranking covers more than 100 schools worldwide.

Similar findings are obtained from the business school rankings of *Business Week*. Gioia and Corley (2002) report that only a very small elite group of schools consistently occupy the top positions and show that, over the twelve years in their study, only fifteen schools have ever been in the top ten. These data reveal a pattern in which a select, predominantly private and well-endowed group of schools consistently score the top ranking positions and are labelled 'winners' by the media. Therefore, we believe that the schools in the top twenty are likely to profit most significantly in terms of status from the brand and reputation effects they have developed over the period of their existence.

Overall, the combination of brand loyalty and reputation effects implies the existence of critical differences between the top twenty schools and those outside the top twenty. We suspect that this could be particularly true with respect to the main European schools. European business schools do not have the same strategic orientation as US schools and position themselves in the marketplace against criteria that more closely reflect the cultural and competitive characteristics of those markets. As pointed out earlier, the analysis in Table 1.6 shows that European schools rate much more highly on international dimensions, career progress and value for money but fall behind on the salary, research and alumni criteria. The latter criteria, of course, reflect longer-established reputations.

Moreover, the perception that high-paying employers have of the quality of particular business schools is itself crucial in deciding the salary offered to new recruits. Those schools that are able to establish a reputation with such employers or place students into 'top flight', fast-track career channels are more likely to create a self-sustaining momentum for success in the 'rankings game'. In general, the more established US business schools in terms of size and endowment clearly benefit from such reputation advantages.

It is also noteworthy that the fourteen schools that remained in the top twenty group for all seven years of the FT rankings (Table 1.5) are all, primarily, US-based (or -modelled) private institutions with large endowments. These well-endowed business schools, therefore, have access to greater financial resources with which to make strategic investments and hire high-quality, research-productive faculty. The lower European faculty salaries and the relative lack of clear and appropriate incentives for research productivity contrast with the strong research orientation and heavy investments in research by top US business schools. This makes it increasingly difficult for European business schools to bridge the research gap between themselves and the top US business schools, if this research standard comes to be evaluated by a standardised norm of predominantly American origin (Baden-Fuller, Ravazzolo and Schweizer, 2000).

However, European schools see such US-dominated rankings as a useful source of market information but not necessarily the ultimate standard to be targeted and scaled. Rather, as van Roon (2003) notes, 'the [European] schools see rankings as a valuable source of business intelligence, that can drive decision-making aimed at developing the school's products and services. Schools, however, say they try hard to resist pressure to radically alter the school on a more fundamental level to cater better to the [FT] ranking's criteria, seeing this as a challenge to their identity and value system.' In essence, both European and US critics would argue that accreditation and rankings are forcing deans to focus on the wrong things – that is, image management – at the expense of focusing on, for example, narrowing the gap between theory and practice, and providing sound advice to professional managers (Zimmerman, 2001).

1.9   SUMMARY

The strengths of the leading US business schools (see also Tables 1.4 and 1.6) derive from the competitive advantages associated with their gains as 'fast first movers' in management education – i.e. product standardisation (e.g. M.B.A.), business school legitimisation, strong and well-established brands and reputations (e.g. Harvard,

Wharton) and, above all, significant financial strength and very large private endowments fuelling their strategic positioning in the marketplace. In essence, as a consequence of rapid standardisation and the rapid adoption of the business school in the United States, monetary resources in abundance 'moved mountains' in establishing US business schools and their curricula, and in developing strong brand images and reputations internationally (see Tables 1.5 and 1.6). Alongside these elite US schools, a cadre of other strong US schools developed in state universities and private schools.

European business schools, on the other hand, have developed strength mainly over the last twenty or thirty years, with the rapid development of business schools in higher education worldwide. The initial shortage of key faculty to staff the schools was solved by sending promising young faculty from European countries to leading US schools to complete their postgraduate study. There were clear initiatives in the United Kingdom (via the Foundation for Management Development) and in France and other countries, through government-sponsored initiatives, to provide doctoral fellowships/scholarships for study in the United States. These newly minted US-trained, but European, Ph.D. students then returned to join home faculties and developed curricula defined and derived, initially at least, from their US experience. However, quite quickly leading programmes in Europe developed their own identity as students and faculty sought to make them more relevant to the business practices and customs in their own countries. As a consequence, 'national' champions and role models developed from the 1970s through to the 1990s (see Tables 1.3 and 1.4), with distinct identities and competitive characteristics, and they have reinforced their reputational position over the last decade (see Figure 1.1 and Tables 1.5 and 1.6). Since they never possessed the abundant financial resources of their US counterparts, the European schools positioned themselves uniquely in their markets as niche, segmented players, targeting their distinctive, national and regional characteristics and the requirements of their management audiences.

1.10 EMERGING ISSUES AND CHALLENGES: RETHINKING THE BUSINESS SCHOOL

Starkey, Hatchuel and Tempest (2004) and Starkey and Tiratsoo (2007) make the case for a reconfigured business school playing a central role in the context of the new economy and knowledge society. Such a school would develop new thinking and knowledge and provide a reflective and reflexive site for enquiry about business management. They contrast this knowledge-based business school with alternative scenarios of *business-as-usual* – i.e. variations of the existing US model of business school practice; *takeover* by management consultants/alternative providers, leading to 'dumbing down' and the commoditisation of programmes; or *more academic models*, focused on either a professional school – i.e. a practically relevant agenda – model or a more rigorous intellectual agenda grounded either in the social sciences or the liberal arts agenda (Ivory *et al.*, 2006).

A dilemma for any business school dean is that of balancing the twin hurdles of academic rigour and practical relevance (Pettigrew, 1997b). On the one hand, business schools must produce academically rigorous and scholarly research, but, on the other hand, they have to demonstrate the impact and relevance of their research to the problems and issues faced by managers in practice. The question is: how can business schools be more relevant to the 'clinical' art that defines the profession of management (Schoemaker, 2008)? Starkey and Madan (2001) argue that the increasing relevance gap needs to be bridged, otherwise it will be filled by rivals and alternative providers, such as consultants or corporate universities. However, the means of bridging this gap are unclear (Grey, 2007), but the best advice would appear to be the proposition that business schools should engage in cutting-edge, rigorous, academic research on management that is informed by the context and practical insights about management gained from engagement with management issues and challenges.

There is also a strong and important debate, inspired by Khurana (2007) and Khurana and Nohria (2008), about the art of management and, in particular, the idea of management as a profession. Although he accepts that it is difficult for business schools to codify and agree a common and acceptable body of knowledge defining management, Khurana maintains that business schools have lost their moral and ethical high ground in educating business leaders. Podolny (2009) echoes this theme, and argues that business schools need to show that they value what society values. They need, inter alia, to reinvent themselves as highly professional scholarly educational service organisations, communicate the view that money is not the only reason to do an M.B.A., redefine what they teach and how they teach it and expel students who violate codes of conduct. In essence, business schools need to critically examine their purpose, which Hay (2008; emphasis in original) argues is 'to create value through three types of value, namely, *academic value*, through research and its dissemination; *personal value*, through their teaching; and *public and social value*, in the form of knowledgeable and skilled graduates and through the way they engage in the societies in which they are based'. Clearly, business schools need to emphasise new directions that provide a sense of identity – moral and intellectual – that will serve society better (e.g. avoid Enron-type management scandals) and produce more ethical, professional, critical and creative business leaders in the future.

I.II   A COMPELLING CONTEXT FOR BUSINESS SCHOOLS AND THEIR LEADERSHIP

It is clear that the history of business schools has been short but significant. In a little over 125 years business schools have successfully established themselves as relevant, renowned academic institutions, whether as part of prestigious universities or as stand-alone management education providers. The pursuit of their initial purpose – to professionalise management, in the process building its own body of knowledge, rules and values – has shifted from a combination of individual insights shared by savvy, veteran managers and practical advice to a more scientific approach that encompasses several academic disciplines. In addition to shaping management practices and knowledge and educating business leaders, their role as liaisons between the academic and business worlds afforded them great visibility and influence. As businesses expanded internationally and American management practices seemed to prevail, the demand for management education became more intense, and new business schools in some European countries and, later, in Asia and Latin America joined the pioneering US institutions in a burgeoning industry. However, business schools around the world soon found themselves confronted by the double hurdle of delivering answers to relevant practical business dilemmas while simultaneously deploying scholarly research to expand and deepen critical management knowledge.

The sweeping forces of globalisation have had an immense impact on business and, therefore, on business schools. Schools have had to decide how to approach internationalisation. Some have remained local, with their activities focused in just one city or country; others have forged partnerships and alliances with schools in other countries; while a few have built campuses in other countries and continents. They have also had to develop the ability to attract and educate multicultural faculty and students. However, probably the most challenging globalisation issue has been incorporating truly international business content and issues into their programmes. As talent development turned into a strategic asset for every organisation over the past two decades, corporations increasingly demanded more and better executive education and training for their hosts of managers worldwide. At the same time, business schools have been required to further customise their programmes, contents and delivery formats, while enhancing their cost efficiency.

Indeed, business schools have become particularly visible and central as the interface between the business world and the academic community. The dramatic worldwide rise in the number of business schools in recent decades clearly points to their significant role: almost exclusively American for some time, they are now found on six continents. Not only has an M.B.A. become the logical next educational step for a large number of university graduates around the world but corporations have entered into a new stage marked by their recognition of management development as a strategic asset to be included in their budgets. This fact also points to their success as higher education institutions, as they have managed to carve not just a sound reputation for themselves but a growing, international market as well.

With the new millennium has come a new stage in business school history. Across the globe, management schools now face truly intense international competition. Marketplaces have become more globalised and demanding, as domestic boundaries no longer fuel preferences or amount to actual barriers. Thus, circumstances are driving business schools to review their academic value propositions so as to cater to more sophisticated audiences and to respond to more taxing and fast-changing needs. Their quest for differentiation has turned into an urgent need that demands enhanced and targeted efforts. In an increasingly mature industry, these institutions are forced to differentiate themselves and to deepen their focus in order to fend off competitors as well as to respond to the shifting requirements of both business and society. Indeed, as the world struggles amid unprecedented economic and financial turmoil, with the fundamentals of capitalism and the free market system shaken and profoundly questioned, business schools are expected to contribute new knowledge and sound management education to help reshape critical aspects of global regulations and policies so as to strengthen, improve and, thereby, relegitimise the free enterprise model.

While critical views have zeroed in on a number of problems and shortcomings that management education institutions need to address immediately, several contributions have been made to help them overcome new challenges and to meet the ever-changing demands of practitioners and scholars alike. Some critics claim that business schools have become too close to the corporate world, abandoning their original and valuable mission of transforming management into a respected 'profession'. Most recently, in his book *From Higher Aims to Hired Hands*, Khurana (2007) argues that business schools have strayed from their intended role as professional schools meant not only to prepare students for managerial positions but also to drive the legitimacy of management as a bona fide profession.

As students seem to pursue an M.B.A. solely as a means of gaining a larger pay packet, and the current financial crisis and business scandals offer highly visible examples of corporate greed and reckless behaviour, some observers have begun to question whether there is sufficient emphasis on ethics and corporate social responsibility in M.B.A. and executive education programmes. A recent survey of the top fifty business schools in the United States found that 'three major features of the ideal M.B.A. curriculum – soft skill development, corporate social responsibility, and a global perspective – continue to get short shrift'.[7]

The critical influence of management education rankings from business publications such as *The Financial Times*, *The Wall Street Journal*, *Forbes* and *BusinessWeek* has increased over the years, making competition even more intense between schools. Rankings are based on the academic quality of business schools and measure several factors, ranging from the estimated return on an M.B.A. education to the opinion of recruiters and overall school reputation. To secure a high-ranking position, a school must produce high-quality research and generate new ideas – neither of which outcomes necessarily translates into stellar classroom experiences for students. This pressure to focus on research in order to remain high in the rankings is at odds with what schools' corporate customers demand – that is, relevant business takeaways. However, for Khurana, while rankings have forced business schools to pay more attention to both their mission and their environment, some institutions have been trapped in the tyranny of these powerful measurements, reshaping their

---

[7] See www.businessweek.com/bschools/content/apr2008/bs20080422_496936.htm.

academic offerings and shifting their focus purely to merit a higher score next time.

Although business schools face the pressures of the business world, such as a need for funding and increased competition, they are also immersed in the idiosyncratic struggles of academia. In this respect, the leadership challenges in business schools are like those in professional service firms and consulting partnerships – namely, achieving a strong balance between enhancing the skills and creativity of academics and leading them to agree on the future strategic pathways for the business school. For example, there are the ever-present, often conflicting pressures to produce scholarly and vigorous research while remaining relevant to corporate customers, who insist upon germane business content. The tension from these two different worlds has created a number of different responses from business schools. For some authors, the trend towards a more scholarly faculty profile has prevailed over business relevance. Bennis and O'Toole (2005) argue that 'business schools are on the wrong track. MBA programs face intense criticism for failing to impart useful skills, failing to prepare leaders, failing to instil norms of ethical behaviour – and even failing to lead graduates to good corporate jobs.' In short, these authors believe that business schools are focusing excessively on research, weakening their ability to teach students how to 'wrangle with complex, unquantifiable issues – in other words, the stuff of management'. Mintzberg's telling comment (2004) is that business schools should be developing 'managers, not MBAs'.

In his book *New Vision for Management Education*, Peter Lorange (2002), former dean of IMD, argues that, as a result of these pressures, business schools often lack strategic focus: they strive to satisfy their stakeholders' every need – delivering M.B.A. and Ph.D. programmes, embarking on scholarly research, designing customised programmes for corporate clients – and simply spread themselves too thin. For Lorange, business schools need to have and pursue a clear and focused strategic direction. In addition, as he puts it, 'strategy means choice': these institutions cannot afford to embrace an opportunistic approach if they are to successfully live up to their mission.

Researchers and industry analysts now feel that the M.B.A. as a product is at a new stage of maturity, with a number of challenges to overcome and different choices to make in terms of content design, length, experience delivered and outputs. In our view, this is just one of the numerous challenges business schools need to confront if they want not only to survive but to contribute to society, by adding real and substantial value to business leaders and organisations at three critical domains: *knowing*, *doing* and *being*. In fact, the academic sector at large is also confronting the challenges faced by business schools.

In conclusion, a range of general leadership issues and challenges that may be faced by business schools in the future are identified below. The issues include the following.

- The urgent need to enhance faculty salaries, given talent supply shortages.
- Broadening the role of research relative to the twin hurdles of rigour and relevance.
- The privatisation of business schools, to improve the financial resource base.
- Building international perspectives.
- Linking entrepreneurship to business education.
- Balancing public and private management skills.
- Defining the role, ethical compass and meaning of management education.

Challenges include the following.

- Rigour versus relevance.
- Research versus professional models.
- Balancing research and pedagogy.
- Understanding cultural differences.
- Building and managing alliances.
- Technology enhancements.
- Fund-raising.

2 Business schools as professional organisations (professional service firms)

2.1 INTRODUCTION

The increasing complexity of the role of the business school dean over time is evident from the rapid competitive evolution of business schools and the parallel challenges of growth (Davies and Thomas, 2009). Indeed, Starkey and Tiratsoo (2007: 55) note that 'forty years ago running a business school was something a senior professor might well take as a matter of duty shortly before retirement. Nowadays deans almost constitute a profession in their own right, a cohort with unique and specialist skills.' As noted in Chapter 1, the current rigours of the deanship role are exacerbated by strong criticisms of the business school and questions as to the legitimacy of business and management as an academic discipline, coupled with increasing globalised competition for experts and students and a diverse range of stakeholder interests.

Typically, in business schools, deans have grappled with the issues of the balance between rigour and relevance (Zell, 2005) and that between academic and professional practice (Grey, 2002), which they have attempted to address by creating scholarly and professional reputations alike. In this respect, deans have to learn to champion both the academic values of the university/academy and the professional values of their external management constituency without appearing two-faced (Fagin, 1997; Gmelch, 2004: 78). This has led several deans to compare themselves to partners in professional service firms (Davies and Thomas, 2009). That is, they argue that they are promoted on the basis of expertise, knowledge and intellectual capital to leadership/management positions, in which their subsequent accumulation of political and social capital then combines to generate economic and reputational – i.e. cultural – capital for the business/professional school (Nahapiet and Ghoshal, 1998).

This chapter explores whether the identification by some deans of a business school as a PSF can be justified from the extensive literature on professional service firms and knowledge-intensive firms. It begins with a classification of the business school as a professional form of organisation (Mintzberg, 2007) and then examines a range of issues concerning leadership and management in business schools through the identification of the key characteristics and decision-making processes of PSFs and KIFs.

2.2   THE BUSINESS SCHOOL AS A PROFESSIONAL SCHOOL

Mintzberg's important work on patterns in strategy formation provides the intellectual background for the examination of the business school as a professional organisation.

In his work on the structuring of organisations, Mintzberg (1979) proposes four types of organisations – entrepreneurial, machine, adhocracy and professional – of which the latter two most closely resemble a business school. They are defined as follows (342).

Adhocracy organisations: characterised by a dynamic external environment and decentralised internal power, and organised around teams of experts working on projects to produce novel outputs, generally in highly dynamic settings.

Professional organisations: characterised by a stable external environment and decentralised internal power, and dependent on highly skilled workers who work rather autonomously, subject to professional norms, mostly providing standardised services in stable settings.

Mintzberg (287–318) has studied the strategic development pathways over time of both McGill University, where he lectures, and himself as researcher and professor in the context of McGill. This involved examining the university's actions over time, investigating their origins and the decisions that lay behind them.

Mintzberg describes McGill University as the classic professional organisation, with a highly trained corps of professors pursuing their own interpretation of the organisation's mission of teaching and researching, with little or no collective strategic planning or strategic learning and with strategic venturing being largely an individual pursuit. These individual professionals researched typically around an established stable paradigm. They shaped their strategies in association with colleagues in their own departments and, just as importantly, in association with their professional colleagues and associations – e.g. the Academy of Management, which sets their standards of practice. Moreover, their individual strategies tended to dominate those of the professional organisation – e.g. the business school – whose overall leadership with regard to strategy formation is found to be somewhat weaker than in the adhocratic form, with its organisation of professionals into teams.

Table 2.1 shows the configurations of the organisational form and the strategy formation process contrasting the adhocracy organisation with the professional organisation (which is most likely to resemble a business school).

However, it should be noted that the adhocratic and professional forms may sometimes overlap, as, for example, when research teams or subject groups – pockets of 'adhocracy' – coexist in professional organisations such as business schools. Further, the relationship of individual professionals with their environments can be similar to project teams, involving processes of constant recycling and feedback. Nonetheless, professional work is often more standardised and established in terms of stable norms than the more innovatory team work of adhocracy teams.

Mintzberg's work on patterns of strategy formation and strategic processes establishes the business school as an exemplar of the professional organisation form, given that its academics operate individually and in a decentralised fashion but with a weaker but supportive leadership involving tacit coordination and supportive and mentoring management styles.

Table 2.1 *Configurations of organisational form and strategy formation process*

	Adhocracy organisation	Professional organisation
Conditions	Innovation, high technology, dynamic environment	Skilled workers, stable environment
Power vested in	Project teams	Each professional
Integration	Loosely coupled	Decoupled
Favoured strategy process	Collective learning (and venturing)	Individual venturing
Strategies	Emergent positions and perspectives	Portfolio of individual positions (deliberate and emergent)
Pattern of change	Cycling in and out of focus	Frequent shifts of positions within overall stability
Environment, leadership, organisation	Environment takes the lead	Professionals in the organisation take the lead
Key strategic issue	Collective mind?	Strategic management in question

Source: Adapted from Mintzberg (1979: 362).

Bryman's (2007) extensive study of the findings of research on effective leadership in higher education also stresses that, in the context of departmental leadership, academic staff (professionals) expect the following supportive management features: the maintenance of autonomy; consultation over important decisions; the fostering of collegiality (both democratic decision-making and mutual cooperativeness); and fighting the department's corner with senior managers and through university structures (3). He also points out that much of the leadership literature suggests that academics or professionals would react against a directive style of overt leadership, since it would interface with their autonomy. Instead, a minimalist leadership style is preferred (Middlehurst, 1993), and this is confirmed by Mintzberg (1998: 143) when he suggests that professional workers expect little direct supervision from managers and require a covert form of leadership involving 'protection and support' that creates legitimacy and reputation for their department. Raelin (1991, 1995) emphasises that central to the leadership and management of academics is the 'management of autonomy'. He also argues that collegiality, in terms of critical debate and open examination, and persuasion should dominate bureaucratic control if processes of strategic change are to be successful in the management of professional academics.

Given this background, therefore, we explore further the conception of the business school as a professional service firm or a knowledge-intensive firm. We first define PSFs and KIFs and then identify their key characteristics (features) and key processes. The linkage between characteristics and processes then leads to a thorough examination of the literature on leading and managing professional service firms. The chapter concludes with a discussion of the main leadership challenges in PSFs and, by association, business schools.

2.3   WHAT IS A PROFESSIONAL SERVICE FIRM?

There is an extremely varied and wide-ranging literature on PSFs and KIFs suggesting that there are strong similarities between them (Løwendahl, 2000; Maister, 1993). One common characteristic is the description of what constitutes a professional service. For example, lawyers, architects and auditors, among others, deliver professional services and are excluded from selling their services if they are not members of the corresponding professional association. Other vocational groups, such as business consultants, have not succeeded in establishing their professional association firmly. There is no set body of knowledge for consultants as such, and, in fact, many management consultants are members of established professions – e.g. accountancy and the legal profession – in addition to being consultants. Moreover, there is no licensing of management consultants, and there is no professional organisation with the right to supervise and potentially exclude consultants from practising.

Løwendahl (2000) does not attempt to classify the people delivering professional services, finding it more meaningful to talk about professional services as a special type of service. Along these lines, she goes on to say that 'management consultants may deliver a service regarded as professional as that of lawyers' (19). In a similar vein, Teece (2003) defines a PSF as an expert services firm – that is, a professional firm whose primary product is the delivery of expert services. He further notes that university faculties have similar attributes to PSFs and argues that 'experts, be they medical doctors, professors…, [d]esire high autonomy and can be self-motivated and self-directed because of their deep expertise. The university environment caters for this magnificently with the tenure system – requiring the discharge of teaching, research, and service obligations by faculty, but allowing the individual faculty member considerable discretion as to whether and when (other than meeting class) tasks are performed' (907).

On the other hand, Alvesson (2004), Blackler (1995) and Løwendahl (2000) offer a range of definitions of KIFs that stress the critical importance of the intellectual and knowledge dimensions of high-quality professionals to the success of those organisations.

- Alvesson (2004) defines KIFs as 'companies where most work can be said to be of an intellectual nature and where well-educated, qualified employees form the major part of the workforce'.
- Blackler (1995) describes KIFs as 'organisations staffed by a high proportion of highly qualified staff who trade in knowledge itself'.
- Løwendahl (2000) argues that there are three generic types of KIF – i.e. client relation organisations, problem-solving and creative organisations and solution and output organisations. Table 2.2 shows the three generic contributions in relation to the internal/external focus aspects of the KIF. A business school, or university department, would probably be categorised in her terms as a problem-solving/creative organisation.

Table 2.2 *KIFs defined by internal/external focus*

External focus / Internal Focus	Clients	Problems/ creative solutions	Standardised/ branded solutions
Organisationally controlled			Solution and output organisations
Individually, team- and organisationally controlled		Problem- solving and creative organisations	
Individually controlled	Client relation organizations		

Mintzberg (1989) also refers to PSFs and KIFs in an inclusive way. He considers the following establishments to be either PSFs or KIFs: universities, general hospitals, accounting firms, law firms and engineering firms, among others. Like most of the authors above, he underlines certain key aspects, such as: a high level of knowledge and skills; autonomy and discretional judgement based on professional expertise; a close relationship between professionals and clients; difficulties in coordination; and duality between the power of the professional and administrative bureaucracy.

Morris and Empson (1998) clearly assert that PSFs (accounting firms and consulting firms, among others) can be considered KIFs even though they recognise that the role knowledge plays in PSFs has received little research attention, and that it might be important in the future to consider it as an objectively definable and key resource for PSFs. We therefore conclude that the terms 'PSF' and 'KSF' can be used, interchangeably, to describe a wide range of professional organisations including business schools.

2.4   THE KEY FEATURES AND CHARACTERISTICS
OF PSFS

Table 2.3 identifies the key features and characteristics of PSFs as proposed by a range of authors. These characteristics are summarised and discussed in the following subsections.

Individual professionals

As Løwendahl (2000: 41) mentions, PSFs provide innovative problem-solving services, based on a high degree of professional expertise and individual judgement. She adds, 'The core of the resource base of the professional service firm resides in the professionals employed and their ability to solve whatever problems the clients may want them to solve.' Therefore, professionals are key resources, and one of the main challenges for PSFs is attracting and retaining the most valuable professionals.

The literature on the subject focuses mainly on three broadly defined unique characteristics of individuals: (1) the need for autonomy; (2) career development focused on professional expertise; and (3) a stronger link to professional standards and values than to the PSF that employs them.

The first characteristic, the professional's need for *autonomy*, is the perceived right to make decisions about both the means and the goals associated with one's work (Bartol, 1979). This implies that professionals require the independence to define problems and generate solutions without pressure from clients, non-members of the professions, or the employing organisation (Hall, 1968; Scott and Scott, 1965).

The second main characteristic of the professional is the focus on *professional expertise* and the desire to avoid repetitive or managerial tasks. Indeed, Hinings, Brown and Greenwood (1991) identify professional expertise as the main source of power in PSFs. This may be the reason a professional's career development is more focused on the level and quality of professional expertise, rather than on progress in the administrative or management hierarchy.

Table 2.3 *Key features of PSFs*

Important authors	Individual professionals	Professional competences	Shared power	Intangibility	Standardisation/ customisation	Trust
Løvendahl (2000)	X	X		X		
Bartol (1979)	X	X				
Bucher and Sterling (1969)	X		X			
Montagna (1968)	X		X			
Hall (1968)	X					
Scott (1965)	X					
Kerr, Von Glinow and Schriesheim (1977)	X					
Hinings, Brown and Greenwood (1991)	X					
Friedson and Rhea (1965)	X					
Goode (1960)	X					
Hrebiniak and Alutto (1972)	X					
Empson (2000)	X	X		X		
Paulin (2000)		X				X
Pettigrew and Fenton (2000)		X		X	X	X

Table 2.3 (*cont.*)

Key features Important authors	Individual professionals	Professional competences	Shared power	Intangibility	Standardisation/customisation	Trust
Maister (1993)		X		X	X	
Aharoni (1997)		X				
Liedtka et al. (1997)		X				
Mintzberg (1989)		X	X		X	
Greenwood, Hinings and Brown (1990)			X			
Mills et al. (1983)			X	X		
Greenwood, Hinings and Brown (1994)			X			
Winch and Schneider (1993)				X		
Larson (1977)				X		
Nachum (1999)				X		
Morris and Empson (1998)					X	
Sharma (1997)						X
Thakor (2000)						X
Bloom (1984)						X
Hill and Neeley (1988)						X
Hill and Motes (1995)						X

Finally, professionals demonstrate a *stronger link to their professional standards and values than to the PSF that employs them*. This can be seen in the importance professionals attribute to their reputation among their peers, professional standards and ethical values (Bucher and Sterling, 1969). This strong link to the profession is particularly relevant for PSFs, since it provides a network and helps its professionals to keep up to date. In the words of Løwendahl (2000: 115),

> The professionals bring to the firm their expertise, their experience, their skills in relationship building and maintenance, their professional reputation, their network of professional peer contacts, and their established relationship with past, present and potential clients. These strategic resources are critical to the success of PSFs, but they are to a large extent owned and controlled by the individual professionals rather than by the firm itself.

In conclusion, it is important to note that academics in business schools clearly demonstrate all the characteristics of individual professionals.

Professional competences

PSFs need individuals with 'professional competences', which include *professional knowledge, skills* and *attitudes* that enable them to develop the required ability to comprehend and analyse the diverse situations that they face with new projects and situations.

Professional knowledge should not just be acquired but constantly updated as well. Knowledge may generally be acquired in two ways: through formal education or by participating in challenging and innovative projects, thus refining the participant's problem-solving experiences. In PSFs the latter is more frequent, and so their ability to generate interesting projects is often the key to attracting and retaining the best professionals. Empson (2000) considers that the PSF's main input is professional expertise, and that the output includes the services or products created to solve clients' problems. However, not only is knowledge based on 'objective facts' but it is also a socially constructed learning process. Therefore, knowledge is altered by beliefs about what is useful and what is not, or about what generates value and what does not: a combination of professional and social institutions legitimate knowledge (Zucker, 1987). Morris and Empson (1998) suggest that knowledge in PSFs can be viewed as 'information which professionals acquire through experience and training, together with the judgement which they develop over time which enables them to deploy that information effectively in order to deliver client service'. This creates information asymmetry between PSFs and their clients, which adds value to PSFs' knowledge base.

On account of the idiosyncrasy of professional services, the degree of information asymmetry varies not only from one client to another but also from one project to another. In such a demanding atmosphere, professionals should always remain one step ahead of their clients with the necessary competence to continue delivering valuable services. Indeed, as Løwendahl (2000: 37) points out, 'the challenges of the knowledge gap between the professional service provider and the client representative(s) lie at the very core of the management of professional service firms, and contain both a fundamental and a strategic dimension'. The strategic dimension can be identified through the type of projects the PSF undertakes. Information asymmetry also involves positioning the firm in relation to the different types of clients, since the delivery process will differ from client firms with specialists on the subject and those that do not have them. Løwendahl suggests that the wider the knowledge gap, the more pedagogical the service provider must be, therefore providing not only a service but also a learning experience to its customer. As a result, information asymmetry requires that professionals possess pedagogical skills in order to guarantee that the knowledge transfer processes are managed effectively.

It should be emphasised that professional skills of individual judgement, and interpersonal and pedagogical skills, have a clear impact. In terms of the client–PSF relationship, they strengthen the link with potential and current clients. Further, in terms of the internal communication processes, they promote interaction and the potential for information-sharing with other professionals, regardless of their area of expertise.

Innovation is also a key competence of the PSF delivery process. Mintzberg (1989: 190) notes: 'In the professional organisation, major innovation also depends on cooperation. The single professional may perfect existing programs, but new ones usually cut across the established speciality...and so call for collective action. As a result, the reluctance of the professionals to cooperate with each other and the complexity of the collective processes can produce resistance to innovation.' The PSF may, therefore, have to design reward systems so as to promote cooperative behaviour among professionals, since cooperation is a key skill for PSF members. In innovatory project situations, the professional's desire for autonomy and the 'dual authority' system sometimes makes it difficult to align and coordinate the actions of all PSF members.

The key attitudinal dimension of professionalism, namely 'ethics', is an essential element of the professional's repertoire (Bartol, 1979). This involves a responsibility to avoid self-interest and emotional involvement with clients in the course of rendering services, as well as being dedicated to providing high-quality service to the client.

Shared power

Another key characteristic of PSFs is the diffusion of power among professionals, who expect to participate in strategic decision-making as a sign of trust and respect from the organisation. The unique characteristics of such a shared power system are its emphasis on collegiality, peer evaluation, autonomy, informality and structural flexibility (Bucher and Sterling, 1969; Montagna, 1968).

An even narrower definition of shared power has been proposed, which focuses solely on 'collegiality, peer evaluation, and autonomy' (Greenwood, Hinings and Brown, 1990: 733). In addition, in PSFs authority is a key component, because of their collegial and fragile nature. Typically, there is only a minimal hierarchy: a chief executive who holds office at the will of his colleagues, and who acts within a system of shared decision-making on all major policy issues.

Authority is generally defined as 'a relationship in which the subordinate voluntarily surrenders his own judgement and ability to make decisions and bases his actions on the commands of his superior' (Bucher and Sterling, 1969). However, the professional's need for autonomy may hinder the existence of this type of relationship. In contrast, power is defined as 'the extent to which individuals and groups can control their working conditions' (Bucher and Sterling, 1969). Therefore, in PSFs professionals are likely to have both authority and power. This shared power may be limited to professional work teams, and is derived from the unique characteristics of professionals – namely their strong need for autonomy, a strong link to professional standards and the importance of reputation and peer evaluation. In this context 'consensus-based decision-making' is usually proposed as the most effective way to make decisions, although it might take more time and require fluid communication channels.

Mintzberg (1989) states that the unique configuration of PSFs resides in their democracy as reflected in the dissemination of power throughout the whole organisation. Power is thus directed to every member and does not reside in the group itself. 'This provides PSFs with extensive autonomy, freeing professionals from the need to coordinate closely with their colleagues. Professionals in these organisations are free to serve clients their own way, they are only limited by professional established standards.'

Therefore, the 'dual authority/power' issue represents a significant managerial challenge for the leaders of PSFs. They are responsible for guaranteeing the alignment and efficiency of the entire organisation in order to fulfil current client demands and to build trust both inside and outside the PSF.

Intangibility

The inputs and outputs of the PSF, as well as its main assets – including professionals' knowledge, skills and attitudes and the PSF's reputation in the marketplace – have the particular characteristic of being intangible.

Winch and Schneider (1993) identify the undeployable and intangible nature of PSF assets as the most striking difference between professional services and other types of service industries. The latter deploy their infrastructure assets, such as production facilities, aeroplanes, hotels or even liquid assets (banks), whereas PSFs focus on two main tasks: first, dealing with the development of people and professional skills and promoting the inimitability of their own reputation and that of their professionals in the marketplace; second, maintaining a balanced 'dual authority' system.

Pettigrew and Fenton (2000: 3) emphasise that the PSF's unique 'people' characteristics 'signal the extreme reliance upon named individuals, rather than the tangible entity of the firm to drive the business in value creation'. Larson (1977) further argues that what distinguishes a professional service from other services is that its 'output or product' is sufficiently intangible to prevent it from being traded as a commodity, yet sufficiently standardised to enable differentiation of the PSF. Because of the intangible nature of PSFs' output, PSFs have focused more on the strategic criteria of quality and reputation than on minimising transactional costs.

Standardisation/customisation

PSFs are highly complex on account of a wide range of factors, including dual authority (professionals and managers), intangible assets (reputation, knowledge, professional competences), intangible output (innovative solutions to clients' problems) and the pressure to be efficient in a competitive and changing environment. One possible approach to the latter factor would be to increase efficiency through standardisation.

Pettigrew and Fenton (2000) define PSFs as 'having a high degree of customisation, relying almost exclusively on the discretionary effort and subjective interaction with the client'. They stress the internalisation of PSFs, and point out that, due to competitive forces, PSFs tend to concentrate on developing either markets or regions, in order to provide specialised services through a standardised delivery process (24).

In order to standardise delivery processes that are customised to fulfil the particular needs of each client, knowledge management is required. Morris and Empson (1998) stress the relevance of knowledge management in PSFs as a central issue for leveraging the knowledge disseminated to each member of the organisation, whether in the same or in different offices, around the country or around the world. The starting point for knowledge management would be finishing every project with an analysis of what has been learnt and how it can be transmitted to the rest of the organisation. However, based on the unique characteristics of professionals, and assuming a lack of incentives to carry out this task, the likeliest outcome is that at the end of a project professionals will become immediately engaged in another project, without taking the time to review their previous one.

Moreover, Morris and Empson (1998) refer to other factors that might jeopardise the transfer of knowledge. One factor also identified by Mintzberg (1989) is the lack of coordination between professionals. Mintzberg notes that innovative problem-solving requires inductive reasoning – that is, the inference of the new general solution based on a particular experience. Since such inference differs from one individual to another, it leads to a lack of coordination and standardisation.

Nevertheless, Morris and Empson propose that appropriate incentives and cooperative behaviour, enshrined within a strong organisational culture, may help the firm overcome these obstacles. Further, promoting knowledge that is both connective – that is, originating either from inside or outside the organisation – and collective – that is, possessed by all members of the organisation – requires all structures and systems, and even the organisational culture, to be aligned so as to foster cooperation between individuals.

Trust

The idiosyncrasy of professional activity together with the intangibility of the assets – such as reputation and credibility – and services of PSFs make it crucial to build up relationships and networks, both internally and externally, as a basis for the creation of trust that will make interaction possible. 'Moreover, these reputations are built up over time and are not replaceable or imitable in the market place' (Pettigrew and Fenton, 2000: 3).

Pettigrew and Fenton state: '[W]e find trust to be the basis of most social and professional relationships... Trust is hard to build but easy to lose.' They also note that reputation is critical in reducing behavioural uncertainty and that it provides the basis for the development of trust.

Thus, the relevance of 'trust building' is directly related to the following factors. First, there is the intangible nature of the PSFs' assets, such as 'reputation', 'professional knowledge' and 'professional competences'. Second, the close interaction between professionals and clients requires trust building. Moreover, the increasing demands for efficiency require fluid communication and excellent coordination between PSF members, so internal trust building is also a key issue. Third, the professional's respect for the norms of the profession implies certain common ideas about how the job should be done. Fourth, 'information asymmetry' between professionals and clients might lead to professionals applying their discretionary judgement with unclear purposes, such as experimenting with new tools or selling solutions that are not actually necessary to solve the client's problem. Finally, client firms might require 'confidentiality' from the PSF; disregarding this issue could be fatal for the PSF's reputation, and therefore building trust with regard to clients also implies managing confidentiality.

Pettigrew and Fenton (2000: 31) suggest that one current issue for PSFs is the shift from 'a highly individualistic culture to a team-based one'. Further, these authors also propose the development of strong ties among professionals as a way of reducing opportunism. Accordingly, the role of organisational culture is extremely important in relation to trust building.

2.5   LINKAGES BETWEEN KEY FEATURES AND CHARACTERISTICS OF PSFS, PROFESSIONALS AND CLIENTS

In the previous section we identified six key features and characteristics of PSFs: individual professionals, professional competences, shared power, intangibility, standardisation/commoditisation and trust (all of which can be identified in the context of academics and business schools). Figure 2.1, is a diagrammatic conceptualisation of the important dynamic linkages between professionals, PSFs and clients.

In a professional organisation, such as a business school, an important dynamic links professionals, professional competences and shared power. Such PSFs should aim to attract and retain the most 'competent professionals', who, in turn, will demand from the organisation professional challenges, personal growth and recognition, along with working conditions suited to their autonomy and discretion in dealing with clients' needs according to their own judgement and expertise.

Professionals are highly qualified people, independent and autonomous, who risk becoming 'free riders' if the congruence between their goals and those of the PSF is not clear. PSFs can deliver accordingly by encouraging and facilitating the development of professional competences in their members. They must also allow considerable decentralisation in order to respect autonomy, discretionary effort and judgement among professionals. If PSFs boost the development of professional competences but lack shared power as a consequence of too much centralisation, they become less attractive for the best professionals, and, in turn, their commitment will fade.

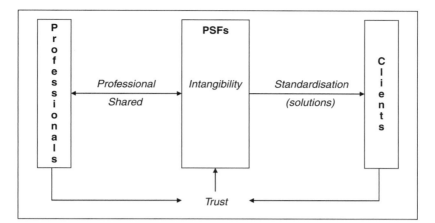

FIGURE 2.1 Dynamic between key features in the context of professionals, PSFs and clients

PSFs should therefore adopt an organisational model resembling Mintzberg's professional or 'adhocracy' forms, in order to provide professionals with the necessary autonomy in relationships with clients and on-the-job design in terms of case diagnosis and solution implementation (Mintzberg, 1989).

Intangibility refers both to the 'intangible' nature of the PSF's main assets, namely the professional competences inside the organisation, and reputation or credibility in the outer external context. However, it also refers to the intangible nature of the services provided by the PSF, since these are 'solutions' to specific and unique problems, rather than products bearing technical and material specifications. Hence the client's trust in the PSF's 'solution' impacts with intangibility. Intangibility, therefore, is inherent in the nature of the business itself, and provides a challenge in setting standards for assessing solution quality and in improving efficiency in using these intangible resources.

As a result, the standardisation/customisation feature becomes more crucial, because of the need for effective knowledge management processes and the ability to set standards. However, inappropriate and rigid standards might jeopardise the level of customisation that clients expect, and also the professional's demand for autonomy and discretionary judgement.

It is important to bear in mind, therefore, that the standard-isation versus customisation debate has an effect both on clients' needs and expectations and on professionals' search for autonomy. However, because of the intangibility of the services delivered, customers need and expect to develop a trust relationship with the PSF with elements including reputation, credibility, quality standards and the expectation of confidentiality in the PSF–client relationship.

Trust is also a key feature in the internal relationship between PSFs and professionals. If we analyse the factors distinguishing 'individual professionals', in terms of their sense of professional reputation and dignity, the need for fair recognition and reward, and the value granted to ethical aspects in order to build long-lasting relationships and to forge 'personal prestige' – not only among com-panies but also among colleagues – then trust is clearly a relevant feature within the professional firm (Pettigrew and Fenton, 2000; Sharma, 1997).

PSFs can enhance or harm trust through different managerial decisions, such as incentive and recognition systems, project assign-ments, the appraisal assessment process, internal promotion criteria, the stress (or lack of it) on professional competence development, the degree of autonomy and discretion for project resolution and execu-tion and, finally, involvement in strategic decisions. Thus, building trust might help to generate more cooperative and long-term-oriented behaviours. The opposite actions would tend to generate more oppor-tunistic and short-term-focused attitudes.

We can conclude that the trust characteristic is the critical, overarching element. It is the consequence of every action of any relevance, both within the organisation – to strengthen the bond between professionals – and with the PSFs, and outside the organ-isation, to build up the prestige and reputation needed to foster rela-tionships with new companies or to strengthen the relationship with current clients. Trust, therefore, can reduce the internal and external transaction costs, facilitating interaction, encouraging cooperative behaviour, building networks and strengthening existing relationships.

We now examine in detail how the characteristics of PSFs should interact effectively with the decision-making processes of PSFs to ensure successful performance outcomes. Here, the complex organisational dynamics of a knowledge-intensive, professional service firm are explicitly linked to the success or failure of the firm. It is these key processes that the leaders of business schools must monitor, anticipate and adjust in shaping the inner context of their organisation. In turn, this inner context must be shaped and evaluated in relation to the outer context of the organisation. For this reason, the intersection of these contextual levels forms the foundation of the strategic leadership process explored in Chapter 3.

2.6   KEY PROCESSES IN PROFESSIONAL SERVICE FIRMS

The examination of 'key processes' involves the analysis of a 'sequence of actions' that influences performance, thereby defining either the success or the failure of a PSF. For the purpose of this analysis, six key processes are examined in detail: (1) governance; (2) strategy-setting; (3) staffing; (4) service delivery; (5) innovation and learning; and (6) knowledge management, and relationship, network and trust building.

Governance

Although governance is a core process in most organisations, the unique characteristics of PSFs have a direct and dramatic impact upon it. First, there is the intangible nature of PSFs' assets: professional knowledge and competences, reputation and trust. Second, professionals, as the most crucial members of PSFs, have a particular need for autonomy and present certain difficulties when it comes to internal coordination. Third, there is the shared power system, which is reflected in consensus-based decision-making. Fourth, there is the 'dual authority' phenomenon that exists between two groups of PSF members: professionals – who possess expertise and therefore power, since expertise is the key asset for PSFs; and managers – who have the authority to coordinate the actions of all PSF members. Hence, governance in PSFs is a complex process that deserves further attention.

However, since we have discussed dual authority and shared power in the previous section, we focus here on the traditional centralisation/decentralisation dilemma and the issue of the most appropriate type of control for PSFs.

In relation to the centralisation/decentralisation dilemma, Greenwood, Hinings and Brown (1990) concentrate on examining which activities should be either centralised or decentralised. They suggest that, since a collegial and consensus-based approach to strategic decision-making best fits the interactions in PSFs, *operational control* – that is, control over professionals delivering solutions to clients' specific problems – should be *decentralised*. However, *strategic control*, which is exercised over strategy setting, policy decisions, the definition of standards, staffing and career design, should be *centralised*.

Mintzberg (1989) agrees that the operational control of PSFs should be decentralised, thus allowing professionals enough autonomy to be creative, apply their discretionary judgement and interact with clients. However, he proposes that control should be exercised through the standardisation of skills, not routines.

Strategy setting

The greater an organisation's complexity, the more it needs a clear direction and vision for the achievement of a particular goal. Moreover, complexity also demands internal coordination to achieve an efficient use of critical resources. Thus, if the organisation is made up of highly skilled and autonomous professionals delivering services in close interaction with clients, then the need for clear direction setting and coordination is correspondingly higher. However, a cursory glance at most business schools reveals a varied and confusing picture. Business schools may be part of a university, independent, publicly owned or privately owned. Let us consider the numerous stakeholders with which a business school has to engage. For example, Warwick Business School's 'Vision 2015' mentions a wide range of stakeholders, including students, academic and supporting staff, internal managers (e.g. vice chancellors and registrars), businesses, public policy-makers, alumni and clients. Further, the additional perspective of the institutionalised position of the business school as a 'cash cow' to fund other university departments is an additional element with which university-based schools must contend (Clark, 1998; Davies and Thomas, 2009; Shattock, 1994b). The mixed, often conflicting, goals that come from this add to the challenge of leading a PSF.

Løwendahl (1997: 168) notes: 'Strategy in the professional service firm, then, involves setting priorities, rather than making plans or developing and maintaining a competitive position.' Given the autonomy of professionals, priorities are required to set a common direction, thereby deciding what to deliver, to whom, where, when and how. She also argues that the higher the degree of autonomy within a PSF, the more important it is for individual professionals to know the strategic priorities of the firm, probably requiring continuous monitoring of the alignment of their decisions.

Mintzberg points out that, in PSFs, strategy setting is carried out by many individuals, including managers and professionals from diverse areas, the latter participating both individually and collectively. While this may lead initially to many largely fragmented strategies, he also finds a range of forces promoting overall strategic cohesion and appropriate strategic alignment. These include the common purposes of managers, the collegial negotiations required for collective decision-making – for example, decisions on new tenure regulations in a university – and even the forces of habit and tradition. The strategies of PSFs therefore tend to show a remarkable degree of stability, since strategic change of a revolutionary nature seems to be discouraged by fragmentation and individual influence within a shared power scheme. This implies a critical role for strategic leadership, as highlighted by Hinings, Brown and Greenwood (1991), as well as by Denis, Langley and Cazale (1996), particularly when there are major changes taking place, environmental uncertainty and strong competition, arising, for example, from the globalised and challenging business school situation at present.

In summary, strategy setting in PSFs is a key process with a twofold impact: internally, it provides the priorities to align individual actions and promote coordination, and, externally, it aligns the PSF with the increasing demands of clients immersed in a constantly changing business environment.

Staffing

Løwendahl (1997) and Maister (1993) both affirm that PSFs face a double challenge, with competition not just in the market for clients but also in the market for talented professionals, who represent their key assets. Morris and Empson (1998) note that PSFs have to resolve client problems effectively and profitably, but to do so they need talented professionals. Winning in the client marketplace implies the generation and maintenance of demand, but winning in the talent marketplace represents the complex challenge of attracting and retaining the best professionals. Chapter 1 outlined the highly competitive operating conditions for business schools, and it is against this background that deans have to manage their key asset: academics. Indeed, the training, hiring and retention of these key workers have received increasing attention in the study of the state and evolution of business schools (AACSB, 2007: 3; Thomas, 2007b). Here we see this challenge as a combination of this intense, globally competitive environment, shortages in the supply of knowledge workers (new academics) and the complexities of managing PSFs.

For leading institutions, hiring the right people is not enough; once they have joined the company and proved themselves to be valuable, the firm needs to retain them – and the critical issue becomes how to do this. Various alternatives are possible. First, they can be motivated by being offered challenging projects. Second, their development can be promoted with the corresponding evaluations, showing them that they have made progress and rewarding them for it. Third, the right incentives can be provided, not only in monetary terms but also, and more importantly, by making professionals feel respected and valued by the organisation. Fourth, professionals can be mentored with regard to their learning and skill development infrastructure needs and their alignment with the culture and values of the firm.

The ultimate aim of all these alternatives is to recruit and retain valuable professionals, mainly by offering them the prospect of a long-term career development full of challenging opportunities and responsibilities, thereby encouraging them to commit themselves to the objectives of the firm. Certainly, within higher education, and within business schools in particular, an ageing faculty profile, a lack of Ph.D. training and a dearth of attractive alternative careers signal a likely shortage of academics in the very near future (Hawawini, 2005; Ivory et al., 2006). This compounds the difficulties of managing and leading the staff, faculty and the relatively few 'stars' and high-quality academics as part of complex, expert-based and knowledge-intensive organisations such as business schools.

Service delivery

Maister (1993) states that there are two fundamental dimensions driving the managerial challenges in PSFs: the high degree of customisation and the strong influence of face-to-face interaction with clients.

Løwendahl (1997) uses Maister's dimensions to derive three fundamental characteristics of PSFs: highly qualified individuals; idiosyncratic client services; and subjective quality assurance. A fourth dimension, also mentioned by Løwendahl (2000: 32), is information asymmetry: 'PSFs primarily create value through processes that require them to know more than their clients, either in terms of expertise or in terms of experience in problem-solving situations.' Thus, it is clear that there are two main issues concerning PSF service delivery: PSFs' output characteristics and the characteristics of PSF–client interaction.

PSF output consists of innovative solutions to specific client problems. Customisation is an intrinsic characteristic of PSF activities, therefore, implying the development of a close relationship with clients. It may often require a non-routine adaptation to client needs in order to solve a problem. In this respect, PSFs must rely on a high degree of discretionary effort and the personal judgement of individual professionals.

Reflecting the intangible nature of PSF output, quality assessment depends to a large extent on clients' expectations. Therefore, unless the client has a clear idea of his/her real needs and the specific service he/she expects to receive from the PSF, the greater the uncertainty for both parties and the more complex the service delivery. One possible way of managing such uncertainty could be to agree ex ante on the quality criteria to be used in assessing the service.

Close interaction between the PSF and client is a critical element of service delivery. Clients participate in the problem definition and in the choice of solution, and often in the process of delivering and implementing solutions as well. Løwendahl (2000: 32) even argues that the more process-oriented the service is, the higher the degree of interaction required. These joint activities between the PSF and the client firm make the 'boundaries between producers and consumers' not as clear as they might be in the case of a manufacturing firm.

Mintzberg (1979) notes that controls within the professional context may sometimes disrupt and obstruct the delicate personal relationship between the professional and the client. As a result, traditional notions of supervision, focused on maintaining adherence to prescribed roles, rules and standards, are not subscribed to within the professional service context. Flexibility, creativity, intellectual analysis and self-management are the most appropriate tools for PSF service delivery. Moreover, the close interaction between clients and professionals in PSFs will lead to further involvement of the latter in decision-making (Manz and Sims, 1981).

Consequently, in this context, the leaders of a PSF require the extraordinary ability to cope with both the complexity and intangibility of its output, self-managed service delivery and difficult quality assessment.

Innovation, and learning and knowledge management

Nachum (1999) describes the PSF production process as one based on the analysis and application of knowledge by professionals or 'highly educated employees' to provide 'a one-time solution to specific clients' problems'. However, Maister (1993) proposes that PSFs can provide more than a one-time solution, as during the delivery process professionals may achieve considerable project success and also identify new client needs that may become new projects for the PSF. Maister's main argument is that the return on investment in marketing for, and nurturing, existing clients brings a higher profit than investment on marketing to new clients. Furthermore, existing clients are more inclined to give challenging projects to a PSF they already know and respect, and the PSF can then offer its professionals new challenges, and foster innovation and organisational development (Maister, 1993: 97).

'Professional competence' is considered to be one of the key characteristics of PSFs. It is evident, therefore, that innovation and knowledge creation, with an emphasis on application, and knowledge development are two important mechanisms for differentiation within PSFs. However, from the firm's perspective, the key issue related to knowledge is knowledge management – the effective dissemination of acquired knowledge among professionals through standardised procedures in order to foster efficiency and enhance learning and innovation – due to its strong impact on efficiency and, accordingly, business performance.

This indicates that the organisational learning process involving the creation and dissemination of knowledge throughout the entire organisation is a critical part of the mission of PSFs. However, the fragmentation of work between individual professionals can jeopardise the link between internal and external knowledge. Consequently, one of the main challenges for PSF leaders is to create an environment that promotes knowledge creation and guarantees effective knowledge management through a strong organisational culture and the adoption of appropriate systems for knowledge transfer.

Relations, networking, and trust building

Networking is a vitally important process in a PSF, in that it is individuals who *produce, deliver* and *improve* the service itself.

Internal networking is necessary for the continual enhancement of knowledge and competence for service delivery through 'connective knowledge'. Meanwhile, external networking provides a strong link with peers – through professional associations – and with clients, mainly during and after the delivery process.

There are also two aspects to the concept of trust. Inside the PSF, trust enables coordination, and thereby improves efficiency. Externally, clients' trust is reflected in new projects and recommendations to other potential clients. In essence, trust is the 'glue' that binds the diverse interactions within the firm and with current and potential clients, and it is the concept that best synthesises the intangible nature of the PSF's assets: reputation, credibility and the like.

2.7   ORGANISING AND MANAGING PROFESSIONAL
      SERVICE FIRMS: LINKAGE BETWEEN
      KEY FEATURES AND KEY PROCESSES

We have just identified six key processes that have a critical influence on the operation and performance of the PSFs: governance; strategy setting; staffing; service delivery; innovation, learning and knowledge management; and relationship, network and trust building. If, as we have argued, PSFs operate using these six processes, then what are the key features of PSFs and what do they look like as organisational forms? The following discussion builds upon the six key processes identified above and focuses on the organisational forms of PSFs.

There is abundant evidence that PSFs are coming under pressure to adopt managerial forms of organisations in response to increasingly demanding clients and intense competition (Cooper *et al.*, 1996; Morris, 1992; Tolbert and Stern, 1991). Indeed, Cooper *et al.* suggest that, for the effective management of PSFs, it is vital to have a coherent set of structures, systems and beliefs that lead to improved configurations or managerial 'archetypes'.

Two such archetypes are analysed by Cooper *et al.* The first is the 'P2' archetype, which is based on a combination of partnership and professional idiosyncrasy, and focuses on uniting ownership and control, within a representative democracy system in which owners get involved in management. It stresses the value of professional knowledge, peer control, strong links with clients, widely distributed authority and minimum hierarchy. However, *strategic control* is vested in the owners, who concentrate on medium- and long-term positioning, thereby interpreting threats and opportunities, building capability and competences and initiating actions to sustain and improve positional fit. Hence, authority is institutionalised in the ownership of the firm. It is worth noting that this structure implies the juxtaposition of two apparently opposite realities: on the one hand, individual, autonomous daily activities; and, on the other, collegial, group-based decision-making. The ultimate effect is a fragile and diffused governance system.

The second archetype is the managerial professional business (MPB) scheme. Although this kind of scheme may also have partnership governance, the difference from the P2 form lies in the fact that partners delegate to an elected committee of partners the daily matters relating to the running of the firm. The MPB model interprets a PSF from a business perspective, emphasising professional skills, providing value-added services and taking technical skills for granted. The emphasis on effectiveness and efficiency leads to the introduction of managers into the firm, although they remain under the supervision of professionals. This might lead to coordination difficulties, since the objectives of managers (efficiency and effectiveness) might not coincide with those of professionals (professional development, challenging projects, and reputation). Hence, the main strategic issues in an MPB structure are management, client service, competition, marketing and growth strategies, rationalisation and productivity. In addition, formalised administrative systems for human resource management and financial control are required for efficiency and effectiveness.

We now examine, in Table 2.4 and the following text, the interrelation and linkages between these 'key processes' and the previously identified 'key features' and characteristics of PSFs (Table 2.3).

As a process, the *governance* system will generate the conditions for 'shared power' to be properly established, balancing the 'duality' between 'centralisation' and 'decentralisation'. It thus defines the degree of autonomy and 'discretional judgement' for each professional to undertake the projects assigned as his/her responsibility. The governance process also determines the overall organisational structure – for example, whether the P2 form is adopted or the more business-oriented MPB form. In the MPB model, rewards are based on performance and results, whereas, in the P2, professionals' and partners' rewards are tied to seniority. In the MPB scheme it is also clear that hierarchy is more significant and there is a demand for business plans per unit, and teams are encouraged to develop 'cross-selling' between specialist areas.

The interpretative scheme of the P2 form is one of a diffuse authority structure that ensures that partners have scope for self-actualisation rather than profit maximisation. This 'shared power' satisfies professionals' creative or altruistic impulses by pursuing assignments or by focusing on activities outside the firm. Empson

Table 2.4 *Linkage between key processes and key characteristics of PSFs*

Key processes	Key characteristics	
	Direct influence	Indirect influence
Governance	Individual professionals Professional competences Shared power Standardisation/customisation Trust (internal/external)	Intangibility
Strategy setting	Professional competences Shared power Intangibility Standardisation/customisation Trust (internal/external)	Individual professionals
Staffing	Individual professionals Professional competences Trust (internal)	Shared power Intangibility Standardisation/customisation Trust (external)
Service delivery	Professional competences Shared power Standardisation/customisation Trust (external)	Individual professionals Intangibility Trust (internal)
Innovation, learning and knowledge management	Individual professionals Professional competences Standardisation/customisation Trust (internal/external)	Shared power Intangibility
Relationship, network and trust building	Individual professionals Intangibility Trust (internal/external)	Professional competences Shared power Standardisation/customization

(2000: 3) believes that the most common control mechanisms in a P2 structure are 'pride and pressure'. The structure also indicates the appropriate professional and organisational competences that need to be acquired and define the culture for 'individual professionals'. This environment should then allow them to operate independently and maintain a stable relationship with their peers, to adhere to the professional regulations and behaviours of their respective professional associations, to obtain fair reward and recognition for their efforts and to generate trust internally and externally.

Strategy setting is another critical process, since it sets clear priorities and hence influences the performance of PSFs in both the medium term and the long term, and also affects their short-term goals in promoting consensus and coordination. Strategy setting in PSFs involves strategic guidelines rather than specific and precise plans. Mintzberg (1989) notes that, in a professional or adhocratic type of organisation such as a PSF, strategy making is likely to be more 'bottom-up' than 'top-down', because the most critical information and participation is provided by the highly competent professionals who have operational control, build customised solutions for client problems and thereby generate trust, goodwill and reputation for the PSF. Further, as noted by Cooper *et al.* (1996), it is common in governance terms for strategic control to be centralised and operational control decentralised.

The staffing process is critically important for hiring and retaining competent 'individual professionals', for developing 'professional competences' and, in particular, for building client 'trust' in the professionalism of the PSF.

The *service delivery* process builds on the professional skills of members of the PSF and client trust, thus enabling appropriate levels of standardisation and service customisation to be determined that ensure effective client solutions and enhanced service quality.

The *innovation, learning* and *knowledge management* process serves as a motivating element for the growth in the professional expertise of individuals, thereby fostering ongoing knowledge, skill,

standard and attitude enhancement, and strengthening organisational and 'professional competences'.

Knowledge management also influences 'shared power', as it
promotes the spread of knowledge among professionals, thus providing a broader organisational knowledge base and promoting internal
trust. It also drives the organisation towards new knowledge creation and acquisition and internal diffusion, both internally and
externally.

The *networking* and *trust building* process is also very important for the success of the PSF, and involves all the key features of a
PSF. In a PSF, reputation reduces behavioural uncertainty and provides the basis for the development of trust (Pettigrew and Fenton,
2000). Reputation promotes further success, reduces the risk of individual opportunism and promotes cooperative behaviour between
different constituent parts. Internal and external networking,
cooperative group behaviour and an increased sharing of information and knowledge promote trust, improve internal efficiency and
generate success in the marketplace, as argued in the P2 model. In
contrast, in the MPB model, concepts of professionalism and partnership are reinterpreted to emphasise efficiency and teamwork,
respectively, ensuring that all professionals work together to pursue the commercial objectives that are defined by the management
group, enforced by control systems.

In summary, our examination of business school organisations and their leadership resonates with the characteristic features
of PSFs. This leads us to regard business schools as a particular form
of PSF. Indeed, we observe that the characteristics of individual professionals, professional competences, shared power, intangibility,
issues of standardisation versus customisation, and trust are all constituent elements in business school organisations. While the P2 and
MPB forms provide frameworks and useful distinction between certain types of PSF, these archetypes are found to be problematic for
the study of business schools, as they do not conform neatly to either
type. Therefore, a hybrid form of managerial structure involving

both the P2 and the MPB forms may be more appropriate in the context of leading and managing a business school. This leads naturally to a much more extensive discussion of issues involved in leading and managing PSFs in general and business schools in particular.

2.8   LEADING AND MANAGING PROFESSIONAL SERVICE FIRMS

Throughout this chapter, the case has been made that business schools share common elements and characteristics with both knowledge-intensive and professional service firms. Using Løwendahl's typology of KIFs, we have identified business schools as 'problem-solving and creative organisations', involving as their internal focus a mixture of individual, team and organisational control alongside a commitment to generating creative problem-solving solutions as their external focus (Løwendahl, 2000). However, in order to understand the strategic leadership processes of business schools we need to combine the features of PSFs and KIFs with the 'inner workings' of these organisations. The P2 and MPB forms of PSF in turn begin to produce the shape and structure of these organisations.

Howard (1991) underlines the importance of leadership in PSFs by pointing out that it is the most critical factor in managing these kinds of organisations, because of their diffuse authority structure, in which professionals typically resist authority and look for independence and autonomy.

The following are some of the more important leadership issues. First, leadership as a social phenomenon is of special importance in PSFs, since they are organisations in which the key resources are people, and the main assets and services delivered are intangible.

Second, the leadership process may be challenged from inside, because of characteristics such as shared power and the spread of authority due to issues of collegiality, partnership and peer reference influence within professional organisations. The autonomy and individual discretionary judgement of professionals occur in parallel with the fragmentation of the work and the 'adhocratic' project-based nature of the work (Mintzberg, 2007). As Denis, Langley and Cazale (1996) point out, the ambiguity of authority in PSFs reflects the duality of power and collegial or consensus-based decision-making, which makes collective leadership both crucial and, at the same time, a tough challenge. This is made more difficult by the fact that most professionals reject management responsibilities, which makes it challenging to find the right person among them to put in charge of these management tasks.

Third, in the increasingly competitive and turbulent outer context, clients demand increasing customisation and high-quality service delivery. Consequently, a strong leadership process is necessary to provide strategic direction in leading change and making key decisions, such as the designation of targets in terms of both markets and clients, defining alliances at international and regional level, improving efficiency by establishing standards, managing knowledge, identifying critical competences, staffing, the use of information technology and the delivery of customised solutions to clients.

2.9   WHAT ARE THE MAIN LEADERSHIP CHALLENGES IN PROFESSIONAL SERVICE FIRMS?

There are, clearly, five main tasks in the leadership process: establishing a vision and setting direction; creating identity and a sense of common purpose and shared values; communicating, motivating and mobilising people; supporting and empowering people; and, finally, aligning and coordinating the organisation. Each of these five leadership tasks is strongly influenced by three critical features of PSFs or KIFs, namely the presence of individual professionals, shared power and the intangibility of inputs and outputs. Table 2.5 identifies the interaction between leadership tasks and the critical elements of PSFs.

Therefore, we suggest that a series of questions should be examined from the leadership process perspective, which should provide insights into the leadership challenges in promoting professional competences, standardisation or customisation, and trust, and into

Table 2.5 *Dynamic between main leadership tasks and key characteristics of PSFs*

Key PSF characteristics / Leadership's tasks	Setting the direction	Common purpose	Motivating and mobilising	Support and empowerment	Aligning the organisation
Individual professionals	X	X	X	X	X
Professional competences					
Shared power	X	X	X	X	X
Intangibility	X	X	X	X	X
Standardisation/customisation					
Trust					

ways of dealing with the other three features that may harm effect-ive leadership action. These questions include the following.

(1) How can professional competences (knowledge, skills and attitudes) be challenged and developed, stimulating innovation and learning, in a changing external environment?
(2) How can a sense of common purpose be created through organisational identity and identification with the company's set of beliefs?
(3) How can trust be built, both outside the organisation, with current and potential customers, and within it?
(4) How can a shared vision be articulated and communicated, providing strategic direction and promoting coordination, autonomy, creativity and discretionary judgement among professionals?
(5) How can efficiency be stimulated through standardisation, promoting knowledge management (connective and collective knowledge) both within the organisation and with the wider environment?
(6) How can a culture of delivering customised solutions for client needs be created and stimulated?

These six questions bear strong resonance with the challenges of managing a business school. The global and fierce competition in the market for higher education (outlined in Chapter 1) com-bined with the organisational dynamics of managing a professional service firm, outlined in this chapter, place the dean as the nexus between the demands of the inner and outer contexts of business schools. It is within this complex assembly that deans have to lead their schools. Figure 2.2 describes the leadership process and chal-lenges in terms of the features that influence these schools from the inner and the outer contexts. The conclusion is that we should try to handle the three key features of the inner context that are in conflict with the leadership task – namely individual professionals, intangibility and shared power – in order to promote and to enhance the other three factors through the entire leadership process.

From our perspective, this is the essence of the leadership challenge in PSFs or KIFs – particularly in classic professional organisations. We argue that this captures the organisation and activities of business schools, in which academics pursue their own

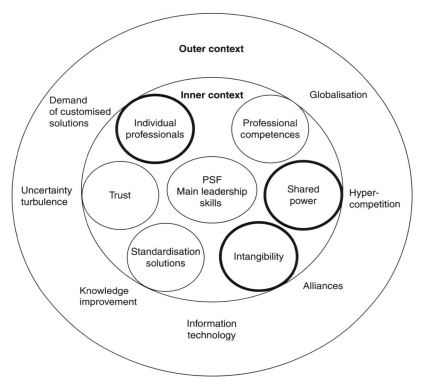

FIGURE 2.2 The main leadership challenges for PSFs within the scope of the inner and outer contexts
Note: The three highlighted circles illustrate the features that are in conflict with the leadership tasks.

agendas and strategies, expect autonomy and consultation but prefer a 'minimalist' leadership style, offering 'protection and support' for their endeavours. Having started to unpack the nature of business schools and their competitive environment – their outer and inner contexts – the following chapter focuses on the strategic leadership process in business schools.

3   The leadership process in business schools

The first three chapters of this book have signalled the compelling context of business schools and their striking similarities to characteristic traits of professional service firms. The combination of these complex organisational dynamics, captured through a knowledge-based view of business schools, with an intensely competitive environment globally presents significant challenges to business school organisations. Further, the chief source of power to rise to these challenges seems to lie not outside but inside these organisations – in their own governance and leadership.

As the first decade of the twenty-first century draws to a close, with the world plagued by unremitting uncertainty and daunting dilemmas, business schools have a historically unique opportunity to make a difference, influencing, shaping and contributing to the ever more relevant role of business in society. At this turning point in their own history, they need to clarify and reinforce their mission, values and purpose in order to enhance and clearly convey their *academic value proposition*. As they tackle these current tests, the most critical challenge faced by business schools relates to their own governance and strategic leadership.

3.1   INTRODUCTION TO THE LEADERSHIP LITERATURE

There is no single definition of leadership, but there is a general consensus over some of the essential concepts that characterise it (Northouse, 2001; Yukl, 1998). Most theorists agree that leadership is a process that involves influencing people's values, beliefs, motivations and behaviour in order to accomplish a particular objective or purpose. However, the emphasis of leadership may be on the influence exerted either by one person or by different people playing their

93

own coordinated roles within an organisation. The latter situation involves a leadership process, in contrast to a view of the leader as a single person playing a unique role.

There are two main theoretical approaches to leadership as a single role. First, there is the *trait approach*, which focuses on the 'traits' that characterise the leader ('what the leader is like') and identifying and understanding leadership in terms of these psychological aspects. Second, the *style approach* examines how the leader does his/her job ('how the leader works' or 'how the leader behaves'). This research approach stresses the impact of the leader's behaviour on the followers, representing an important step towards the issue of 'context' in understanding the dynamics of the leadership phenomenon.

Two other approaches focus more closely on context. First, there is the *situational approach*, which identifies the different types of behaviour the leader adopts depending on the circumstances and considers how that behaviour could become more effective based on the demands of a particular situation. Second, there is *contingency theory*, which emphasises the importance of matching a leader's style to the demands of the underlying circumstances.

Although these approaches provide important findings, such as those relating to a better understanding of leadership skills and types of behaviour and how a person could improve his/her style of leadership or way of behaving, there is a gap in building up knowledge about 'leadership as a process' and 'leadership development' within the organisation.

Leadership can also be viewed as a process of influence that occurs within a social system and is spread among its members (Yukl, 1998; Northouse, 2001). In studying different PSFs, Pettigrew (1992) and Denis, Langley and Cazale (1996) underline the importance of considering leadership more as a process, in which different actors with different skills handle alternative aspects of the change process but work together as a group. They also suggest that collective leadership in terms of a group of people, with different weight and influence in the process, could play a more effective leadership role than a single leader with great power. Further, this type of collaborative leadership can be particularly valuable in organisations with ambiguous authority, because it is legitimised by the approval of the entire group.

Kotter (1990) suggests that leadership and the management process should be considered separately, based on the various tasks and objectives and different competences (skills and attitudes) needed. The management process is viewed as a deductive procedure intended to introduce order, planning and coordination within an organisation with the objective of reducing risk, organising work and establishing goals. The leadership process is then examined through a more inductive process that is focused on interpreting the future, finding new strategic paths, defining broad guidelines and motivating people. Thus, the leadership process is designed to change, mobilise, inspire and coordinate people, take risks and generate breakthroughs within the organisation. Finally, the leadership process functions more in terms of cultural aspects such as values and beliefs. However, few theorists agree on the value of differentiating leadership and management processes. The distinction between both processes is therefore seen as simplistic and unnecessary (Mintzberg, 2007; Yukl, 1998).

There are many studies on the process of leadership. For example, Alvesson (1995), referring to Selznick's view of the institutional and human relations tasks in management, suggests that there are three types of tasks involved in the leadership process (Selznick, 1957). First, *institutional leadership* considers the purpose of the organisation and its basic values. Second, *structural leadership* concentrates on organisational design, planning and control. Third, *social leadership* focuses on human relations, communication, supporting subordinates and job satisfaction. Selznick stresses that these three forms of leadership are not mutually exclusive, but that the 'leader', depending on the particular circumstances of the context and on his/her competences, will probably conform to one or two of them.

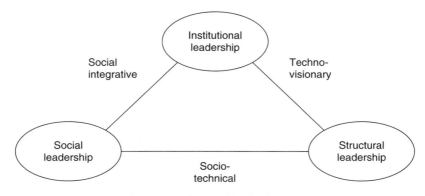

FIGURE 3.1 Alvesson's scheme of leadership tasks
Source: Alvesson (1995: 177).

The most interesting aspect of Alvesson's suggestions is his identification of three processes corresponding to the leadership tasks mentioned above. These processes are: *social integrative leadership*, linking the institutional and social leadership tasks; *techno-visionary leadership*, combining the institutional and structural leadership tasks; and, finally, *socio-technical leadership*, linking the social and structural leadership tasks.

This can be examined graphically in Figure 3.1, in which the three main leadership tasks suggested by Alvesson are linked with the three main processes of leadership mentioned above.

Using Alvesson's framework, we can now identify the most critical *tasks in the leadership process* as follows.

3.2   THE INSTITUTIONAL LEADERSHIP PROCESS

Setting the direction

Normally this task is executed through the development, articulation and communication of a *shared vision*. This vision should have some clear and broad image corresponding to what the company wants to be in the future, answering the questions 'When?', 'Where?' and 'How?'. It is critical in creating the sense of challenge that the organisation will need to face in order to achieve that future vision. Encouraging change and assuming risks are typical elements of this task. The vision will create a kind of 'tension' that will help to concentrate and focus the organisation on a more concrete and better future stage. In this sense, Richards and Engle (1986) assert that leadership consists of 'articulating visions, embodying values, and creating the environment within which things can be accomplished'.

According to Yukl (1998), a vision should be simple and idealistic, not a complex plan with quantitative objectives and detailed steps for action. It should appeal to the values, hopes and ideals of the members of the organisation and other shareholders whose support is necessary. It should also be challenging, but feasible. A vision should address basic assumptions about what is important for the organisation, how it should relate to its environment and how people should be treated. Moreover, a vision should be sufficiently focused to guide decisions and actions, but at the same time sufficiently general to allow initiative and creativity in the strategies used in attaining it.

The visioning process is critical for strategic change and is complemented by the strategic planning task, involving the analysis and definition of objectives, targets and goals, in terms of the future steps and resources that need to be defined in pursuit of the vision.

Creating the sense of a common purpose, and shared values and beliefs

It is important at this point to define and communicate the company's mission, values and beliefs in order to create an organisational identity and sense of belonging among its employees. Schein (1992) underlines the fact that leadership creates, communicates and sometimes destroys cultural values and beliefs in organisations through a range of decisions, such as rewarding, promoting, hiring and firing people. These critical decisions become more important in defining the organisation's culture than any statement purporting to establish organisational cultural values

3.3   THE SOCIAL LEADERSHIP PROCESS

Motivating and mobilising people

The effective communication of the vision and values of the company is an important process, informing and enhancing every member of the firm, and also confronting assumptions of the different constituent parts within the organisation, including the top management team. Formal and informal communication can be used in clarifying purpose, meanings, objectives and targets, but the pattern in the stream of decisions and actions is the most effective channel in communicating the values (Mintzberg, 2007).

Supporting and empowering people

Supporting behaviours develop knowledge, skills and attitudes in a PSF. As Yukl (1998) points out, important actions include showing acceptance and positive regard, bolstering self-esteem, providing recognition and reward for achievements and contributions by each employee and mentoring and clarifying career paths. These processes and behaviours foster cooperative relationships between members of the organisation.

3.4   THE STRUCTURAL LEADERSHIP PROCESS

Coordinating the organisation

This task is related to shaping structures and systems consistently with the vision, culture, shared values and strategy of the company. It is directly related to all critical aspects of control, incentives and rewarding systems, but also, and importantly in PSFs and KIFs, with the knowledge management systems for organisational learning. In particular, in PSFs it involves creatively designing and managing a flat and flexible professional structure to support the organisation in the current globalised and ever-changing environment.

Organisational archetypes for the PSF, such as the P2 and MPB forms (Cooper *et al.*, 1996) need to be fully examined here. We now use the elements of the leadership process framework in Figure 3.1 to examine the critical challenges faced by business schools in their own governance and strategic leadership.

3.5   GOVERNANCE AND STRATEGIC LEADERSHIP

Because of the richness and value of the numerous sources dealing with the many challenges that business schools currently face, the focus here is not on what these institutions need to do or change to overcome them. Rather, we try to contribute to clarifying *how* business schools and, in particular, deans and other influential actors and key stakeholders should address these dilemmas, anticipating and overcoming resistance or opposition from within and securing buy-in across their organisations in pursuit of their goals. Specifically, we focus on the leadership process and the role of deans as strategic leaders or champions for their organisation.

In our experience as deans and our conversations with colleagues from a number of institutions around the world, we have come to realise how decisive it is for business schools to *shape* and *articulate* three critical and essential elements in order to succeed in delivering their *value proposition* in an effective and sustainable way. These *basic* but *key* elements are: the academic model, the economic model and the strategic agenda (see Figure 3.2).

First and foremost, business schools' primary driver is their *academic model* – the *engine* that drives their sheer existence, embodying their aspirations to contribute to business leaders' development in the three critical dimensions of *knowing, doing* and *being*. In a setting that features, as described previously, fierce, widespread competition against a backdrop of critiques questioning their identity and actual contributions to management advancement and professional legitimacy, it becomes crucial for business schools – and other higher education institutions and professional service firms – to revisit their academic model. Specifically, they should look into

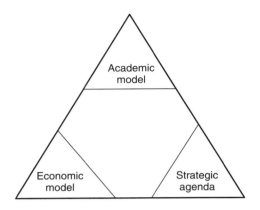

FIGURE 3.2 Business schools'
core drivers

their teaching, knowledge development and research standards and
their particular emphasis by exploring basic questions. What kind
of teaching will they offer? What type of learning experience will
they deliver? Who will be considered as their prime target? How
will they position themselves in terms of academic rigour and business relevance? What research activities will they pursue? Will the
school reach out to businesses, focusing on management needs; will
it adopt a more academic approach; or will it try to strike and maintain a balance between corporate and scholar engagement? Finally,
how are they going to reach these goals?

Once schools have reformulated their academic model so as
to respond to current market needs and challenges, they need to
determine the kinds of critical resources that will be required to
pursue that model. Particularly key are definitions regarding business schools' core asset – their faculty. Schools need to map their
faculty's profile, background, teaching skills, research competences
and needs, finding the way to attract, recruit and compensate the
academics who meet those requirements. In addition, business
schools' overall research capabilities, facilities and technology will
all contribute to enabling business schools to fulfil their mission
of knowledge production and educating business leaders within the
path chosen by each.

Therefore, to achieve their academic vision, schools need an explicit and realistic definition of their *economic model* to support their academic model. How will they generate the sustainable financial resources – the *fuel* needed for business schools' engines to run? Indeed, it may be argued that some of the inconsistencies currently besieging business schools and exposing them to harsh criticism from both academia and corporations have stemmed from their efforts to turn a sound academic endeavour into a sustainable, enduring business venture. In this pursuit, they have sometimes embarked on opportunistic initiatives with a view to short-term returns that were actually inconsistent with their true missions and visions.

Traditional, university-based business schools, particularly in the United States, have tapped into their large endowments and taken the lead in building full-time faculties, investing heavily in research with a strong academic background and research skills. As a result, academic research has flourished and expanded – though not always with impact in relevant business issues. However, their European counterparts lack endowment funds and and have to contend with declining state support, in real terms, for their sustained development. These institutions have therefore come to rely heavily on tuition revenues. In Asia, Latin America and, more recently, parts of Africa, there has been little government support and scarce private sector donations to build endowments, adding to the challenge of building a consistent economic model to ensure local business schools' survival and success. The issue of economic sustainability looks likely to remain critical and complex around the globe, due to rising competition not only to secure revenues but also to raise funds from governments, private foundations and wealthy individuals.

As a result, having a sound and robust economic model becomes a critical source of competitive advantage for consistent academic value delivery. Business schools seem to struggle with several business issues, ranging from defining their cost structure (faculty compensation and other critical expenses) to designing, delivering and positioning their programmes while renewing their fund-raising efforts in the search for donors who want to contribute to society's well-being by supporting business education.

Once a school has built its academic value proposition (academic model) and has determined where it will obtain the necessary financial resources to support that proposition (economic model), it needs to establish its strategic priorities and initiatives. In an extremely uncertain and highly competitive environment, business schools are compelled to set a clear and focused strategic direction that is, at the same time, broad enough to enable and enhance creative and thoughtful engagement from academics, pursuing it consistently and relentlessly. Their *strategic agenda* –the *road map* plotted to reach business schools' intended destination or mission – also needs to rely on an open mindset, combined with assertive and focused decision-making and execution. In a nutshell, schools' strategic agenda needs to be built with initiatives that match their academic model and executed with means provided by their economic model. As Lorange (2008: 215) concludes, 'There are so many different directions that a business school could potentially follow. A clear focus seems paramount, i.e. to choose a destiny and develop a consistent, simple strategy that will enable the school to stay focused and through this create strong academic value.'

In this context, we are going to concentrate on the role of strategic leadership in achieving focus and success. The role of deans is to champion their schools' leadership processes – in other words: to manage, build and execute schools' strategic agenda over time. Nonetheless, as readers know only too well, some specific organisational characteristics of business schools are strongly embedded in these institutions and clearly influence nearly every one of them, as well as other higher education institutions and professional service firms at large. Features such as shared power, dual authority (academic and managerial staff), collegiality and deans' rotation schemes add to the inherent difficulty of leading these institutions. Indeed, the main purpose of this book is to improve the understanding of *how* strategic leadership works in the specific organisational setting of business schools. Three world-class European business schools – LBS, INSEAD and IMD – have been studied to analyse how their strategic agenda with particular reference to internationalisation was built and executed over the period 1990 to 2004. The purpose is to shed some light on the strategic leadership process required for business schools to build and execute a suitable and successful strategic agenda that will guide them to their intended destination.

We discuss and examine the leadership process as a sequence of events, decisions and actions triggered by top-down, bottom-up and horizontal forces. These forces are embodied in the people and features that constitute an organisation's inner and outer environments. Regarding leadership as a collective – shared – process puts people at the centre of this phenomenon. Leadership is, accordingly, construed as a social influence process, in which there is no single actor shaping and executing the school's strategic agenda individually. The diversity of key actors involved, their specific roles, backgrounds, perspectives and concerns, combined with limited resources, in a specific organisational setting brings about a shared leadership process that unfolds over time to respond to challenges, internal and external alike.

3.6   LEADERSHIP AS A PROCESS IN CONTEXT

In the abundant literature on leadership, authors often refer to leadership styles – types of leaders, leadership traits – partly because most of the existing works on this topic approach leadership by focusing on leaders as individuals and the way they relate to others. Many have written about what leaders do and how they do it, including political and religious leaders as well as a number of legendary business moguls, and they have regaled readers of all walks of life with their stories of corporate exploits. Over time, academic studies on leadership have evolved from this individual perspective – grounded primarily in psychology and concentrating on leaders' traits and style, though later expanded to incorporate a situational perspective of their behaviour in different scenarios – toward a relational focus that, based on a sociological approach, zeroes in on the roles of followers and team members. Viewed as a social influence process, leadership refers not only to leaders themselves but to those who follow them as well. Moreover, new leadership theories award the same, if not a more relevant, role to followers and leaders. These theories also consider whether it is leaders who attract followers or followers who create leaders by projecting their own values, beliefs and aspirations onto those individuals. Clearly, there is no leader without followers.

Nevertheless, this social influence process is also embedded in a *context*, which conditions its development. Indeed, context-free approaches to leadership seem to disregard important questions – such as: in what way do internal and external constituencies influence leaders and followers? These questions are the first steps towards the consideration of the influence of context on leadership processes. More evolved leadership theories contemplate the *contextual variables* that influence strategic decisions, including organisations' inner and outer environments and their specific features. These factors are likely to impose different demands on leaders and to require specific leadership behaviours (House and Aditya, 1997). Within an organisation, decision-making is influenced by a number of people and features from its inner and outer contexts, including organisational culture and climate, history, systems, structure, financial resources, performance, competition, economic conditions and customers. Leaders will influence and be influenced by their organisations' environment. In other words, the impact of leaders' actions in an organisation is related to the influence of the organisation on the tasks facing leaders, and vice versa. Key actors' decisions are often constrained or enhanced by factors in their inner and outer environments, organisational inertia resulting from fixed costs and prior commitments, and their own limitations. These constraints and organisations' specific characteristics – including people, the prevailing culture and other organisational features – affect leaders' decisions and behaviours and are influenced by them as well.

Why approach leadership as a process? The driving assumption behind process analysis is that social reality is not static: it unfolds as a dynamic process. Process analysis enables us to *catch reality in flight* (Pettigrew, 1997); it is designed to account for and explain the 'What?', 'Why?' and 'How?' of the links between context, processes and outcomes. Such an approach highlights the complex pattern of interlocking, sequential and simultaneous value-added activities of leadership at different levels in the organisation. It helps explain paradoxes, vicious circles, dilemmas and tensions that derive from the activities of key actors and leaders who hold different positions in the organisation and respond to different external and internal pressures (Burgelman, 2002). This process outlook on leadership focuses primarily on what leaders do to mobilise others in a system of interrelationships, and it visualises the tactics that leaders use to influence the course of events as well as the types of organisational outcomes they promote. It also shows how leaders respond to the results of their past choices and to new developments in their organisations' environment, adjusting their behaviours and future decisions.

The study of leadership advanced here does not view it just as the activity of a single individual or group of people – the top management team – but as a dynamic, ongoing collective process that unfolds across a specific organisational setting and incorporates organisational theory into the overall picture. This processual approach to leadership rebuilds the important link between leadership and strategy that seemed to have been lost over the years in the study of both phenomena. For some authors, leadership studies and research were eventually captured by psychology and sociology scholars, while the focus on strategy appeared to be seized by economists. This gradual estrangement of strategy and leadership issues left managers with no guidance when it came to successfully executing the strategies formulated by their organisations. Leaders knew what they had to do but had no help in figuring out how to do it. In fact, in recent years, business leaders' unmet needs in this regard fuelled the publication of a large number of books and articles focusing on execution.

The processual approach offers a significant opportunity to recapture the link between leadership and strategy in an organisational context in order to get a holistic grasp of strategic challenges, their formulation and their execution. Viewing leadership as a collective, organisational process also enriches strategy formulation and execution with additional communicational and motivational insights. Thus, by means of this contextual and processual approach, we come to focus on the *leadership of organisations* rather than *leadership in organisations* (Bryman, 1992, 1996; House and Aditya, 1997; Hunt, 1991). This broadened approach to the study of leadership regards leadership as an organisational process that influences superior performance in organisations. Performance is thus largely determined by strategic choices and other major organisational decisions made within the organisation (Finkelstein and Hambrick, 1996). The term *strategic leadership* is used because the decisions made by these leaders influence their entire organisations and their destiny. Indeed, the strategic leadership approach responds to this need to 'put top managers back in the strategy picture' (Hambrick, 1989).

While leadership is seen as the process through which leaders influence the attitudes, behaviours and values of others, strategic leadership refers to leaders' or key people's ability to anticipate, envisage, maintain flexibility and empower others to create strategic change as necessary (Hagen, Hassan and Amin, 1998). Strategic leadership is the variable that brings about organisations' strategy formulation and implementation process, and it is indicated by the direction, purpose, adaptation to the environment, and the allocation of resources present in the organisation (Parham, 1994). We define the *strategic leadership process* as 'the set of decisions, actions and events produced by the whole set of key people in providing direction, influencing big strategic choices and implementing them, in order to achieve the organisational mission, over time' (Boal and

Hooijberg, 2001; Collins and Porras, 1994; Dutton, 1986; Grint, 2000; House and Aditya, 1997; Kotter, 1990; Pettigrew, 1973, 1997b; Schein, 1992). This outlook offers a broader understanding of the nature and dynamics of effective leadership, revealing the sequence of roles and events involved in the process, as well as interplays between actors and features influencing decisions over time.

The study of strategic leadership processes in organisational settings is intended to shed light on the set of decisions, actions and events involved in providing direction – *strategic agenda building* – and influencing major strategic choices as well as implementing those choices – *strategic agenda executing* – in order to achieve an organisational mission over time. However, this set of decisions, actions and events is shaped and constrained by contextual factors provided by an organisation's inner and outer settings. Indeed, business schools have a specific organisational context, characterised by key traits and groups of stakeholders that are shared with other higher education institutions and have parallels with the context of professional service firms, as we discuss next. It is necessary to understand how these inner and outer context forces and actors interact in the specific setting of business schools and similar organisations.

3.7   A CONTEXTUAL APPROACH TO STRATEGIC LEADERSHIP PROCESSES IN BUSINESS SCHOOLS

Like most higher education institutions and professional service firms, business schools are loosely coupled organisations, with a set of distinctive traits and characteristics that conform to a highly unusual organisational setting. It is a well-known fact that leading a business school is not the same as leading a corporation. In most academic institutions and professional service firms, leadership roles are not viewed as career aspirations, unlike the coveted CEO position in most business companies. Rather, professional and academic career paths tend to revolve around building and consolidating a specific expertise and reputation – for example, as an academic by

securing tenure, succeeding as a scholar, conducting groundbreaking research and publishing the relevant findings.

The dean of a business school is sometimes seen by its internal
constituencies as 'first among equals', as he/she is elected directly
or indirectly by the faculty to serve for a specific term, eventually
rejoining the faculty when his/her term concludes. The dean is rarely
viewed as the boss; rather, he/she is regarded as more of a colleague.
Antonio Borges, INSEAD dean from 1995 to 2000, remarked, 'So the
dean, to a certain extent, is also accountable to the faculty, having
been elected by them. And there are some intermediate structures of
management that also re-emphasise the role of the faculty.' This is
even more the case in institutions featuring a tenure system: while
deans may be ousted by faculty members, they can seldom remove
professors from their chairs. Like senior partners in professional service firms, and unlike top executives in corporations, faculty members 'believe they have a right to question, debate, and even oppose
initiatives with which they disagree – and often do so' (Lorsch and
Tierney, 2002).

Collegiality is undeniably a distinctive trait that characterises
the academic and professional service worlds. Unlike most business
executives, academics do not generally report to a hierarchical superior, but refer mostly to their colleagues for approval, recognition and
respect. This culturally embedded phenomenon seems to shape the
way power flows in these organisations. Indeed, power tends to be
shared and diffused, residing largely in professional and intellectual
expertise as well as in personal prestige, although there is a managerial scheme with formal authority assigned for administrative
and resource allocation purposes. However, some business schools
are shifting towards a more managerial style of governance in an
effort to deal with the increasing competition and market demands
of management education. These institutions seem to pursue a more
business-oriented leadership approach, with the dean – sometimes
an experienced former executive or management consultant – resembling a regular CEO in more aligned organisations. Though still

incipient, this governance scheme seems to be permeating the world of business schools – albeit with varying formats – as they struggle to find new ways to address the current challenges. In these institutions, making decisions and setting the direction are predominantly top-down processes that reflect more of a business mindset than the horizontal, collegial idiosyncrasy of academia, but they still require bottom-up and horizontal inputs stemming from academic and research needs. These organisations are likely to be more market-responsive and entrepreneurial in their undertakings and goals.

Dual authority accounts for another distinctive characteristic of business schools, as academic and managerial roles need to coexist and interact in the same organisation, with different agendas and goals. This dual authority scheme compounds the complexity of strategic leadership – mostly for deans, who need to ensure the effective integration of both business and academic worlds across the organisation in order to lead successfully. As Lorange (2008: 183) writes, 'Business school leaders need to balance their time between the classic leadership focus on top- and bottom-line performance and a broader set of objectives.' These objectives typically and notably include academic excellence – a primary concern for faculty members.

In order to gain a better understanding of the contextual approach to strategic leadership as a process in business schools, Figure 3.3 shows the key actors involved in shaping schools' strategic agenda over time. It also presents the critical features of schools' inner and outer contexts that influence key actors' decisions and actions as they interact to build and execute their organisations' strategic agendas.

The three key actors in business schools are all 'influencers', who shape and guide their institutions' decisions and actions. The *dean* is generally entrusted with the mission to secure the school's sustainability and strategic performance, taking the lead in the process of building and executing its strategic agenda. The *board* is responsible for ensuring the school's long-term governance,

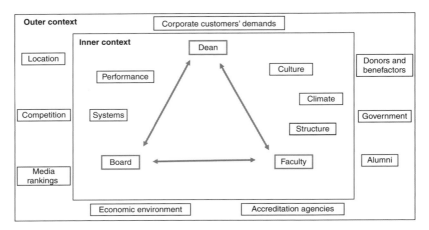

FIGURE 3.3 SLPs' extended contextual framework

sustainability and reputation (note that, in university-based business schools, the 'board' includes the university president and the board of trustees (sometimes a university council) as well as the school's advisory board). Both the dean and the board stand at the school's strategic apex, and their decisions bear an impact on the entire organisation, since they constitute its highest formal authority. The *faculty*, with no official governance role, bears a natural influence on long-term academic and institutional decisions affecting the school's performance and reputation.

As George Bain, London Business School's experienced dean (principal) between 1989 and 1997, recalled, '[M]y real boss was the faculty... I was sort of the "first amongst the equals", so I wasn't too worried about the governing body. The governing body would always say, "George, you are the chief executive – just like the chief executive of a company." And I'd say, "No, no, no, I'm not... At best, think of me as the managing partner of a law firm or a consultancy."' On account of the specific idiosyncrasies of academic organisations, faculty members' support and contributions to building and executing the school's strategic agenda are crucial – much in the same way as professionals enjoy substantial influence in any professional service firm. In all fairness, at some business schools, key staff members may be viewed as a fourth group of influencers, with a bearing on their organisations' strategic agenda building and executing processes, though that is not the case in most institutions.

An organisational approach to strategic leadership in context requires not only consideration of people or groups of people and their capacity to influence, but also factoring in some critical features from both organisations' inner and outer contexts that constrain or facilitate key actors' activities over time. Figure 3.3 shows the most salient inner context features – namely organisational culture and climate; systems, especially faculty's academic promotion, tenure and compensation schemes; and schools' performance – that influence and are, in turn, influenced by strategic leadership processes in business schools. As several deans, board and faculty members included in our study (of LBS, INSEAD and IMD) have emphasised, performance became instrumental to gaining credibility in order to raise groundbreaking initiatives to their organisations' strategic agendas. In the same vein, early wins prove very useful to bolster new deans' credibility and power. For LBS's George Bain, there is a 'honeymoon period. You've got six months, eight months, a year at most, to bring the big changes in. [...] I am a great believer that you've got to get some quick wins.'[1] It is worth noting that we refer to performance here in a very general fashion, engulfing financial results as well as reputation and positioning in both academic and business spheres. Finally, within business schools' inner context, structure plays a critical role, given the idiosyncrasy of academic organisations, traditionally characterised by the existence of boundaries between academic groups, tenure track hierarchies and collegiality.

Business schools' strategic agenda building and executing process is also conditioned by external factors and developments as well as by inner context features. Their outer context, depicted in Figure 3.3, includes nine major elements: location, competition,

---

[1] Interview with George Bain, former LBS dean.

media rankings, economic setting, accreditation agencies, corporate clients, alumni, donors and benefactors, and the local government. We have discussed some of them already – including fierce competition, as well as the emergence and rapidly growing influence of management education rankings – when we looked at the current challenges faced by business schools in an increasingly globalised world. As for location, despite common traits and tests shared by business schools around the globe, each one's geographical setting bears an additional, specific impact on its performance and growth potential. Indeed, historical events also influence business schools' strategic leadership processes, just as they shape the destiny of all human organisations. In fact, throughout the span of our study over the 1990–2004 period, a number of developments truly changed the world in many ways, including the Gulf War and the subsequent recession, the advent of the worldwide web, the dot.com bubble collapse, Asia's financial crisis, the attacks of 11 September and the avian flu outbreak in Asia, to name but a few.

Individuals think differently and want to act differently. Alone or in groups, they struggle to pursue and serve their interests. In loosely coupled organisations such as business schools, diverging interests come into conflict. Whether acting autonomously or as members of a coalition, key actors latch onto issues and use their power to place their interests on the school's strategic agenda (Dutton, 1986). The size of the agenda, determined by the schools' limited resources, forces actors to engage in negotiation and consensus-building activities to ensure that their *main generic interests* (MGIs) secure a place in the school's strategic agenda and are effectively pursued by the organisation. We intend to concentrate on key actors' MGIs – that is, those that apply to each influential group or role and affect the school's strategic agenda building and executing process – as revealed by the study conducted at INSEAD, IMD and LBS over the period from 1990 to 2004.

Even though main generic interests depend on key actors' roles and are always present in their agendas, some of those interests often

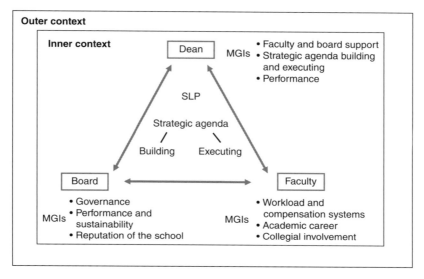

FIGURE 3.4 SLPs' core contextual framework

take precedence over others as a result of environmental, demographic or other conditions. Thus, for example, the dean may prioritise the school's financial performance over other long-term goals in the institution's strategic agenda-building and -executing process in times of economic unrest. However, MGIs are not prioritised and pursued solely in response to specific external or internal features but also as a result of personal characteristics – background, leadership style, skills and values – that also affect key actors' decision-making. Figure 3.4 shows business schools' key actors with their respective, role-based main generic interests, introducing strategic leadership as a strategic agenda-building and -executing process that results from the interplay between key actors. MGIs are prioritised according to key actors' characterisation and key features of both the outer and inner contexts, which act as hurdles and enablers of the strategic leadership process over time. Key actors' MGI prioritisation impacts strongly on the initiatives that become part of schools' strategic agendas.

It should be noted that the underlying study of these business schools is not intended to analyse every interest of every key actor in business schools, but only those interests that are specific to their individual roles. It should also be recognised that the interests considered are generic – that is, they are applicable to an entire class or group that is differentiated from other groups. Among key actors' generic interests, this study focuses on those that are most important, because they affect schools' strategic agenda-building and -executing. Findings have shown that deans' main generic interests include faculty and board support, as they need the approval of both groups to legitimate their decisions; strategic agenda building and executing, as they view the SLP as a long-term, decisive process; and performance, as they are indeed responsible for ensuring school sustainability. Boards, instead, are mainly concerned with issues associated with schools' governance, performance, sustainability and reputation. In turn, faculty interests mostly focus on workload and compensation systems (transparency and fair rewards), academic career development (long-term professional growth) and collegial involvement (participation in shared power).

As Figure 3.4 suggests, in business schools – and in most higher education institutions and professional service firms, as well – strategic leadership involves complex, collective ongoing processes that unfold in an elaborate, unique organisational setting. In other words, strategic leadership processes feature political and social influence activities, and they are shaped by the interplay between key actors with different roles and interests, who share limited resources and a single strategic agenda. While the dean is usually the school's strategic champion, he/she is not the only individual framing its strategic agenda. Additionally, as noted by Lorsch and Tierney (2002: 170), exercising this type of leadership is 'exceptionally challenging because the position lacks the inherent power and control that CEOs of traditional companies enjoy'. Although these authors are referring to the responsibilities of professional service firm managing partners, we feel that their description fits the leadership requirements of business schools' leaders as well. Indeed, they also point out that 'leadership in this context has a lot more to do with the details of managing a complex organisation and economic system effectively than it does with delivering the occasional inspiring speech' (171).

As key actors in business schools interact in different roles and with differing interests, strategic leadership processes call for a combination of negotiation skills and power. Although an organisation's members may agree on the goals to be included in its strategic agenda, establishing priorities and allocating limited resources accordingly can be daunting. Diversity in actors' roles and positions, backgrounds and interests introduces a political dimension into SLPs. In addition, the choice between alternative paths of action usually hinges on the power relations between key actors. INSEAD's former dean, Antonio Borges, has noted, 'You have to first build the consensus and get support, make sure that everybody is going to follow you, and, then, once you do that internally, you also have to do that with the board, and with the alumni, and with all the supporters, all the donors that provide the capital support for the school.'[2]

A political approach therefore proves very useful, in viewing leadership as an interplay between several actors with different interests competing for scarce resources and influence on the scope of the strategic agenda. The political analysis focuses on how divergent interests give rise to visible and invisible conflicts that individuals within the leadership constellation solve while trying to further their collective interests. As Laura Tyson, LBS dean from 2000 to 2005, has pointed out, 'The main thing that I think a dean is trying to do is actually trying to represent the institution to the different groups that don't quite see the institution in the same way. So you're standing for the collective interests and the future of this institution.'[3]

---

[2] Interview with Antonio Borges, former INSEAD dean.
[3] Interview with Laura Tyson, former LBS dean.

3.8   STRATEGIC LEADERSHIP PROCESSES IN
BUSINESS SCHOOLS: A POLITICAL APPROACH

To study organisations, authors often use metaphors or images that provide part of the picture in understanding organisational phenomena. Organisations may be viewed as machines and regarded as *bureaucracies*, consisting of interlocking parts that each play a specific role. They may also be studied as *organisms*, with special attention being paid to how organisational needs and environmental relations are understood and managed. When organisations are considered as *brains*, studies focus on information-processing, learning and intelligence, providing a set of principles to create 'learning organisations'. In approaching organisations as *cultures*, analysts focus on values, ideas, beliefs, forms, rituals and other patterns of shared meaning that guide organisational life.

Finally, when the *political* metaphor is used, the focus is on the different sets of detailed factors, such as interests, conflicts, and power plays, that shape organisational activities. It should be noted that the political approach to the study of organisations can create powerful insights that also become distortions, so that the 'way of seeing becomes a way of *not* seeing' (Morgan, 1986; emphasis in original; Allison and Zelikow, 1999). However, by enabling us to visualise the 'underweaving' of social actions, the political approach facilitates the understanding of power and influence processes.

The political organisational construct regards organisations as pluralistic entities divided into various subunits, which are wedded to their own goals, interests and subcultures. Basically, it assumes that power and politics are facts of life in organisations, and, as a result, that these are not issues that can be easily dismissed or ignored. This political model enables us to visualise the diversity of interests at play when people think differently and want to act differently, and it shows how this diversity gives rise to wheeling and dealing, negotiation and other processes of coalition building and mutual influence within any organisation.

In organisational settings, the political approach focuses on three elements: contextual factors, structural conditions and content of influence. *Contextual factors* refer to environmental conditions determined by the outer context, such as the political, social and legal environments, cultural and historical trends and economic setting. These factors also include organisations' inner context features, including their people, background, culture, values, coalitions, policies, systems and business performance. *Structural conditions* point to the power distribution patterns triggered by the disparity of roles and functions of organisational constituencies (such as the board, the CEO, committees) and their influence on leadership. Both contextual factors (the outer and inner contexts) and structural conditions determine how key actors obtain their influence, which is constrained and limited by the influence of others – the *content of influence*. Key actors' power sources are provided and restricted by the setting, but their power mobilisation depends on their will and skill to transform their potential power into power in action (see Figure 3.5).

Thus, a political analysis within organisational settings entails the identification of different roles for the key actors (structural conditions) in a particular environment (outer and inner contexts), an assessment of the scope of their power (content of influence) and an analysis of the nature of their influence (power sources) and the strategies employed by these groups as they translate power into action (power uses) in the form of political behaviour. In other words, the political perspective within a specific organisational context requires an understanding of the interests and demands that result from individual functions and responsibilities, values and perspectives and scarce resources to determine how demands are generated and presented as well as how power is mobilised around demands to build support, to overcome resistance, to resolve conflicts and to produce desired outcomes.

As already stated, business schools – like most professional service firms and other higher education institutions – are loosely

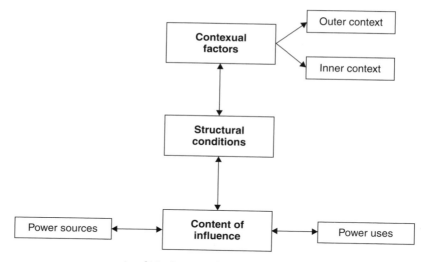

FIGURE 3.5 A political approach to organisations

coupled organisations, in which power tends to be shared on the basis of personal expertise and reputation. In fact, as readers are surely well aware, in these organisations managerial authority refers to formal authority rather than to real power. To regard business schools as a political arena, it is necessary to understand how demands stem from different interests that, in turn, result from the diversity of functions and responsibilities held by key actors within each organisation. Further, we need to look at how key actors mobilise power to gain support for their demands and produce desired outcomes, and how conflicts of interest are ultimately solved.

Key actors in business schools – the dean, faculty and board – interplay to shape their organisations' strategic agendas and to set priorities, competing for economic and other critical resources. Their diverse interests – resulting from their different roles, demographics, cultures, backgrounds and mindsets – make this process even more complex and dependent on their ability to build, use and mobilise power as well as to rally consensus around initiatives. A political analysis of SLPs seems to facilitate the observation of these phenomena as social influence processes that unfold among constituents in organisations. This political approach serves as a lens focusing on the generation of diverse interests and demands that result from the division of work, scarce organisational resources and the disparity of perspectives. Moreover, this lens centres attention on human action: in essence, how conflicts are overcome through the use of power. In observing strategic leadership from a processual perspective in an organisational setting in which power tends to be shared and collegiality permeates the way in which academics relate to each other, a political analysis zeroes in on power mobilisation issues associated with building and executing the strategic agenda over time.

The full scope of potential decisions and actions taken to address strategic issues 'falls along a continuum ranging from modest, small-scale change to far more extensive radical and dramatic changes' (Dutton and Duncan, 1987: 286). Strategic issues involving a turning point in the strategic agenda of the organisation produce *breakthrough initiatives* that bear a significant impact on the organisational agenda. In contrast, strategic issues that pursue strategies that have been set previously produce only *incremental initiatives.* Breakthrough initiatives imply a turning point in schools' strategic direction, altering their resource and organisational capability allocation patterns as well as bearing an impact on their culture, systems and structures. Obviously, these groundbreaking projects require effective issue selling and a thoughtful consideration of potential supporters and opponents.

In order for deans to lead their schools' strategic agenda successfully, they need not only to articulate and communicate their vision and key initiatives effectively but also to identify possible champions and supporters to move forward, overcoming hurdles and resistance from other key actors who may oppose critical decisions. Using an American football analogy, Bain, of LBS, has remarked that deans need political support to make sure they have 'the backing' required to get their initiatives through. Bain explains that he dealt with opposition first 'by building coalitions and making sure that what was coming up would have fairly broadly based support'.[4] This was even more the case in the event of breakthrough initiatives, which call for substantial communication and persuasion efforts, with a significant use of power by deans and their supporters, as they involve significant changes that affect their organisations' culture, future and identity. Incremental initiatives, on the other hand, are usually less controversial and easier to sell across the organisation, for they revolve around or further strategies that have already been formulated and pursued with sufficient consensus. These initiatives basically continue previously established strategies, and, as such, involve less dramatic changes and need lesser selling effort.

Indeed, power appears to be a critical concept in carrying out a political analysis of strategic leadership within organisational settings. As a relational phenomenon that seems to be generated, maintained and lost in the context of relationships with others, power has to be exercised in order to have an effect on outcomes, influencing who gets what, when and how (Morgan, 1997). Power is a relative concept that can be explained only in a particular context; if it is displayed on one occasion, it may not be transferable to other settings. Key actors may hold power for a limited period of time and in a specific situation, but such power may not last, since power distribution varies over time. Thus, since power is inherently situational, dynamic and potentially unstable, it has to be understood in its political context – i.e. power distribution throughout the organisation – and in its historical context – i.e. its specific time frame. It should be noted that, in this book, power is viewed as a neutral or value-free concept. It refers to the capacity to influence people and make things happen. It can be used either to attempt to fulfil one's own responsibility and duties or to manipulate other people. This makes it crucial for key actors to understand the nature and purpose of power: what it is, how it is built and how it is lost when abused, used when it is not necessary or vice versa.

---

[4] Interview with George Bain, former LBS dean.

As already mentioned, power is conditioned by contextual and structural factors in every organisation. In business schools, given their idiosyncratic characteristics, some inner context features – such as performance, culture, coalitions, personal background and reputation – are particularly relevant. Structural conditions associated with position, role and formal authority, though clearly significant, are not as decisive as they usually seem to be in corporate or more hierarchical organisations. On the contrary, informal power sources, such as networking, academic standing and prestige, resource allocation and reward or punishment schemes, become essential to build power in business schools. However, power sources account only for the initial conditions in terms of exerting influence on others. Will and skill become key drivers for power mobilisation, through the use of behavioural or relational tactics that include information management, assertiveness, rationality, coalition building, ingratiation and exchanges. All the same, personal values such as integrity, personal commitment and consistent behaviour are instrumental in reinforcing credibility and securing support.

Key actors exert influence through power mobilisation in order to prioritise some issues and to incorporate them in their organisations' strategic agendas. The analysis of IMD, INSEAD and LBS over the 1990–2004 period that serves as a backbone to this book intends to identify *how* different key actors build and use power to influence strategic agenda building and executing over time, showing, at the same time, *how* inner and outer context features alike both shape and are shaped by strategic leadership processes.

Nonetheless, leadership is not just about getting things done or getting other people to do what is wanted to be done. To lead is also to motivate and inspire others. In the words of Bain, '[L]eadership is the ability to get someone else to do – delegation – what you want done – direction – because they want to do it – motivation.'[5] These three elements – delegation, direction and motivation – are

---

[5] Interview with George Bain, former LBS dean.

critical elements in any leadership task. We have characterised leadership as a social influence process; as a result, and as readers probably know only too well, motivation plays a central role in leadership.

We have also defined leadership as a collective process, in which several people or groups of people interact in different roles, with different interests and perspectives, to raise their issues to their organisation's strategic agenda. In this process, the motivational component of leadership is brought about by actors' efforts to legitimate each initiative to be included in the agenda. As John Quelch, LBS dean from 1997 to 2000, has remarked, 'Everybody wants to be a part of something that they feel is energy, is on the move, is successful, and my job was really to create the energy, the atmosphere.'[6]

Throughout the analysis of the three business schools studied in depth here, several elements have been explored to assess key actors' approach to issue legitimation: issue sponsorship and selling, agenda structure, the alignment of MGIs prioritised and inner and outer context features. In all three cases, deans were found to be the key initiative sponsors. However, while they were the highest formal authority because of their position in their schools' structure, the particular characteristics of business schools as higher education institutions (shared power and dual authority) made it necessary for deans to secure the support of other key actors. Issue legitimation therefore complements power mobilisation throughout strategic leadership processes. Legitimation occurs when key constituents to be affected by new initiatives 'buy' them, or at least recognise their value for the organisation and for themselves.

Power mobilisation and issue legitimation are both crucial parts of the SLP, yet there are no fixed rules to guide or constrain this process. Clearly, the struggle to legitimate a new and bold initiative leading to significant organisational change will be substantially

---

[6] Interview with John Quelch, former LBS dean.

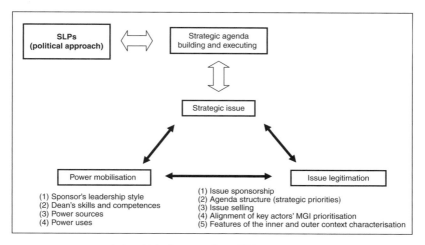

FIGURE 3.6 A political approach to SLPs

greater than the one needed to push through an incremental initiative that does no more than continue the pursuit of a strategy already
embraced by the organisation. Breakthrough initiatives require committed, consistent issue legitimation efforts to sell, articulate and
communicate them in a transparent, attractive and eloquent way,
not only to minimise resistance or opposition but also to motivate
all stakeholders by appealing to their aspirations, values and beliefs.
These initiatives also call for sponsors to fully exploit the entire
range of their power sources – both structural and personal – and
power uses so as to ensure successful execution. Figure 3.6 shows
how SLPs work from a political perspective.

The contextual and political approaches to SLPs that we have
discussed so far complement each other, offering a combined, well-
rounded overview of how these processes unfold in organisational
settings. In fact, it is hardly possible for key actors to move forward
with their issue legitimation and power mobilisation efforts without a clear, thorough understanding of their organisations' outer and
inner contexts. Figure 3.7 combines both perspectives to show how
the two complement and reinforce each other as people and organisational features change over time.

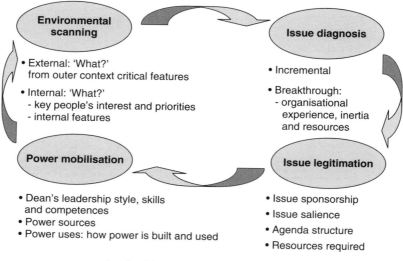

FIGURE 3.7 Leadership process dynamics

Direction setting results from a combination of strategic choices that are constrained by environmental forces (Lorange, 2002). Organisations usually seek to interpret these forces by looking into their internal and external environment. Bain explains, 'I'm a pretty good listener and I took on board everybody's points.'[7] This managerial activity of learning about events and trends in the organisation's environment is defined as *environmental scanning* (Hambrick, 1981). Environmental scanning can be conceived of as the first step in the ongoing chain of perceptions and actions by which environmental data and stimuli are translated into focused issues. These strategic issues become relevant because they are likely to have a significant impact on the organisation's present and future strategies. Indeed, former IMD dean Peter Lorange asserts that, in order to be able to adapt to the signals that come from the marketplace and, thus, create value, business schools have to be demand-oriented and externally focused, rather than supply-oriented and internally focused. It is by carrying out environmental scanning that they can understand the

[7] Interview with George Bain, former LBS dean.

growth segments. As Lorange puts it, '[T]he external environment is critical. It is a "raison d'être" for the whole organisation.'

However, identifying strategic issues through the diagnosis enabled by environmental scanning does not rely solely on the observation of the external setting. It also builds on existing openings in the organisational context. Moreover, given the impact of the organisational context in shaping issue interpretations, several studies support the idea that it is an important influence on decision-makers and refer to three major aspects of organisational context: organisational experience, inertia and resources (Capelli and Scherer, 1991; Denison *et al.*, 1996). Through environmental scanning and issue diagnosis, key actors – deans in particular – collect relevant information to identify trends and opportunities, threats and obstacles in their organisations' external and internal environments in order to formulate either breakthrough or incremental initiatives for schools' strategic agendas.

This political perspective on the study of the SLP in business schools facilitates the observation of how people use and mobilise power to influence decisions. Such a perspective enables us to visualise different *interests* and *demands* that arise and compete for organisational attention and resources. Given the distinctive idiosyncrasy of these loosely coupled organisations in which power tends to be shared between the dean, the faculty and other key constituencies, a political approach enables the observation of strategic leadership as a social influence process with a contextual approach. The political perspective brings this dynamic process into sharp focus. From this perspective, the content of strategic decisions is viewed as an outcome of transactions of power and influence. The implication is that an examination of strategy content alone is insufficient to explain strategic choices. Only by investigating the 'organisational processes out of which strategies emerge...can one understand and explain why they come to be' (Narayanan and Fahey, 1982). That is the purpose of the journey across three leading international business schools over a fifteen-year period, as described in the next chapter.

3.9   A GLANCE AT STRATEGIC LEADERSHIP
IN PRACTICE

To illustrate the notions discussed in this chapter and to gain a better understanding of SLPs, a series of longitudinal and comparative
case studies of IMD, INSEAD and LBS were conducted over the
1990–2004 period. Longitudinal design permits the study of long-
term processes in context, with insights into variable order eventually facilitating causal inferences. As a result, causation and
connectivity can be determined, while patterns are easily identified
and explained. The case study method is a 'research strategy [that]
focuses on understanding the dynamics present within single settings' (Pettigrew, 1992), tracing processes in their natural contexts
(Eisenhardt, 1989; Pettigrew, 1992; Van de Ven, 1992; Yin, 1994). This
research methodology proves suitable for an in-depth exploration of
strategic leadership processes in business schools, describing and
explaining the sequence of events, interconnections and behaviour
patterns involved in SLPs. Finally, given that the case study method
essentially generates theories about specific phenomena, a multiple
sample increases the study's external validity and helps to prevent
observer bias. Thus, each case study serves to confirm or challenge
the inferences drawn from other cases. Comparing strategic leadership processes at three business schools provides a springboard for
theoretical reflections on the issues discussed above.

In line with process research practices, a temporal bracketing
strategy is employed here. This study breaks down the chronological
data identified in each business school into successive time periods
or phases that become comparative units of analysis. Phases are
defined so that there is context and action continuity, with boundaries marked by turning points or 'social dramas' (Pettigrew, 1979).
Changes in the three schools' deanship, as well as their initiatives
to become top international business schools, are analysed to determine how strategic leadership processes unfold through strategic
agenda building and executing. Comparisons between these strategic

initiatives undertaken by each deanship and between all three business schools over this period of time favour pattern identification.

Data were gathered from multiple sources: semi-structured ninety- to 120-minute interviews with members of schools' key constituencies: boards, deans, faculty and staff; documentary and archival data from all three business schools, including books on their history, brochures, speeches, presentations, annual reports, minutes, *Business Week* and *Financial Times* rankings, materials published by AACSB and EQUIS; and statistical data on the evolution of schools' inner and outer context key features – e.g. faculty, board and students' and major stakeholders' profiles.

This study, fully discussed in Chapters 4 and 5, examines the SLPs of these three top European business schools in terms of the following questions.

(1) Who are the key actors in each case? How do they interplay in exerting influence to shape and execute their school's strategic agenda while raising their own interests?

(2) What are the main features of each school's inner and outer contexts that influence its strategic agenda building and executing over time, and what is their respective influence?

(3) How do key actors mobilise (build and use) power and legitimate issues in order to successfully shape strategic agenda building and executing over time?

To answer each of these analytical questions, this study first identified key constituencies within each business school and their main generic interests over time. It did not focus exclusively on deans but also on other people who influenced the process of these organisations' strategic agenda building and executing; in other words, boards and faculties were also surveyed. Moreover, this study also identified key actors within these constituencies to determine who had the most influence and to establish how they prioritised their main generic interests over time.

Next, critical features of schools' outer and inner contexts influencing these strategic agenda-building and -executing processes were also studied so as to determine how these characteristics affected interest prioritisation and legitimation throughout the study period. In order to understand how key actors mobilised (built and used) power to raise or block initiatives and how they legitimated or de-legitimated other strategic issues, influencing schools' SLPs, the study explored the power sources and uses that helped them to prevail over time. Initiatives were categorised as breakthrough or incremental, and their development was analysed in terms of issue legitimation, based on issue sponsorship and selling, the alignment of key actors' MGI prioritisation, the agenda structure and the characterisation of features of both the outer and inner contexts. Finally, the study focused on power mobilisation according to sponsors' leadership style as well as deans' skills, competences, power sources and power uses. Findings were compared within each business school and across all three over time. Similarities and differences could therefore be identified, and patterns could be established regarding the strategic leadership process as a social influence process in the specific setting of business schools.

4 Strategic leadership in practice: leading the strategic process in three top business schools

4.1 INTRODUCTION

The previous chapter explained the logic of the processual approach to studying the strategic leadership process. In order to understand the SLP in context, this chapter examines the efforts deployed by three leading European business schools, IMD, INSEAD and LBS, to compete in the international business school market. This analysis also provides a historical account of the events that determined these schools' evolutionary process against the backdrop of the significant developments that changed Europe – and the world at large – in the late twentieth century and early years of the third millennium.

IMD, INSEAD and LBS were studied over the period from 1990 to 2004. To explore SLP practices, the study focused on several initiatives launched by all three schools over these fifteen years to address a specific strategic goal: *consolidating their standing as top international business schools*. The purpose of this study has been to follow some of the initiatives pursued by these schools to accomplish this aim, using them as vehicles to analyse the SLP in context from a political perspective. Their strategies and actions were approached and analysed from a contextual approach, explained in detail in particular in Chapter 3. After identifying the prevailing aspects shaping their external contexts and the key actors interacting in their internal contexts at each stage within the study's time span, our analysis zeroed in on the contextual features that influenced – and were influenced by – each school's strategic agenda building and execution over time. Finally, adopting a political perspective, the study surveyed how key actors built and used power to raise, prioritise and legitimate their strategic initiatives in order to support their schools' progress towards successful internationalisation.

The study unfolded in three stages. First, it identified some of the key strategic initiatives undertaken by each school during the 1990–2004 period to enhance and consolidate their international positioning. Next, the study explored each school's agenda-building and execution efforts, organising them sequentially under each deanship and studying how contextual factors and actors shaped their development and were, in turn, affected by them. In its third and final stage, the study focused on issue legitimation and power mobilisation practices, examining sponsors' leadership styles, deans' skills and competences, and key actors' power sources and uses to understand how and why some strategic initiatives were successfully incorporated into schools' strategic agendas and effectively pursued while others failed to make it through.

A combination of a longitudinal approach and a comparative case study was employed to depict the course of events in the schools' external and internal contexts in order to establish patterns and to examine temporal interconnectedness, looking at past, present and future developments. The study sought to explore how strategic agenda-building and execution processes unfolded over time as IMD, INSEAD and LBS, each with its distinctive features, set out to consolidate their positioning as a top international business school. The strategic issues prioritised by each school were examined through the sets of initiatives or episodes that triggered decisions and actions to achieve them. The case study research design called for the utilisation of three primary data sources from each business school: nearly thirty semi-structured interviews with members of all key constituencies at every school; documentary and archival materials; and quantitative and statistical data. All three schools were extremely helpful and generous with their information and in terms of their willingness to collaborate.

4.2 IMD, INSEAD AND LBS: CONTEXTUAL COMMONALITIES AND SPECIFICITIES

The period from 1990 to 2004 was a time of major geopolitical and economic changes that reshaped the world at large and the European continent in particular. All three schools faced an increasingly competitive market, both at home and abroad. The introduction of numerous newcomers and new rules of the game unfolded as a result of the dramatic historical developments that rearranged the global landscape. Events such as the fall of the Berlin Wall, with its political ramifications, a worldwide economic crisis brought on by the Gulf War, the growth of the European Union and the overarching trend towards globalisation engulfed all human endeavours, but they had a more tangible effect on business management. The worldwide consequences of the devastating terrorist attacks in the United States and Europe had an impact on these three schools as well, demanding new approaches to their strategic agenda building and execution in order to respond to the new challenges confronting them.

As the European Union consolidated after the 1992 Maastricht Treaty, its member states embraced common policies on a number of significant fields in addition to monetary and market unification, including citizenship, foreign affairs, continental security and labour regulations. Other regional markets were also being built in the Americas and Asia. Escalating global trade was intensified by new technological developments, such as the advent of the internet, which fuelled a revolution in communications. Technology created the possibility, and even the likelihood, of a global culture, as the internet and global communications swept away geographical and cultural boundaries (Castells, 2000).[1] A myriad of potential opportunities emerged for new businesses and investments, leading industries of all kinds to reformulate their operations so as to adapt to

---

[1] See also 'Globalization and culture' at www.globalpolicy.igc.org.

these profound changes that transformed domestic and regional markets into a global marketplace.

While the 1991 Gulf War and several financial crises around the world added turbulence to the global scene, Europe itself underwent remarkable political changes in the 1990–2004 period. Although the bulk of the eastern European countries that had formerly been in the Soviet Union's sphere of influence did not join the European Union until 2004 and a few are still candidates awaiting approval, the events following the fall of the Berlin Wall in 1989 both inside and outside Russia brought about a new stage in worldwide and European geopolitics. Barriers fell and new markets emerged, with unprecedented growth potential and speed, as a result of technological breakthroughs. The process that unfolded in that period has brought the European Union to where it stands today: twenty-seven member states with a total population of some 500 million 'united in diversity' – as its motto proclaims – to jointly produce an estimated 30 per cent of the world's nominal gross product. Indeed, even the European states that have chosen not to join the grouping, such as Switzerland, have also adhered to most of its cornerstone principles and policies.

However, globalisation has also dramatically altered the way business is done around the world. The business community has been forced to adjust to this new scenario. The creation of worldwide brands, a truly global market and the ability to move money around the world in nanoseconds required a new education to help managers to navigate this tumultuous environment successfully (Wankel and DeFillippi, 2004: 305). Business executives had to be able to think internationally, taking into consideration the state of the world at large in the implementation of strategic decisions. They needed management education to acquire the competences required to anticipate and exploit new trends. At the same time, the marketplace for business schools became ripe, with relentless change and fierce competition for the same, now global corporate clients. The three schools in this study, all top-tier institutions in Europe, were no longer competing only with their leading European counterparts, such as Spain's IESE, but also with the prestigious American Ivy League pioneers, such as HBS and Wharton. As the worldwide demand for business education increased, new programmes emerged in response, and the range of options available to those who looked for answers on the management education industry broadened. As a result, business schools were urged to shift their focus in order to respond to the new priorities and demands (AACSB, 2002; van Baalen and Moratis, 2001).

However, there is one element in these three leading European schools' external contexts that differed and posed specific challenges for each of them. IMD, INSEAD and LBS shared several environmental components – increased competition, global corporate and private customers, more prominent media rankings, similar or common regulatory frameworks, a growing number of international accreditation agencies – that clearly determined many of their features, opportunities and threats. Nonetheless, their individual locations accounted for some specificities that have challenged and favoured each one of them in different ways. In the 1990s INSEAD was located in Fontainebleau, a commune in the metropolitan area of Paris. This large Parisian suburb, a favourite weekend getaway for city dwellers, is 55 kilometres (34 miles) away from the centre of the French capital. In turn, Lausanne, IMD's home town, is the capital of the Vaud canton in Switzerland. This French-speaking city on the shores of Lake Geneva is located some 50 kilometres (31 miles) north-east of the Swiss capital and houses such international institutions as the Olympic Committee and the Court of Arbitration for Sports. Finally, LBS is based at the heart of one of the world's undisputed political, cultural and business hubs, constantly attracting people from virtually every nation on the globe. Their dissimilar surrounding geographies have unquestionably marked the immediate physical external contexts of these three schools, bringing to bear an undeniable impact on their evolution and strategies, even though their big-picture challenges have rendered them akin.

Table 4.1 *All three schools in executive education rankings, open enrolment programmes*

Source	Business school	2000	2001	2002	2003	2004
Financial Times	IMD	4	5	11	6	4
	INSEAD	15	11	15	9	11
	LBS	11	4	14	7	7
Business Week	IMD	–	8	–	8	–
	INSEAD	–	2	–	5	–
	LBS	–	7	–	10	–

Sources: www.ft.com; www.businessweek.com.

Table 4.2 *All three schools in worldwide M.B.A. rankings*

Source	Business school	2000	2001	2002	2003	2004
Financial Times	IMD	11	11	14	13	12
	INSEAD	9	7	6	6	4
	LBS	8	8	9	7	4
*Business Week**	IMD	4	–	3	–	2
	INSEAD	1	–	1	–	3
	LBS	2	–	4	–	5

Note: *Non-US business schools only.
Sources: www.ft.com; www.businessweek.com.

Both to illustrate our sample schools' performance in recent years and to justify their choice as leading institutions in their field, Tables 4.1 and 4.2 show their positions in worldwide executive education rankings published by the United Kingdom's *Financial Times* and the United States' *Business Week*.

After this brief overview of the external context that exerted its influence on all three business schools in the 1990–2004 period, the following sections describe the case studies, with each school's evolutionary periods determined by the turning points (*social dramas*) that propelled significant changes in its direction. In these detailed presentations, internal context features and key actors predominantly hold the spotlight, as they characterise the specifics of strategic leadership processes at each school over time.

4.3   IMD

The Institute for Management Development was founded in 1990 in Lausanne through the merger of two Swiss business schools, Geneva's IMI (International Management Institute) and IMEDE (Institut pour l'Etude des Méthodes de Direction de l'Entreprise) in Lausanne. Its parent foundation's board consists of fifty executives elected from leading client firms around the world. In its short history, IMD has become a major international player in management education, building a global reputation for its executive programmes and full-time M.B.A. courses. Despite the difficulties the school had to overcome in its inception process, the fact that IMD is the result of a merger between two institutions with different cultures – IMI's focus on geopolitical issues and the international environment, and IMEDE's case-teaching approach to management skill development – has enriched both its background and its potential, making its case all the more interesting for studying strategic leadership as a social influence process in context over time.

Our study divides IMD's evolution into three periods, marked by specific episodes that changed the direction of the school. The first period, 1990 to 1992, covers a number of strategic initiatives undertaken by the then dean, Juan Rada, to ensure the success of the IMI–IMEDE merger. The second period, the transition stage between 1992 and 1993, encompasses the initiatives carried out by Xavier Gilbert as IMD's interim dean to restore the school's financial health. Finally, the third period unfolds between 1994 and 2004, shaped mostly by dean Peter Lorange's initiatives to consolidate IMD's success and reputation.

Table 4.3 *IMD's evolution, 1990–2004*

Strategic goal	Becoming a top international business school		
Period	1990–2	1992–3	1993–2004
Dean	Juan Rada	Xavier Gilbert	Peter Lorange
Set of initiatives and objectives	Making the IMI and IMEDE merger successful	Restoring the school's financial health	IMD's consolidation and success in top-tier management education

The merger (1990–2)

Several unsuccessful attempts were made to merge IMI and IMEDE after 1957. However, it was not until December 1988 that a merger was discussed in earnest as a way to build a large, internationally relevant and financially and academically sustainable institution. Although IMI and IMEDE each enjoyed considerable success and reputation on their own, their size and financial sustainability proved insufficient to meet market demands and to secure a competitive position in the emerging global higher education market. The decision was made to base the resulting school in Lausanne, where IMEDE's campus was located. To compensate IMI for this location choice, Juan Rada, its director general, was to become the new IMD dean.

In the following years IMD's strategy focused on 'responding to client demands and achieving excellence'[2] by 'strengthening the partnership with the industry and adding organisational learning to management development'.[3] The school's board and dean worked together to set up its governance structure, policies, rules and strategies. However, the fact that faculty members had not been involved in the merger decision brought great discontent to the school, and

---

[2] 'IMD strategy 1991–1995' – archival material.
[3] 'IMD executive summary, October 1, 1990' – archival material.

the impact of the former schools' long-standing rivalry was some-what underestimated.[4] 'There were two radically different cultures. [...] I realised this during the merger process. IMI had been founded by Alcan, a business that focuses on long-term return on investment and, therefore, is interested in geopolitics and social stability. [...] IMEDE was founded by Nestlé, which is a business of short-term cash flow, with an interest in management functions – and market-ing in particular.'[5]

These differences translated into dissimilar faculty compo-sitions, teaching methods and programme offerings. Indeed, these dissimilarities shaped many of each founding school's internal con-text components – their key actors' features and background, their organisational climate, culture and shared goals. After the merger IMI's faculty members had to move to Lausanne, while IMEDE's faculty were expected to work with a new dean from a formerly competing school. Rada realised he was facing an enormous chal-lenge as head of a start-up school. In fact, some IMD faculty mem-bers recalled a growing tendency towards individual agreements, which contrasted with the values that IMD intended to instil and, instead, created an atmosphere lacking in transparency, trust and understanding. As the board focused strongly on IMD's perform-ance, Rada concentrated his efforts on successfully completing the merger, unifying the school's faculty and developing his vision for its new profile.

Although IMD's financial performance was excellent in its first year, the school posted an operating loss of Sfr 880,000 in 1991. As a result of an economic downturn caused by the Gulf War, most customised programmes were cancelled, causing a shortfall of Sfr 1.2 million in programme revenues that was only partially offset by better non-programme revenues. Nevertheless, the school's overam-bitious plans led to an unhealthy increase of manpower and total

[4] Interviews with former and current IMD faculty members Jim Ellert, Xavier Gilbert, Derek Abell, Kamran Kashani, Jan Kubes, Juan Rada and Fred Neubauer.
[5] Interview with Juan Rada, former IMI faculty and former IMD dean.

operating expenses.[6] The chairman of the board, Kaspar Cassani, announced, 'Efforts will be sustained to streamline the portfolio and reduce overheads.'[7] Stringent measures, such as a hiring freeze, a headcount reduction and operational cutbacks, were enforced, while revenue sources were stimulated in the hope of achieving a modest surplus.

Growing discontent drove the school's faculty to create a committee called the faculty college, 'a "think tank", which – while not being a decision instrument – could influence the orientations and decisions'.[8] Excluded from its inception process, IMD's dean was 'invited' to join the committee's monthly meetings but not to chair it.

The differences between the priorities of the board, which focused primarily on the school's operating budget, and the dean's agenda, which prioritised IMD's strategies, triggered additional confusion and dissent. Rada's decisions were usually thwarted by the chairman of the board's actions, and, despite the dean's persistent efforts to achieve consensus, decision-making and execution processes became slow and difficult. Moreover, the school's financial performance in 1991 confirmed that its increasing costs were not matched by rising profits. Rada's troublesome relationship with the board compromised his authority, while unwavering faculty discontent only compounded his challenges. He decided to resign, and outlined several suggestions for changes to IMD's governance structure. Xavier Gilbert, an IMD faculty member, was asked to step in as interim director general until the search committee could appoint a new dean.

IMD's transition period (1992–3)

IMD's faculty college met and accepted Gilbert's appointment. The board entrusted him with the task of restoring the school's financial

---

[6] Minutes of the executive committee of the IMD foundation board meeting on 15 October 1992 – archival material.

[7] Fourth meeting of the IMD foundation board, 7 November 1991 – archival material.

[8] Ibid.

strength. A French national and former IMEDE faculty member, Gilbert was viewed as a man of strong personality, very determined and committed to the school. He was respected by his fellow professors, who thought of him as a faculty leader.

By 1992 IMD was besieged by confusion as a result of a lack of leadership and strong management. Its deteriorating finances called for an urgent turnaround, and its faculty were divided as to what the school ought to be and do. A group of professors, known as 'the farmers', concentrated on teaching the IMD regular curriculum, while another group, 'the hunters', ventured outside the school, working with companies and delivering their own programmes. This division hindered the development of IMD's own identity. Clearly, there were two tiers of knowledge work – IMD teaching and external corporate venturing – going on, and in addition there was a lack of the well-defined professional identity that is critical to the management of a PSF such as a business school.

The board's focus was set on IMD's governance, its finances and short-term alignment, while Gilbert was determined to bring IMD to the fore, although he knew it was not an easy task given its lack of identity. He felt that 'his' school needed some radical 'surgery'. He had to restore the school's financial health, but his grasp of the school's actual financial outcomes and performance was not as thorough as he desired. He proceeded to keep a close tab on IMD's private programme portfolio and its relationships with companies, as he engaged in rigorous expense management to gain control and strategic direction of the school's financial performance.

Towards the end of Gilbert's deanship, IMD was indeed able to reverse its negative financial performance, averting the threats to its short-term viability. As a consequence of cost-cutting and the creation and installation of proper operating management systems, the school's focus shifted towards revenue creation. Most importantly, by 1993 IMD's annual expenses had decreased by approximately Sfr 1.8 million.

IMD's consolidation and success (1993–2004)

After having assessed no fewer than eighty-five candidates,[9] IMD's search committee appointed Peter Lorange, a Norwegian with extensive academic and managerial experience. A Harvard graduate with a Ph.D. from IMEDE, he had been a faculty member at MIT's Sloan School, Wharton and IMEDE. He served as dean of the Norwegian School of Management from 1989 until 1993, when he was appointed president of IMD.

A harsh reality awaited Lorange at IMD. 'I was not aware of how bad it was. When I arrived, I felt that the school was much more uneven than I'd thought.'[10] With its future still uncertain, IMD's image was somewhat tarnished in the management education environment. Although Gilbert had managed to mitigate IMD's financial distress, the school's revenues still failed to meet expectations, and costs remained high. IMD's restless yet expectant faculty wanted to overcome the merger process, and 'needed a strong outsider who could come in and put the place in order'.[11] All the same, some faculty members were still eager for a more collegial participation in school management.

Based on his management experience in academic institutions and some advice he had received from Rada, Lorange secured the board's support: he wanted to be fully responsible for school management. In a brief introductory address to the IMD board, Lorange stressed four focal points he intended to zero in on. First, IMD's finances had to be kept sound; second, the school needed a clear vision; third, IMD was to forge a mutually beneficial partnership with business; and, fourth, he saw a need for close attention to the school's critical resources – faculty and administration. In turn, to muster the faculty's support, Lorange wrote a personal letter to every

---

[9] Interview with Xavier Gilbert, former IMEDE faculty, former IMD acting director general and IMD faculty.
[10] Interview with Peter Lorange, former IMD president.
[11] Interview with Philip Rosenzweig, IMD faculty.

professor, and, based on their feedback, he identified three key priorities: faculty strengthening, the programme portfolio and marketing efforts.

As IMD president, Lorange's formal authority was robustly established, but he realised that having the faculty on his side was crucial. 'He said quite clearly, "I cannot do the job alone. I need the faculty." '[12] Lorange was also determined to bring different perspectives and experience to the table, so he drew on key faculty members originally from IMI and IMEDE to create IMD's management committee.

Building IMD's culture and identity

Lorange felt he needed to promote new values and behaviours based on IMD's ethical standards as well as institutional ownership, teamwork, transparency, responsiveness, world-class teaching and programme delivery, and meritocracy. As he believed that '[t]eamwork is the focus of IMD's culture' (Lorange, 2002: 360), he set out to encourage teamwork by innovatively breaking away from existing academic traditions, thus avoiding the previously mentioned two-tier management problem of 'hunters' and 'farmers' in the 1992–3 transition period. He established a non-departmental academic structure, with neither tenure nor titles, in order to avoid faculty hierarchies. This bold move found some support among faculty members: 'It's been very surprisingly helpful keeping politics out' was one response[13] However, not all IMD professors were as keen on this new system. In Lorange's words: 'It was a matter of asking a number of professors to leave. People who did not live up to the guidelines were asked to leave. [...] Several faculty left by themselves.'[14]

The new dean knew that the key to faculty strengthening lay in the school's ability to attract and retain the best faculty possible – in other words, outstandingly successful people who had the ability

---

[12] Interview with Fred Neubauer, former IMI faculty and former IMD faculty.
[13] Interview with Tom Malnight, IMD faculty.
[14] Interview with Peter Lorange, former IMD president.

to deliver business-relevant research in the classroom. However, to attract and retain the best faculty, an academic institution has to be an eminently attractive and interesting place. Lorange adapted the workload system in order to develop more transparency among IMD's professors. Faculty workload was allocated to three broad categories: teaching, research and citizenship. Transparency was a key feature: 'Everybody knew what the other was teaching. That immediately meant that we got a lot more capacity built.'[15]

In the following years compensation systems were adapted so as to stimulate a partnership between IMD and its faculty. 'When I came and I thought: "We can only have fixed pay," but, then, a chairman of the board who came from Caterpillar, Vito Baumgartner, insisted that we should have bonus pay like in business. Today we have a very big bonus pay – partly a group bonus, so that everybody shares as a team, and partly an individual bonus based on research output, teaching excellence and citizenship.'[16] A 'buy-back' arrangement was designed for the school, to buy professors' time beyond a threshold of programme delivery workload. This buy-back scheme was intended to expand faculty capacity to meet institutional demand in good years, optimise the utilisation of physical space, leverage secretarial support and contain fixed costs generally, while also safeguarding IMD's break-even in slower years.[17] If IMD met its surplus objectives it distributed these back to the faculty, but, if its budget showed a deficit, year-end bonuses were reduced.[18]

Shaping IMD's vision

In describing the way in which IMD shaped its strategy, Lorange asserted that it was built around four elements. The first element was 'real life, real learning',[19] and it implied a practical focus on learning,

[15] Ibid.
[16] Ibid.
[17] Buy-back provision for capacity adjustments – archival material.
[18] Ibid.
[19] Interview with Peter Lorange, former IMD president.

based on thought leadership, clear business trends, quick transformation from research to programme delivery ('leading through research and being behind to adapt it to the practice'[20]), a pedagogical focus on 'action-learning' and world-class faculty. IMD committed itself to cutting-edge research, with an emphasis on business relevance, to share the latest trends with customers through good teaching programmes. As such, its research needed to have a strong impact, not just in the academic world but also among the business audience.

The second element was 'the global meeting place'.[21] IMD's answer to globalisation trends has been to 'stand alone', bringing the world to its campus in Lausanne and providing a global meeting place – a unique place where clients can find an international faculty, student body and programmes. Thus far, this approach has proved successful: executives from all over the world learn side by side at IMD – 50 per cent from Europe, 27 per cent from Asia, 10 per cent from North America, 10 per cent from Latin America and 3 per cent from Australia and Africa. Similarly, IMD's fifty-member faculty includes nationals from nineteen different countries. This second element also permeates IMD's clear business trend, with its growth in Asia, its new research centres – e.g. the Evian Group – and its expanding Learning Network of around 170 companies.

The third element was the notion that 'all learning is lifelong learning',[22] which became more relevant as alumni wished to remain in contact with IMD after completing their programmes. Webcasts were set up so as to provide weekly updates for everyone at the companies engaged with IMD's Learning Network and its alumni. Every week some 25,000 people log in to these webcasts.

Finally, the fourth element, 'a minimalist organisational approach',[23] translated in practice into no academic departments, no

---

[20] Ibid.

[21] 'Latest strategic development at IMD' – archival material; interview with Peter Lorange, former IMD president.

[22] Ibid.

[23] Ibid.

titles, no tenure, and market-driven internal processes.[24] According to Lorange, 'simplicity is absolutely critical' to preserving the school's trend focus. Some faculty members still question whether these elements are just slogans rather than a strategy. Others argue that, given the idiosyncrasy of academic institutions, these elements play the role of clear, broad 'guidelines' that are more suited to knowledge-based organisations.

Two years into Peter Lorange's deanship, IMD's revenues began to increase, and the school managed to grow steadily, until its revenues had almost tripled by 2004, rising from Sfr 35 million in 1993 to Sfr 97 million. Likewise, IMD's reputation enjoyed an unprecedented boost within the international management education industry. 'IMD is a leader in executive education, with a very strong leadership and management focus and deep connections into the European business community.'[25] Its financial sustainability was ensured: the school now boasts ten endowed chairs, and it recently completed a new Executive Learning Centre. Completely debt-free, IMD is now expanding its premises with no external funding.[26] Figure 4.1 shows IMD's revenue growth since its inception until 2004. In the 1993–2004 period IMD not only consolidated its viability and success but increased its revenues by nearly 280 per cent.

IMD's success and recognition as a leading business school has been reflected in international management education rankings. In recent years a consistent pattern of excellence has raised the school's profile and strengthened its brand, as evidenced by leading publications such as *The Financial Times* and *Business Week*. Top business schools in the United States and Europe view IMD as an innovative, reputable key player in the management education industry. Its highly productive, fifty-two-member full-time equivalent faculty appears to capture worldwide interest with its work, affording more visibility to IMD's relatively strong

[24] Ibid.
[25] Interview with Donald Lessard, MIT Sloan deputy dean.
[26] Second EQUIS self-assessment report, IMD 2002 – archival material.

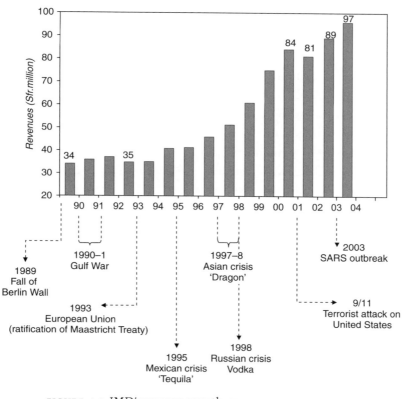

FIGURE 4.1 IMD's revenue growth, 1990–2004
Sources: Faculty retreat, December 2004; auditors' report to the IMD
Foundation board, Pricewaterhouse Coopers; archival material.

brand for its originality rather than its size.[27] The school's Learning
Partnership Network, comprising some 170 leading global corporations, is stronger than ever and continues to bolster the IMD brand.
The network ensures that IMD's research agenda keeps its focus on
critical management issues, and it also provides regular feedback
on the quality of the school's knowledge creation activities. As a
result, IMD's revenue and profit growth has been impressive for
the past five years.

[27] Ibid.

Future challenges

According to the overall perspective of our interviewees, IMD's future posed three key challenges, relating to faculty recruitment, IMD's business model and Lorange's succession.[28] These are very dynamic, rapidly changing times. In order to teach something worthwhile, business schools need to be ahead of the game, envisaging the future, anticipating trends and spreading knowledge. Attracting world-class faculty members who are committed to both teaching excellence and relevant research has been a major focus for IMD. However, nowadays, as a result of its extraordinary reputation in the management education industry, IMD has around '250 to 300 names per year to quickly look at'.[29] Recruitment is one of the school's chief strategic priorities.

There are two key aspects to faculty recruitment: attracting experienced individuals who are able to raise the average quality of the school's faculty by virtue of their superior teaching skills and their focus on relevant research; and recruiting people who can develop a sense of belonging to the school and cohesiveness towards its faculty in order to lead IMD into the future with its unique organisational model intact. The fact that IMD does not offer tenure affects new candidates' careers: driven out of the mainstream system, they have to consider IMD as a place to stay for quite some time.

Lorange's view was that IMD should remain a world-class, 'boutique-style' institution, with top-quality faculty, heavy on research but practitioner-oriented, emphasising teamwork and entrepreneurship, and limited to one site – 'the global meeting place'. However, Lorange also believed that it was vital to keep re-examining IMD's 'business model', to continue pushing for cutting-edge learning value creation in order to find new ideas for the specific business model that would facilitate IMD's enduring success.

---

[28] All the interviews were carried out prior to Lorange's resignation in 2008.
[29] Interview with Peter Lorange, former IMD president.

The careful alignment of IMD's culture, its structures and systems to its strategic direction, and the dean's leadership style, made the school's success possible. In facing the prospect of Lorange's succession, the challenge lay not only on what business school model IMD should pursue but also on its future leadership scheme. Talking about his future successor, Lorange asserted, 'We have very clear guidelines here. We have a faculty search committee, consisting of three professors and three board members, and they will find my successor. I don't think I should be very active there. It's an institutional process.'[30]

4.4 INSEAD

Founded in 1957 in Fontainebleau, the Institut Européen d'Administration des Affaires is today one of the world's foremost graduate business schools, with two complete, fully connected campuses in Europe and Asia. Both campuses are regional hubs in the school's emerging Global Learning Network. A pioneer in one-year M.B.A. programme format delivery, INSEAD offers a large portfolio of executive development, executive M.B.A. and Ph.D. programmes at both campuses, supported by fifteen research centres.

Over the last half-century INSEAD has grown and developed major strengths in business disciplines, focusing on innovative learning methods. To enhance its research and teaching relevance, the school emphasises the development of close partnerships with leading firms around the world. It provides a unique international learning experience: faculty and students interact in a truly multicultural environment, gaining essential insights into global business practices. Currently, INSEAD relies on a 144-member faculty with nationals from thirty-one countries to teach some 900 M.B.A. programme participants, 7,000 executives and seventy-one Ph.D. candidates.[31] None of the ninety nationalities present in these

---

[30] Ibid.
[31] INSEAD executive education brochure 2005 – archival material; available at www.insead.edu.

programmes exceeds 10 per cent of the total student body. The school's ever-growing community of over 32,000 alumni around the world creates lifelong opportunities for professional development and networking.

INSEAD's mission is 'to promote a non-dogmatic learning environment that brings together people, cultures and ideas from around the world to develop responsible, thoughtful business leaders and entrepreneurs, whose actions create value for their organisations and communities, and to create and disseminate management knowledge, expanding the frontiers of academic thought and informing business practice'.[32] Its values uphold *diversity* as a source of learning and enrichment, *independence* as a governance principle, *rigour and relevance* in teaching and research, *closeness* to the international business community and *entrepreneurial* spirit.

In short, INSEAD stands out among top-tier business schools on three counts. First, it is widely recognised as the world's most global business school, being the only leading school with fully integrated twin campuses in Asia and Europe, while its alliance with Wharton – a global elite competitor – creates additional opportunities, particularly in the United States. Second, INSEAD is the only top business school offering an intensive one-year M.B.A. in international business administration – a highly valued asset in the marketplace. Finally, INSEAD's multicultural diversity ensures that no single nationality, style or dogma prevails, either within its faculty or among students, making for a unique global management learning environment.

To explore strategic leadership processes at INSEAD fully from 1990 to 2004, this period has been divided into three time units marked by turning points that have driven significant changes in the school's direction. The first period encompasses the co-deanship of Claude Rameau and Ludo Van der Heyden, from 1990 to 1993,

---

[32] INSEAD executive education brochure 2005 (company-specific programmes) – archival material.

Table 4.4 *INSEAD's evolution, 1990–2004*

Strategic goal	Becoming a top international business school			
Period	1990–3	1993–5	1995–2000	2000–4
Dean(s)	Claude Rameau and Ludo Van der Heyden	Ludo Van der Heyden and Antonio Borges	Antonio Borges	Gabriel Hawawini
Set of initiatives and objectives	Deepening the school's research strategy and profile		Launching a second campus	Making Singapore work

followed by the co-deanship of Ludo Van der Heyden and Antonio Borges from 1993 to 1995. The second period, with Antonio Borges as dean, lasted between 1995 and 1999, while the third period covered Gabriel Hawawini's deanship until 2004. The study focused on this school's consolidation as a top international business school, with four sets of initiatives based on guidelines that had been set previously by Philippe Naert and Claude Rameau during their co-deanship from 1986 to 1990 (see Table 4.4).

INSEAD's background

INSEAD was founded in 1957 as a privately funded, independent European business school. Its founder, Georges Doriot, was a French-born Harvard professor who wanted to provide cross-cultural business education and to help rebuild war-torn Europe. A pioneer in management teaching and research, he introduced the critical path analysis case study method in France in the early 1930s. The inspiration to build a global business school in Europe first came to him during World War II. Amidst a cataclysmically destructive war that had little respect for borders, Doriot realised that the tremendous challenge of European reconstruction would require entrepreneurial and visionary leaders who would need to navigate seamlessly across language and culture boundaries. Envisaging an institution that was as grand in its scope and as malleable in its programmes as the changing world itself, Doriot wanted INSEAD to be a global business school based in Europe for executives around the world. Thus, internationalisation lay at INSEAD's core from its inception. In the words of Hawawini, 'It is what INSEAD is all about. This is our fate. It's in our genes.'[33]

It was an exciting time: people believed in Europe's renaissance; strong economic growth provided a very favourable setting; and INSEAD graduates were coveted in the labour market. Very soon INSEAD became the school that everybody wanted to attend, with its M.B.A. programme acting as a magnet for faculty as well, luring professors with American Ph.D. degrees to create high-quality, cutting-edge programmes. For many years INSEAD's primary goal 'was to attract great teachers and have great programmes'.[34]

In the 1970s the school introduced executive education and fostered faculty relationships with companies so as to become a dominant player in the European management education industry. In 1975, under the leadership of Henri-Claude de Bettignies, INSEAD started to offer executive programmes in Asia, mainly in Japan and Pacific rim countries, marking the onset of a key strategic approach to that region, which also included the creation of the Euro-Asia Centre in 1980. This centre paved the way for INSEAD's twin campus in Singapore, launched in 2000.

By the mid 1980s INSEAD's scope and scale growth had turned it into a leading business school in Europe, characterised by an innovative and entrepreneurial spirit. Two specific events revealed INSEAD's standing. First, in early 1984, a European Union summit was held to determine a calendar for the creation of a single European market.[35] The summit's press conference took place at INSEAD's

---

[33] Interview with Gabriel Hawawini, former INSEAD dean.
[34] Interview with Antonio Borges, former INSEAD dean.
[35] It was during this summit that the date of 1992 was established for the single market; the official announcement of the accord was made in the school; see Barsoux (2000).

main auditorium, where French president François Mitterrand presented the first European passport. In May 1988 *Fortune International*
featured Antonio Borges, head of the school's M.B.A. programme,
on its cover, hailing INSEAD as the top-ranking business school in
Europe (Barsoux, 2000). Both events fuelled a renewed and steadily mounting interest in INSEAD across Europe and beyond, as 'the
school that virtually invented the concept of international business
education [–] the Rolls-Royce of European Business Schools'.[36]

However, as the European Union swept away economic barriers on its march towards 1992 and the single market, companies
increasingly sought managers unfazed by linguistic and cultural
boundaries.[37] They expected business schools to become academic
centres that attracted the brightest professors and programme participants. To respond to these demands, by the end of the decade
INSEAD recruitment efforts focused on faculty candidates with outstanding research performance in order to bring 'a new wave of more
academic-oriented people that provided a lot of renewal'.[38]

During the 1990s technological developments, including the
advent of the internet, with its breakthrough in worldwide communications and connectivity, drove INSEAD to adjust to new environmental trends. Nearing the end of the decade, in order to remain
faithful to its international destiny, the school proved its determination to stay on as a top international and multi-cultural business
school. In the words of Borges, 'This is one of the main reasons
why we also went to Asia.'[39] In 2000 INSEAD launched its second
campus, in Singapore. In a nutshell, over four decades INSEAD was
able to become and remain a world-class business school, turning 'an entrepreneurial venture into an internationally regarded
institution'.[40]

---

[36] See *Fortune International* (1988) and Barsoux (2000: 175, ref. 37).
[37] Barsoux (2000).
[38] Interview with Antonio Borges, former INSEAD dean.
[39] Ibid.
[40] See Barsoux (2000: 175, ref. 37).

INSEAD's co-deanships, 1990–5

In the late 1980s, as INSEAD pursued a more research-based approach, Claude Rameau and Philippe Naert were the school's co-deans, from 1986 to 1990. It was Rameau's second period. He was an entrepreneurial businessman who had reinforced the school's executive orientation and driven INSEAD 'to establish a very strong and effective economic model'.[41] An academic of considerable research experience, Naert upheld the school's responsibility to innovate and to assert leadership in the creation of new concepts and ideas, in order to advance European management thinking and knowledge.[42] His main thrust was to secure a better balance between 'the *transfer* and the *production* of knowledge'.[43]

In his presentation to the board in March 1986, Naert explained what he viewed as INSEAD's lingering weaknesses: its inadequate per capita research output and its poor standing in the 'academic community'. He advocated a 50 per cent increase in faculty members and the creation of a doctoral programme.[44] By the end of the decade INSEAD had overcome several obstacles and successfully launched its doctoral programme, its Euro-Asia Centre and numerous new executive programmes, while also producing a mass of cases and working papers and recruiting thirty-four new Ph.D. professors, bringing its faculty up to seventy-nine.[45] INSEAD's significant research capabilities and its newly developed ability 'to recruit in a very, very systematic manner' embodied Naert's legacy for the school.[46]

In 1990 Ludo Van der Heyden, the former head of research and development (R&D) head, replaced Philippe Naert as co-dean, alongside Claude Rameau. With complementary traits, the co-deans were

[41] Interview with Antonio Borges, former INSEAD dean.
[42] Minutes of the board meeting, 18 March 1988; in Barsoux (2000: 179–80).
[43] *Financial Times*, 9 November 1987; in Barsoux (2000: 179; emphasis in original).
[44] Minutes of the board meeting, 10 March 1986; in Barsoux (2000).
[45] Minutes of the board meeting, 9 March 1990; in Barsoux (2000: 187).
[46] Interview with Antonio Borges, former INSEAD dean.

expected to manage the school's academic, administrative, business and cultural development. A member of INSEAD's founding group, Rameau was a businessman and a consultant with an INSEAD M.B.A. He loved the school, but he was hardly an academic. In contrast, Van der Heyden was an academic with very little business experience. His job was to ensure the success of INSEAD's Ph.D. programme and new faculty, building a 'model of synergy'[47] with a good blend of relevance, rigour and revelation.[48]

However, his appointment was followed by several new internal and external challenges for INSEAD. Internally, the arrival of new, more research-oriented professors led to the development of two distinct groups within the school's faculty. Externally, a worldwide recession caused by the Gulf War prompted the cancellation of customised programmes as well as a significant drop in applications and admissions for both INSEAD's executive and M.B.A. programmes. As a result, revenues plummeted, and the school posted its first losses in over a decade.[49] The situation worsened as the drop in market demand was emphasised by heightened competition in the management education sector. This critical scenario affected INSEAD's research budgets and teaching loads, while faculty compensation fell, jeopardising INSEAD's appeal for 'top-flight'[50] academics. In fact, the recession served as a potent reminder of the school's lingering financial vulnerability.

Nonetheless, some faculty and board members were reluctant to embark on fund-raising activities. In March 1992 the board agreed to conduct a feasibility study for a capital campaign, which revealed that school supporters would back INSEAD if it presented a clear and convincing development project.[51] The school's first development campaign, from 1993 to 2000, proved a huge success, raising

---

[47] Interview with Ludo Van der Heyden, former INSEAD co-dean.
[48] See Barsoux (2000: 175, ref. 37).
[49] Minutes of the board meeting, 6 March 1992; in Barsoux (2000).
[50] See Barsoux (2000: 175, ref. 37).
[51] Ibid.

€120 million and substantiating its credibility with the business community.

In September 1993 INSEAD's advanced management programme ranked first in *The Wall Street Journal's* worldwide executive education ranking. In addition, research centres were developed, and their outputs were immediately transferred to the classroom. By that time Rameau's tenure had come to an end, and Antonio Borges, former M.B.A. associate dean, was appointed to share the deanship with Van der Heyden. Even though the two men respected each other and agreed on the school's overall strategic direction, their styles were not complementary. Borges had spent three years away from academia, as deputy governor of the Bank of Portugal. He was forceful and determined, while Van der Heyden, with his purely academic background, was more questioning and consensual, viewing himself as a 'primus inter pares'.[52]

Borges was able to use INSEAD's financial distress to press for some urgent changes, including staff salary freezes and a headcount reduction, a slowdown on investments, tightened cost control and a block on recruitment.[53] Although Borges was expected to focus on INSEAD's external work while Van der Heyden handled its internal affairs, it mostly 'turned out to be the reverse'.[54] It appeared that the combination of business and academic skills that had been displayed by the former co-deanship was no longer at work with the current co-deans.

The main virtue of the co-deanship scheme was held to be that both deans had more time and energy to devote to a very demanding task. Some viewed this scheme as a key element for the school's delicate balance of interests and constituencies – the embodiment of a collegial style of decision-making. Others felt it was inefficient and ineffective, compounding INSEAD's current financial difficulties; in short, a luxury the school had been able to afford only in more

[52] Ibid.; 201.
[53] Minutes of the board meeting, 2 December 1994; in Barsoux (2000).
[54] See Barsoux (2000: 175, ref. 37; 200).

prosperous times. INSEAD's internal context was torn between its rising frustration with the decision-making delays and ambiguous authority resulting from its co-deanship scheme and its concern that a single dean would hold too much power.[55] When Van der Heyden's term came to an end, he made it very clear that he did not wish to be considered for a second deanship, while Borges stated, 'If you want me to continue, I want to be a single dean.' It was at this point that faculty members agreed that it was time to move to a more traditional structure, with one person in charge.

Antonio Borges' deanship, 1995–2000

In 1995, after taking over as dean, Borges felt that INSEAD needed to 'be as good as the Americans'. He recognised that the school had to raise its academic standards to reach the bar set by leading US business schools – not only in teaching but, notably, in research. To this end, INSEAD pursued an aggressive strategy based on hiring faculty with strong research skills. Faculty grew at a steady rate of 13 per cent per year during Borges' deanship. To help attract and retain research-oriented professors, a number of systems and incentives were introduced or changed. Chairs, professorships and research support were granted to faculty members who showed an interest in developing relevant, world-class research work. A strong programme of sabbaticals was instituted to further promote research. This bold shift towards a more research-oriented profile caused unrest among incumbent faculty members, who had devoted themselves to the superior teaching that had made INSEAD a top-ranking institution.

Driven by Professor Henri-Claude de Bettignies' vision, INSEAD started forging its relationship with Asia in the 1970s. De Bettignies persuaded the school's board to create a special unit, called the Euro-Asia Centre. This centre was designed to build a base of knowledge to enhance the ability of European and Asian businesses to work together through research, public and company-specific

---

[55] Ibid.

executive programmes, publications and annual forums. Faculty trips financed by INSEAD were also organised to enlighten the faculty on activities in the region and further develop their interest.

Towards the end of the 1980s an Asian economic crisis impacted the centre. Nevertheless, under Gabriel Hawawini's leadership from 1988 to 1995, the development of the Euro-Asia Centre gained momentum: executive programmes conducted in Asia grew significantly, and by 1994 INSEAD had become the largest provider of executive education in south-east Asia.[56] When Hawawini pitched his idea of moving INSEAD's Euro-Asia Centre to Asia to deliver executive education programmes 'on-site', Borges took the project a step further: 'Let's take all of INSEAD there, because the only way we are going to get faculty abroad is with the M.B.As. abroad.'

Borges had no experience in Asia, but, stimulated by the so-called Asian miracle as well as the emergence of China, he became increasingly interested in the region. In 1996, under the direction of Arnoud De Meyer, the East-Asia Centre opened an office in Singapore. However, on examining Asia's market potential more closely, de Meyer realised that the East-Asia Centre did not have enough capabilities to seize these growing opportunities.

New campus launch

In the 1990s globalisation trends drove American business schools, such as HBS, Wharton, Chicago and Kellogg, to forge alliances or open research centres in distant countries. At an INSEAD faculty meeting, Borges introduced the idea of building a second campus to respond to global market demands. This initiative divided the faculty into three different groups: an enthusiastic group (15 per cent of all faculty members), with expertise in Asia, which supported Borges' idea; another 60 per cent of INSEAD's professors were concerned about the project's risks; while the remaining, more conservative faculty questioned whether this initiative would fit in with

---

[56] Ibid.

the school's strategic vision. Even so, they admitted that '[i]f one had asked so many questions, INSEAD would have never existed', in the words of the former dean of the INSEAD M.B.A., Antonio Fatás.[57]

Knowing that he had the full support of the chairman of the board, Claude Janssen, Borges summarily discussed the topic at a faculty meeting and, without taking a vote, decided to go ahead with the project. In 1997 a feasibility study was conducted, and Peter Jadersten, the marketing director of the Euro-Asia Centre, was assigned to research Asia's business education market. Based on the feasibility study and Jadersten's findings, INSEAD's top management team recognised that the key challenge for the potentially successful Asian project would lie in rallying the support of its faculty. The school organised several trips for faculty members to visit the area in the hope of bolstering their support for the new campus project.

At a faculty meeting in late 1997 Singapore emerged as the site of choice for INSEAD's Asian campus. During a visit to Fontainebleau earlier in the year, Singaporean officials had shared their plans to become an educational hub for Asia's Pacific rim region, and, soon thereafter, they submitted an attractive proposal for INSEAD, showing Singapore's commitment to the venture by helping to arrange meetings with a number of senior government officials, local universities and business leaders. However, the crash of the Thai baht in July that year had been followed by a number of regional currency crises, a collapse of banking systems and corporate bankruptcies in several Asian nations during the subsequent months. Several of INSEAD's major executive education customers were badly hit as a result of structural deficiencies in these so-called 'tiger' economies. While the school's board continued to support the Asian project, its top management team was instructed to adjust the business plan to the increasingly worsening conditions in Asia. Borges felt that the crisis would end shortly, and companies would need INSEAD executive programmes to recover. The end of Borges' mandate was

---

[57] Interview with Antonio Fatás, former dean of the INSEAD M.B.A.

imminent, though, and it would be Gabriel Hawawini's mission, as the incoming dean of INSEAD, to oversee the launch of the new campus.

Gabriel Hawawini's deanship, 2000–4

Hawawini had joined INSEAD in 1980, and eight years later he had been appointed director of the Euro-Asia Centre. In 1995 he returned to the faculty as finance department head, and, in 1998, he was appointed Ph.D. programme dean for a year and dean of development, to be in charge of the fund-raising campaign until 2000. By September 2000 Hawawini had a sound performance track record spanning two decades at INSEAD and the support of almost the entire faculty. Borges' bold agenda to turn INSEAD into a more research-oriented institution and his initiative to open a second campus in Singapore had stretched the organisation to its limits, sparking both support and opposition across its key constituencies. The choice of Hawawini as dean can be construed as the faculty's attempt to seek a more consensus-oriented and participative leadership style, founded on the strong reputation as a very effective and focused manager that Hawawini had earned at the helm of INSEAD's Euro-Asia Centre and its development campaign.

Dean Hawawini's key task was to ensure the success of the Singapore campus. Despite some pressure from the more conservative faculty members, Hawawini had been told by the chairman of the board, in no uncertain terms, that he could not 'go back on Singapore'. He knew that stopping the project would dampen INSEAD's growing ambition and inherent entrepreneurial spirit. Nonetheless, multiple unforeseen challenges tested Hawawini's determination to make the Singapore campus successful. In 2001, with Asian economies still struggling amidst a persistent downturn and terrorist attacks around the world threatening to preclude all travelling, an outbreak in Singapore of the respiratory disease SARS added a new source for concern. However, the overall idea of being able to go to Asia was still attractive for students. The school did as much as it could to offer an outstanding experience. In time, faculty members who agreed to teach in Singapore for a few weeks expressed their desire to stay for a couple of months and, later, for an entire year. With its Singapore campus up and running, INSEAD was able to increase the share of Asians on its M.B.A. programme sharply, from 6 per cent in 1998/9 to 25 per cent at present.

After his appointment as dean, Hawawini was approached by the dean of the University of Pennsylvania's Wharton School to build an alliance between INSEAD and Wharton. A partnership of this kind would provide Wharton with a much-needed international scope, and it would offer INSEAD the opportunity to have both global reach and intercontinental endeavours with an already well-known partner. Although the school's faculty supported this initiative, the board disagreed. Hawawini managed to persuade board members, and, in March 2001, the INSEAD–Wharton alliance was announced, the intention being to contribute to advancing scholarship and business practice. From the start it focused on education, with the purpose of developing knowledge to meet the challenges of the changing global business environment. However, after several years, some felt that the alliance was not satisfactory for INSEAD, as its faculty was providing Wharton with much more original thinking than it was receiving from that school. Additionally, as most of INSEAD's professors were educated in the United States, they did not need the alliance to develop contacts there.

Hawawini envisaged a third INSEAD campus in the United States. He managed to get the support of Janssen, the chairman of the board, in the hope that this would secure the approval of the entire board. However, Janssen was soon replaced by a new chairman, Cees van Lede, a Dutch INSEAD alumnus, who was unwilling to make any such significant decisions so early in his term.

As the election to renew Hawawini's mandate as dean drew closer, he made it clear that he still planned to build INSEAD's third campus in the United States. He hoped that his track record and his relationship with the school's faculty would provide him with a strong vote of confidence and support to secure the board's approval. Indeed, his re-election became a referendum for this project. He had announced that he would stay only with a majority vote of support. However, although he was re-elected, Hawawini decided not to serve as dean for a second term. While his drive for a third campus was consistent with INSEAD's global network vision, the institution and its constituencies were somewhat reluctant to embark on another highly demanding project.

4.5 LBS

LBS was founded in 1964 as the London Institute of Business Management, a graduate college of the University of London. Currently, it offers graduate, doctoral and executive education programmes. Its M.B.A. has consistently ranked among the world's top ten programmes and the first or second outside the United States in the annual rankings published by *Business Week* or *The Financial Times*. Though entitled to issue degrees by its Royal Charter of 1986 and its status as a full college of the University of London since 1996, LBS continues to award University of London degrees,[58] despite the fact that, for all intents and purposes, it operates very much like a stand-alone private business school – unlike its domestic competition in the United Kingdom.

Created to help develop a sound domestic management profession, and after concentrating on British managers during its early years, LBS gradually shifted towards a broader and more international scope in the late 1980s. The school's demographics have shown a steady and remarkable increase not only in the number of non-UK students, with their share rising from 51 per cent of the overall student population in 1989 to 77 per cent in 2004, but also in its foreign faculty, which grew from from 18 per cent to 74 per cent in the same period. Since 1990 LBS has clearly adopted a global outlook, enhancing the quality of its research to meet international standards

---

[58] EQUIS report, LBS 2003.

and delivering programmes that appeal to students around the world.[59]

LBS's executive programme portfolio has also become distinctively international and is viewed as central to the school's future development – as well as a significant source of revenues. In addition, LBS has forged several strategic alliances in key locations, including the United States, India and the Middle East, to expand its global reach. Its international drive is reflected in both its vision and mission statements: 'to be *a pre-eminent global business school,* nurturing talent and advancing knowledge in a *multi-national, multicultural learning environment',*[60] and 'to provide students with the knowledge, skills, values and networks – *the global business capabilities* – required for leadership and success in the global economy; and to foster outstanding research that is rigorous, relevant and innovative on the dynamics of global business for students, business leaders, and government leaders throughout the world'.[61] To accomplish its goals, LBS is determined to build on its strengths: world-class faculty and students; relevant, influential research; a broad portfolio of degree programmes; outstanding executive education; global learning opportunities; professional management, staff and services; and its unique location – London, a hub of global business, finance, technology and culture, is unquestionably a key asset.

LBS continues to be subject to the HEFCE's five-yearly Research Assessment Exercise[62] and the standards set by the QAA. Its top score enables LBS to access a block grant to fund its academic endeavours. However, only 5 per cent of the school's total revenues (around £4 million a year) come from government funding, making it, essentially, a private management school. LBS draws most of its income from programme fees and research grants from alumni and corporate sponsors. Without an endowment fund to rely on, the

---

[59] Ibid.
[60] Ibid.: 3; emphasis in original.
[61] Ibid.; emphasis in original.
[62] Higher Education Funding Council for England; see www.hefce.ac.uk.

Table 4.5 *LBS's evolution, 1990–2004*

Strategic goal	Becoming a top international business school		
Period	1990–7	1998–2001	2002–4
Dean	George Bain	John Quelch	Laura Tyson
Set of initiatives and objectives	Making LBS a top-league international school	Deepening the strategy of internationalisation, faculty transformation and enhancing LBS's visibility and revenues	Enhancing LBS's visibility and fund-raising activities

school is challenged to consolidate its positioning among the world's top-tier business schools. Its strategic shift in the late 1980s and early 1990s to seize international leadership dramatically reshaped the school's character, and required tough decisions.

Major developments revealing the strategic leadership processes that unfolded at LBS as it pursued a top international positioning between 1990 and 2004 have been reflected in our division of this time into three periods, encompassing the successive deanships of George Bain, John Quelch and Laura Tyson. The first period discusses a number of initiatives undertaken by Bain to initiate LBS's move beyond domestic management education, luring foreign students and faculty with relevant research and solid academic offerings. The second period describes the strategic initiatives carried out by Quelch in order to deepen LBS's internationalisation strategy through faculty transformation, enhanced visibility and new revenue sources. Finally, the third period explores Tyson's initiatives to expand LBS's global reputation as well as its corporate and private fund-raising activities (see Table 4.5).

George Bain's deanship (1990–7): turning LBS into a top international school

In the mid-1980s, as old political barriers fell and new markets emerged, the world showed signs of significant economic, technological and geopolitical changes. In the United Kingdom, Margaret Thatcher's Conservative government took the lead in broad deregulation and privatisation efforts intended to reduce state expenses. As part of these reforms, business schools were increasingly expected to stand on their own, and public funding for British students was gradually removed. In 1988 *Fortune* ranked London Business School second only to INSEAD, the number one school in Europe. This came as a huge shock to the LBS community.

As a result, the faculty rebelled against the re-election of LBS's incumbent dean. Realising the need for a new vision and fresh ideas, the school's governing body decided to look for a new dean outside the school – a distinguished and successful individual with an entrepreneurial outlook and a background either in business or management education, who combined academic qualifications with leadership and general management ability and who could position LBS as one of the world's top centres of management education and research.[63] In late 1988 George Bain, chairman of Warwick Business School, was appointed principal of LBS.

Born in Canada in 1939, Bain graduated with honours at Winnipeg State School in 1961, majoring in economics and political science. In 1964 he earned an M.A. in economics from the University of Manitoba, followed by a Ph.D. in industrial relations from Nuffield College, Oxford, in 1969. Although he was appointed LBS dean in November 1988, he did not take over until August 1989. For him, this 'actually turned out to be a huge advantage', as he took that time 'to start seeing all of the faculty'.[64] He also visited a dozen American business schools, trying to get a sense of what was happening in the management education industry.

By the time he arrived at LBS, Bain had come to understand that the school needed to bolster its reputation after ranking second to INSEAD. He realised that LBS suffered from a 'disciplinary

---

[63] See Barnes (1989).
[64] Interview with George Bain, former LBS dean.

imbalance',[65] with its economics and finance areas upstaging all other business disciplines. He could also see that the school was predominantly British, as nearly 75 per cent of its students and 90 per cent of its faculty were UK nationals. Finally, LBS's financial sustainability was at stake, as a result of the government's decision to reduce its funding for higher education. Bain presented his agenda for change, organised in a document called 'Bias towards a strategy', compiling the changes expected by LBS stakeholders in a coherent, focused way. With this document, Bain intended to provide the basis for a strategy – a set of guiding principles – that could be used to develop a series of operational objectives. He addressed four basic goals: disciplinary balance, a more international profile, greater scope in terms of portfolio, and financial sustainability.

The faculty welcomed Bain's document with a sense of relief. They felt they had been drifting aimlessly for years, but now they knew what the school's direction would be. The new dean knew he would not be able to implement changes on his own. The creation of the management committee enabled Bain to identify key faculty members and to build sufficient consensus. This group of four or five people would clearly be actually running the school on a day-to-day basis.

Leading change at LBS

A critical early task involved the development of a world-class faculty with US research standards and teaching disciplinary balance. Faculty dean Paul Marsh reviewed LBS's faculty human resources (HR) policy. Faculty compensations were separated from the UK university salary scale so as to move to a scheme that could compete with American faculty salaries, in order to facilitate recruitment. However, this new system sparked some opposition, as it gravitated towards performance-related pay. When he looked back on his tenure, Bain said that it was the internationalisation of LBS's predominantly

[65] Ibid.

British faculty that had been the greatest challenge he faced during that time.

Recruiting a world-class faculty would allow LBS to attract foreign students, but that would not suffice in itself to turn it into a top international business school. As Bain himself put it, LBS had 'a dreadful image' with potential students and a bad reputation amongst employers, 'because LBS was not taking executive education seriously'. Some faculty members believed that executive education should be kept as a minority activity. LBS treasurer Gerry Quincey addressed the arguments opposing the development of a larger executive education programme portfolio with a very straightforward approach: 'We have faculty salaries going up in a rapid way, and, if we don't expand executive education, will somebody tell me where the money is coming from?'

With its plans to develop its faculty, to enlarge its student body and to expand its executive education offerings, LBS would be forced to tackle facility restraints. To address the school's financial constraints, Bain set out to streamline fund-raising, creating a development office and hiring a development director. LBS managed to raise around £2.5 million during Bain's tenure for the building of a new library.

In sum, Bain turned LBS into an international player with global ambitions. 'He made it a global player by exploiting important contacts, by cultivating the academic and by having a vision.'[66] He managed to restore the school's economic health, even though its business model was not transformed. Nonetheless, Bain noted, 'If I deserve any credit, it was probably to have picked some very good people to be champions of products, of policies...'[67]

John Quelch's deanship (1998–2001): furthering LBS's transformation

John Quelch, a London-born graduate of Oxford University (B.A. and M.A.), University of Pennsylvania's Wharton School (M.B.A.),

[66] Interview with Saul Estrin, former LBS faculty dean.
[67] Interview with George Bain, former LBS dean.

the Harvard School of Public Health (M.S.) and Harvard Business School (D.B.A. (Doctor of Business Administration)), was appointed to succeed George Bain as LBS dean. At that time, Quelch was the Sebastian S. Kresge professor of marketing and co-chair of the marketing area at HBS. His vision was to create the most important and respected international business school; his mission, 'transforming the futures'. This entailed ensuring that LBS's 1,300 students, 450 staff and 15,000 alumni were professionally and personally transformed by its brand and its learning experience. The overriding goal guiding the school's operations was to fund growth and improve quality, while its core values were those captured in the LBS spirit: scholarship, professionalism, innovation, relevance, internationalism and transformation.[68]

The new dean did not embrace a conventional leadership style. He focused on expanding LBS's international visibility and profile. First, Quelch strengthened the school's financial soundness, developing its faculty size by transforming LBS's systems and policies according to the typical US elite business school model – a strategic focus on strong faculty recruiting and HR, significant marketing investments and the reinforcement of the school's brand through alumni and fund-raising activities. Then he increased its executive education offerings dramatically and made them profitable, boosting the LBS brand with regional advisory boards and alumni clubs. To pursue these goals, he relied on three key actors: Saul Estrin, dean of faculty; Rob Goffee, dean of executive education; and Jeffrey Devries, secretary and treasurer. Estrin modified the recruiting system to facilitate the hiring of world-class faculty. As a result, the school hired sixty people over five years (mid-1997 to mid-2002). Although salary changes were important, introducing tenure and titles had a greater impact on faculty recruitment. LBS's faculty grew by 60 per cent during Quelch's deanship.

---

[68] Personal note by John Quelch, entitled 'London Business School 1998–2001: a resource to the world' (May 2001).

Quelch believed there was still much to be done to 'market the place'.[69] Specifically, LBS had to leverage its London location worldwide: 'Because London is a highly competitive city, like New York, you have to be out there every day doing something. Top-of-mind awareness is very important.'[70] The first results of the school's new branding thrust were shown in the *Financial Times* rankings, in which LBS held the eighth position for three years starting in 1999.

Quelch took advantage of prosperous market conditions not only to push price rises but also to increase the scale of LBS's programmes. Second and third streams were added to the school's M.A. in finance and executive M.B.A. programmes, while a global executive M.B.A. was launched through a strategic alliance with Columbia Business School. This partnership also enabled both schools to bid jointly for large-scale executive education contracts. In addition, the school also developed distance-learning courses to expand its global reach. As a result, LBS degree programme revenues increased by more than 54 per cent, to £18 million, while executive education revenues grew by 75 per cent, to over £19 million. One-half of LBS's revenues came from overseas earnings, with western Europe accounting for 32 per cent, North America 30 per cent, Asia-Pacific 12 per cent, eastern Europe 6 per cent and Latin America 4 per cent. With a larger number of streams, LBS's alumni population grew, and the dean invited them to join alumni clubs and regional advisory boards in order to motivate international research and to expand the school's presence around the world.

For its size and resource base, LBS was transformed into an outstanding knowledge advancement institution, ranking third in *The Financial Times* survey's research category. The school started to apply strong scholarly standards in recruiting and promoting practices. Quelch's key objective was to increase the number of A journal

---

[69] Interview with John Quelch, former LBS dean.
[70] Ibid.

articles published by LBS faculty every year. During Quelch's tenure, LBS's Global Entrepreneurship Monitor research project assessed entrepreneurship in thirty countries. LBS became a leading innovator in entrepreneurship teaching, research and business creation. Twenty start-ups led by LBS alumni operated at the school's new business incubator, supported by seed funding. A joint venture with the Centre for Scientific Enterprise enabled scientific innovations to be marketed with LBS know-how. Finally, an office was established in Silicon Valley, and a unique entrepreneurship summer school programme was launched.

Despite his determination to boost LBS fund-raising activities, Quelch was unable to launch the campaign he had planned before taking over because the chairman of the board who had approved his project then left the school. In terms of corporate subscriptions, LBS expanded its fund-raising from an annual total of about £100,000 to £1,000,000. 'There were twenty corporate sponsors of the school at £5,000 a year when I arrived, and, when I left, there were around sixty-five at £15,000 a year,' explained Quelch. Each graduating class was encouraged to make a gift to the school, and, during Quelch's first year as dean, MBA graduates donated £100,000 to LBS. 'Then it went up to about £300,000.'[71] Quelch approached the older alumni, saying: '"Our graduates are giving LBS £300,000. How come you can't give us £5,000 or £10,000?" So the idea was to shame them into giving'.[72]

Quelch left as dean before the end of his term; Estrin, the faculty dean, served as acting dean until Laura Tyson took over in mid-2002. For Quelch, '[i]t was a big step up for London Business School to get Laura Tyson to be dean. She's changed international to global, and my impression is that she has not been a radical change agent but, rather, a good consolidator. And the rankings have improved since she's been there.'

[71] Ibid.
[72] Ibid.

Laura Tyson's deanship (2002–4): consolidating LBS as a 'pre-eminent global business school'

Born in the United States and educated at Smith College (B.A. in economics) and MIT (Ph.D. in economics), Tyson was appointed dean of the Haas Business School after serving as faculty member and research director at Berkeley. Tyson was a member of several corporate, academic and editorial boards, and she had served as an economic adviser to President Clinton. When she arrived at LBS she had limited knowledge of the school, although she had visited the school during Quelch's tenure. Tyson had been interested in making programmes more international and building executive education at Haas, but she 'had not been able to. They weren't at all interested in executive education at Haas, but I knew this school did a lot.'[73]

When she arrived at LBS, Tyson realised that the school had a strong operational team with a different viewpoint from the faculty's. 'There was an "issue of shared responsibility". [The governors, senior management and the faculty] are really quite separate... You have to work right away to bring them together.'[74] Booz-Allen consultants had been commissioned to work on LBS's strategy for 2010. For the new dean, the consultants' report revealed 'nothing surprising. We want to be a great business school – an academic, research-based global business school.' LBS differentiation among the world's leading business schools rested on two pillars: the fact that the school was located in London – 'a real advantage, as there aren't any other global business schools in London' – and LBS's drive to develop its 'global research capability'.[75]

With its fragile financial structure, LBS found it hard to sustain the excellence it had achieved during the past years. However, Tyson now realised that LBS was not ready to undertake a fundraising campaign: 'We hadn't developed the network; we didn't have

[73] Interview with Laura Tyson, former LBS dean.
[74] Ibid.
[75] Ibid.

a statement of what we wanted the money for.' LBS needed to develop a process before launching a fund-raising campaign. Tyson laid out a plan: 'Hire a high-ranking associate dean for external relations; put him or her in our management committee; recruit several additional fund-raisers; and then convince the faculty, our alumni and everybody that this had to be a major issue for LBS.' At that time, LBS's offerings were the most expensive programmes in the world. Tyson decided that the school would no longer seek revenue growth through price increases. In order to support its newly recruited research faculty, who expected global compensations, the school would need to boost its fund-raising activities.

Tyson focused on developing the school's faculty, continuing to improve quality and increase size. She set up a new committee – a sort of central faculty hiring. 'I decided not to go through the faculty dean any more, because I felt that the hiring decisions in the school were too decentralised and that faculty were blocking decisions that should be good for the school for their own interests. [...] I took over that.' As for the faculty dean, the role was 'critically important, because the faculty dean is the one that ultimately has to be responsible for tracking the temperature of the faculty, knowing what the issues are because the dean is doing all the representational stuff. You have to have a very powerful faculty dean."[76]

Looking ahead

Tyson pointed to three major challenges for LBS in the future. The first referred to the school's economic model: 'The question is, how do you finance this kind of knowledge generation? That's a very big issue for any business school.'[77] Tyson recognised that the school's current financial model did not match its future expectations, unless fund-raising returns were significantly increased. The second challenge hinged on faculty development. While older faculty members

[76] Ibid.
[77] Ibid.

viewed LBS as being heavily involved in executive education teaching and 'academic entrepreneurship', new generations seemed interested only in 'academic reward'. 'So, the issue then becomes the next generation of leaders in these institutions, and who's going to be the great executive education teachers, or who are going to be the ones that are going to develop a new programme because...they want to be left alone to do their research. They really do not have any interest in governance, in capacity building. On the other hand, if you try to bring somebody from the outside to do that, they are very concerned that their power might be eclipsed. So they have power, but they don't want to exercise it.' Finally, Tyson believed the school faced a third challenge: M.B.A. devaluation as a result of programme proliferation and the utilitarian motivations driving young professionals to business schools. She argued that, as 'M.B.A. programmes are ranked deliberately on the increased salary that a student gets by going onto an M.B.A. programme, the whole M.B.A. programme as an academic learning experience is being reduced; it is totally instrumental'.[78]

Summing up her contributions to LBS, former acting and academic dean Saul Estrin reported that Laura Tyson brought 'fantastic visibility to LBS. The school gained a lot in terms of the brand, and she has been very good at handling the relations with the governors, the relations with the students... She's visibility, she's image.' Tyson herself elaborated, 'When I came back from government, I knew I had a certain set of skills which, maybe, would mean I could do this job well. You know, I can generate enthusiasm for things, I can mediate other hard, complicated critical processes – sort of bring people together who can deal with all of that stuff.'

4.6   CONCLUSION

To summarise, this chapter has described some strategic leadership processes at three major European business schools, focusing

[78] Ibid.

specifically on their internationalisation strategies and linking them to the roles and leadership of deans in these schools. Each case illustrates the different cultures and contexts influencing the school's emergent strategies.

What transpires is a complex landscape for decision-making in and the strategic leadership of these organisations. The combined challenge of reconciling the competitive environment of business schools (Chapter 1) with their nuanced organisational forms as professional service firms (Chapter 2) vividly depicts the intersection of outer and inner contexts faced as part of the SLP (Chapter 3). Building on the case studies of internationalisation presented here, the following chapter addresses the main conclusions that can be drawn from the SLP studies in these schools and pays particular attention to the role of deans in strategic agenda building.

5 Strategic leadership in practice: the role of the dean

In March 2009 *The Financial Times* published an article saying: 'Andrew Likierman has taken on what might seem a veritable poisoned chalice. He has been appointed dean of London Business School after a troubled 18 months that culminated in erstwhile dean Robin Buchanan moving to the newly created and part-time role of president. All of which makes Sir Andrew the fifth dean in 11 years at the UK's most well-known business school' (Bradshaw, 2009b). This paragraph alone eloquently portrays how critical, complex and challenging strategic leadership is at any professional service firm, including world-class business schools such as LBS. Indeed, the role of the dean seems to lie at both ends of a spectrum, stemming from the very idiosyncrasy of these institutions: a dean is both 'first among equals' and a regular CEO in charge of setting and implementing his/her organisation's strategic agenda.

This article also reveals the central influence exerted by internal contexts on business schools' leadership. In these organisations, many actors and constituencies have an outspoken role in agenda building. This book approaches strategic leadership as a deeply embedded, collective process that both shapes and is shaped by people and features from inside and outside organisations – a notion that seems instrumental to understanding how this process actually works in business schools. The fact that these organisations are characterised as 'organised anarchies' (Cohen, March and Olsen, 1972), in which it is often the case that key actors with no formal authority have an influential say on strategic decision-making and execution, further proves this point, and, at the same time, reinforces their managerial uniqueness.

The cases of LBS, INSEAD and IMD provide an opportunity to highlight the texture of strategic leadership processes at business

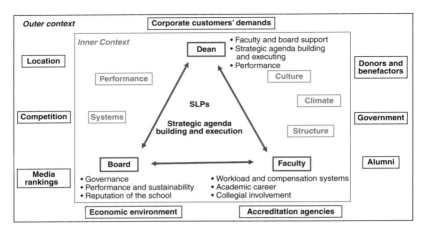

FIGURE 5.1 A contextual framework for understanding SLPs at business schools

schools in order to understand them as ongoing, dynamic processes that involve interactions between key constituencies with different outlooks and interests and explore the influence of critical features in organisations' internal and external contexts. Figure 5.1 illustrates how these interplays and environmental factors determine which strategic issues are incorporated into organisations' strategic agendas and, eventually, which are successfully executed or painfully blocked and ultimately set aside. How and why does this happen? Who sponsors these initiatives? Whose support or opposition becomes decisive for their fate – and that of the organisations as well? By comparing the strategic initiatives designed and pursued – or abandoned – by these three European institutions in the 1990–2004 period to consolidate their positioning as leading international business schools, SLPs can be explored in the very specific and unique setting of professional and academic organisations.

5.1   A CONTEXTUAL ANALYSIS TO IDENTIFY KEY FORCES AT PLAY

The fact that all three schools were established in Europe from inception enables a rather straightforward comparison of their paths to a more international positioning as a result of shared external context features, such as increased competition, new corporate customer demands and overall economic environment, and even some specific cultural characteristics, that shaped their challenges. Indeed, INSEAD, IMD and LBS all faced the need to attract faculty members, students and corporate clients from the United States, Asia and Latin America in order to enhance their standing on a worldwide basis. All three schools also needed to internationalise their programme contents and research activities, while they were equally challenged by Europe's lack of cultural and tax incentives for private and corporate donations to create large academic endowments such as the ones favouring their American counterparts. Traditionally, European educational institutions used government funding for their research efforts, scholarship schemes and infrastructure projects. However, since the 1980s, especially in the United Kingdom, where Thatcher's Conservative administration had driven severe public funding cutbacks, business schools were increasingly left to their own resources, relying on tuition revenues to grow. As former LBS dean George Bain succinctly noted, 'We don't have an endowment – as simple as that. We pay our way.'[1] This took a heavy toll on their economic models and placed an additional burden on their leaderships.

Created as a stand-alone institution, with very little support from the French state, INSEAD was forced to rely heavily on tuition, corporate support and private donations in order to grow. Early in the period studied, the school experienced a period of strong growth, and its ongoing development called for increased fund-raising. Co-dean Claude Rameau recalled, 'We wanted to have more faculty, because we were stretched in terms of faculty. We knew that fast faculty growth would be impossible without some new type of financing.'[2] Realising that more executive education programmes would not suffice to secure the funds needed for a push in faculty recruitment,

[1] Interview with George Bain, former LBS dean.
[2] Interview with Claude Rameau, former INSEAD co-dean.

INSEAD launched an audacious and successful fund-raising campaign that engaged most faculty members and raised nearly €120 million.

IMD's founding schools, IMEDE and IMI, enjoyed strong financial leverage from their major corporate sponsors, Nestlé and Alcan, respectively. However, after the merger, IMD was also challenged to find new ways to ensure its sustainability and develop its learning network so as to secure regular yearly revenues and to deepen its ties to the corporate world. Indeed, when Xavier Gilbert took over as interim dean of IMD after Rada's resignation, the school's board explicitly included 'ensuring IMD's financial health and viability' among his key responsibilities.

In turn, in the late 1980s and early 1990s, when state funding shrank considerably, LBS had to proactively seek financial resources to recruit foreign professors and to lure students from abroad in order to bolster its international reputation and appeal. 'Most British students would get their fees paid by the government, and they would also get a grant for doing an M.B.A. And this was quite generous funding, and the school would also have funding which came from the university funding council – the Universities' Grants Commission. But the government stopped or almost threatened to stop aiding business schools.'[3] Under Bain's and Quelch's deanships, LBS expanded its executive education offerings massively, while creating regional boards and alumni clubs to boost school revenues. Clearly, the successive deans leading these three business schools in this study quickly came to the realisation that their organisations needed to strengthen their financial footing and revenue streams if they intended to compete successfully with other top business schools in the international arena.

Despite the many similarities and commonalities these three schools shared in their external settings, radical differences can be found when looking at their internal contexts. To understand how

---

[3] Interview with Paul Marsh, former LBS faculty dean.

and why strategic choices are made over time, a number of internal issues should be factored in. In other words, the fabric of leadership is not woven with isolated thrusts; rather, it results from a sequence of events forged by key actors' character and behaviour, the organisation's background and the beliefs and values embedded in its culture and identity.

At the outset, it is important to recognise that the origins of these three institutions were different in terms of their historical roots, which, in turn, shaped their respective strategic leadership processes. INSEAD was created as a pan-European school unattached to French culture; in fact, English became its official language early on, while an international focus, cultural diversity and entrepreneurship were upheld as core foundational values. In turn, LBS began as a British school intending to enhance management quality in the United Kingdom. It was only in the early 1990s, with George Bain at its helm, that LBS shifted gears to compete internationally with Europe's INSEAD and the top US business schools. As noted previously, IMD was the result of the merger between two Swiss schools in the early 1990s. Under the strong leadership of its president, Peter Lorange, IMD set out to become 'the global meeting place' for management education, expanding both its reach and reputation on a worldwide scale.

In all three schools, strategic leadership processes were framed to respond to and exploit growing business globalisation trends. They were also influenced by their individual histories, as well as their respective key decision-makers and their organisational features. For example, board composition was a paramount ingredient in the content and focus of schools' strategic agendas. While INSEAD's board was committed to an entrepreneurial, international direction from its inception, the board at LBS featured mostly renowned British business leaders who were determined to build the best business school in the United Kingdom in order to provide world-class management skills and knowledge to local executives. IMD's board was clearly dominated by managers from multinational companies, such as Nestlé and Alcan, the founders of the two original schools. Its base in Switzerland, a small country in the heart of Europe, explains the school's desire to cater to the needs of business practitioners in international companies.

Faculty demographics and skill sets are also important in understanding strategic change. At IMD, the only sentiment that escaped the cultural divide that separated the original faculties from both merging schools was their shared resentment at having been uninvolved in the whole merger process. Two cultures – from the original IMI and IMEDE schools – remained pervasively distinct-ive, with IMEDE's culture prevailing as most of the new school's professors came from its home town, Lausanne. 'Faculty members were quarrelling and fighting, and they were not thinking about the customer. [...] It was a very inward-looking thing. There was a lot of fighting and distraction.'[4] Lorange helped IMD's faculty to come together by promoting a new, team-oriented culture resting firmly on an innovative organisational scheme, abolishing academic departments and tenure to foster a more professional partner-like and team-oriented atmosphere among professors.

Antonio Borges' drive to take INSEAD a step beyond its well-established European higher education pre-eminence by bol-stering its research capabilities was met with mixed feelings by the school's faculty. Some of those who had been at the school for many years found it hard to adjust to the new focus and believed that it had been their sustained commitment to top-quality teach-ing that had funded newcomers' more research-dedicated roles and efforts. Now it seemed that the school was shifting its focus, and Borges was quoted as telling faculty members 'not to overinvest in teaching'.

At LBS, a historically strong faculty played a key role in the school's evolution, with its large finance department drawing add-itional power and influence from its ability to generate superior

---

[4] Interview with Peter Lorange, IMD president.

revenues. Upon his arrival as dean, Bain found this 'disciplinary imbalance', which he described later in the following terms: 'The strength of LBS on those days were two areas: economics and finance. Strategy, marketing, operations – what I would call the central business disciplines – were very weak.' He realised that the school required further development in other academic areas to strengthen both their internal standing and profit creation capability. Later, John Quelch and Laura Tyson continued to enhance LBS's faculty by recruiting a vast number of professors educated at top US universities and by further transforming LBS's compensation and tenure systems. Indeed, at one point or another, the deans in our study have all emphasised how instrumental faculty support is to getting strategic initiatives onto the business school agenda and in executing them effectively.

As Figure 5.1 also suggests, the overall performance of a business school, in terms of revenue growth and market positioning, as well as delivering academic excellence in teaching and research, is critical in shaping its strategic agenda. At INSEAD, Borges managed to render its initiative to bolster the school's faculty research profile viable by simultaneously strengthening its financial health through increased revenues and a fruitful capital campaign. Similarly, at LBS, Quelch effectively furthered the strategic shift initiated by his predecessor and set out to expand the school's programme portfolio, increasing revenues from tuition and fund-raising activities, to make it possible for the school to compete with its leading US rivals. However, IMD's initial stage after the IMI–IMEDE merger was quite rocky as a result of the school's failure to improve its bottom line – a key priority for its board. Dean Xavier Gilbert's ability to focus the entire organisation with clear guidelines in order to regain its financial strength afforded him widespread respect and credibility, despite his interim dean status. Finally, Peter Lorange, IMD's president, kept a keen eye on school finances, strengthening its economic model to ensure sound profitability and continued sustainability without the help of an endowment fund.

Organisational systems – such as faculty and staff compensation schemes, recruiting and promotion practices – and structures
also account for critical internal features that influence – and, in
turn, are influenced by – organisations' strategic choices. Business
schools typically adopt traditional academic tenure systems, with
a hierarchical structure stemming from academic ranks and a dis-
cipline-driven departmental scheme that bears an extraordinary
impact on their leadership. How do deans lead people who are not
only their peers, with remarkable academic standing in some cases,
but also the ones who elect them to office? As former INSEAD dean
Borges candidly put it, 'There is the board, which ultimately makes
the decisions. There is the dean, who is the CEO, important to the
Board. But there is also a very powerful faculty – very, very powerful, because they elect the dean. So the dean, to a certain extent, is
also accountable to the faculty, having been elected by them. And
there are some intermediate structures of management, which also
re-emphasise the role of the faculty.'[5]

However, IMD's academic model constitutes an exception, for
it has neither academic departments nor a tenure system. As a result,
the school excels at cross-field teamwork – a practice also encouraged by IMD's current buy-back compensation policy for academic
overloads. When he arrived in 1993, Lorange found IMD plagued by
a profound crisis, which enabled him to do 'certain things, a deep
cut fairly immediately. [...] It was perhaps an unclear process, but it
became very clear. The board was very much with me, that we could
not have tenure.'[6] The school has also done away with titles, academic departments and fixed pay.

On the other hand, in the 1990–2004 period, INSEAD and
LBS shifted to a scheme more resembling that of top US schools and
introduced more attractive faculty remuneration packages in order to
compete with those institutions also in talent recruitment. INSEAD
went from a co-deanship scheme to a single-dean structure. Despite

[5] Interview with Antonio Borges, former INSEAD dean.
[6] Interview with Peter Lorange, IMD president.

the fact that '[t]he dual structure was bringing some common sense at the top, because you had two different viewpoints',[7] as INSEAD faced a more complex competitive environment, 'the disadvantages overtook the advantages of having two people that are co-responsible and can share the tasks'.[8] The school realised that '[t]he benefit of the single-dean structure was rapid decision-making, speaking with a single voice',[9] and agreed that it was 'time to go to a more traditional structure, with one person in charge'.[10] At LBS, organisational changes during this period essentially strove 'to create a seamless platform between LBS and US systems.'[11] However, at both INSEAD and LBS, more traditional, streamlined systems unquestionably influenced these schools' cultures and internal constituencies' motivations – at least, throughout these years.

Finally, each key actor's main generic interests can be viewed as a critical component of the internal context influencing the strategic leadership processes. MGIs (whose elements are outlined in Figure 5.1) are prioritised by leading actors according to their personal preferences and in response to specific or changing circumstances over time. For instance, although business school boards usually tend to focus on governance, performance and sustainability issues, IMD's board prioritised the school's short-term sustainability during its merger period, critically influencing dean Juan Rada's relationship with this governance body and eventually leading to his resignation. Rada was determined to make the merger work, by engaging faculty members from both IMI and IMEDE in the new school's strategy and policy formulation processes. Nevertheless, the Gulf War's recessive aftermath hit IMD's finances severely, and the internal mismatch between the dean's and the board's priorities precipitated Rada's departure. Lorange, the IMD president during most of the period in question, sums up his views on MGIs thus (2002: 208): 'Above all,

---

[7] Interview with Ludo Van der Heyden, former INSEAD co-dean.
[8] Interview with Arnould de Meyer, former dean of the INSEAD Asian campus.
[9] Interview with Ludo Van der Heyden, former INSEAD co-dean.
[10] Interview with Arnould de Meyer, former dean of the INSEAD Asian campus.
[11] Interview with Saul Estrin, former faculty dean at LBS.

it is the faculty's individual interests and motivation for academic work that matter: commitment to the discovery process, transformation of research into terms that can be shared with others, dissemination of the results through writing and teaching, discussions with colleagues and supervision of students.'

Another example of clashing interests on the part of a school's dean and its board was found at LBS. After LBS had substantially increased its revenues, Quelch believed that the school needed to build an endowment fund to pursue its strategy further in order to compete with its leading US counterparts. Quelch decided to leave his deanship after three years, as he realised the school's board would not provide enough support for his fund-raising efforts: 'I knew it was going to be a short deanship; I wasn't sure if it would be five years or three years, but I was not interested in staying more than five years.'

This analysis of three business schools' external and internal contexts, with their salient traits, as well as their key stakeholders and their respective motivational drivers, has provided the necessary background to study strategic leadership phenomena in specific organisational settings – rather than in isolated vacuums. Moreover, our INSEAD, LBS and IMD case studies spanning fifteen years (1990 to 2004 inclusive) also afforded an opportunity to trace the linkages between actors' interests and priorities with organisational features (performance, compensation, recruiting and promotion systems, structure, background and culture) and environmental factors (competition, corporate customer demands, economic conditions, etc.). Thus, strategic agenda building and execution can be construed as a dynamic, interactive process that greatly exceeds the influential figure – however striking – of a leader or a top management team. This systemic approach to strategic leadership in context over time offers a better understanding of how agendas are built and executed both in business schools and professional service firms.

5.2   WHY IS CONTEXT SO IMPORTANT?

An analysis and comparison of the evolution of these three schools could highlight the set of actions required to ensure or, at least, facilitate success in leading an organisation's strategic agenda and provide a useful but rather unoriginal *checklist* for leaders in academic institutions. However, the entire study of the leadership process is enriched when approached from a systemic, holistic and comprehensive view of leadership in a specific type of organisation, such as a business school, with a distinctive environment. It becomes even more enlightening if it does not focus on the isolated actions of one individual but on the interconnected succession of events, moves and decisions that involves several actors with different roles, aspirations and perspectives, who are affected by other inner and outer context features and, in turn, influence them as well. This is the underlying notion of strategic leadership as a process in context that drives our business school research.

This approach to leadership seems somewhat lacking in current literature. Nye's recent book, *The Powers to Lead*, proves to be a refreshing exception, devoting an entire chapter to what the author calls *contextual intelligence*. Nye (2008) clearly states, 'Leadership is a power relationship between leaders and followers, but power depends on context.' In the 'interactive art' of leadership, leaders 'dance' with contexts, problems, factions and objectives. Mayo and Nohria, of HBS, also use the concept of contextual intelligence to explain why some firms respond more successfully than others to changing markets. These authors define contextual intelligence as 'the ability to understand an evolving environment and to capitalise on trends' (Mayo and Nohria, 2005).

Effective leaders need to identify meaningful trends in their organisations' environment in order to shape developments by using the flow of events to pursue a specific strategy. In addition to the political skills required to read into and factor in stakeholders' concerns and traits, contextual intelligence also hinges on a disposition to take into account the needs of others. A keen understanding of outer and inner context features helps leaders to determine the kind of leadership and the type of strategic initiatives that each situation demands. This understanding should also enlighten leaders as to how to use their power both to accomplish the appropriate leadership style and to execute that type of necessary strategic initiative successfully.

5.3 USING A POLITICAL APPROACH TO EXPLORE STRATEGIC LEADERSHIP PHENOMENA

In the analysis of SLP as an ongoing process or sequence of decisions and actions affecting and being affected by organisations, their organisational settings and key actors, it is crucial to understand the forces that drive people's decisions and actions, building an interplay that ultimately determines which initiatives make it into the organisation's strategic agenda, while others are blocked or discarded. This process bears significant relevance at professional service firms, such as business schools, in which power tends to be shared as formal managerial authority is eclipsed by professional collegiality, expert knowledge and personal reputation. As a result, a political perspective becomes especially helpful in exploring how organisations' strategic agendas are formulated and pursued over time.

As noted earlier, in Chapter 3, a political approach to SLPs hinges on two primary activities carried out by key actors to prioritise their initiatives in their organisations' strategic agendas: power mobilisation and issue legitimation. Through these mechanisms, decision-makers seek to rally the support of their organisations' constituencies for their initiatives and to overcome any opposition from other actors whose initiatives may be also competing for scarce resources and a place in organisations' limited agendas. However, this political outlook on strategic leadership processes is not very popular in current literature, possibly because power is often construed as a somewhat *dark side* of leadership, despite the fact that most experts and experienced practitioners agree that leadership is indeed a 'social influence process'. Clearly, both power and influence are central to leading any organisation, and, thus, it would be wise to understand how power is built, used and, eventually, lost. To concentrate on what can be learned about SLPs from a political perspective at INSEAD, IMD and LBS as all three schools set out

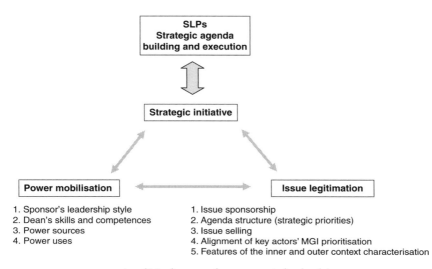

FIGURE 5.2 A political approach to strategic leadership

to consolidate their international positioning from 1990 to 2004, it is useful to revisit the political approach outlined in Chapter 3 (see Figure 5.2).

As shown in Figure 5.2, power mobilisation efforts are characterised by sponsors' leadership styles, deans' skill and competence sets, personal power sources and their utilisation of power. The use of power may involve coalition building, information leverage, resource allocation, compensations, ingratiation, goodwill creation, etc. The other mechanism used to garner support for strategic initiatives is issue legitimation, which encompasses leaders' endeavours to sponsor and sell their priority issues to as many people in their organisations as possible by articulating and communicating the value of their initiatives for the successful pursuit of an organisation's mission, vision and strategic goals. Issue legitimation also involves three critical contextual factors: alignment with key actors' MGI prioritisation; proper consideration of organisations' salient inner and outer context features; and their size and structure. Bain's wise definition of the purpose of leadership as 'producing more leaders, not more followers' seems to highlight leaders' ability to sell their initiatives so effectively that others become true sponsors of those initiatives once incorporated in their organisations' strategic agendas, championing their execution to ensure their success.

Nonetheless, as a result of their particular organisational nature, business schools require leadership processes that not only factor in critical internal and external features, as with any other for-profit or non-profit organisation, but also include the sharing of some key information with other members of the organisation – faculty in business schools and senior partners in professional service firms. These organisations have no room for more command-like leadership styles, with leaders issuing orders to be executed unquestioningly. As a faculty member at IAE Business School in Argentina noted, 'Introducing an issue to the faculty only marks the beginning of the debate for direction setting'.[12] This is true, and probably healthy, considering the mindset of professional and academic organisations. Collegiality involves a dual challenge: providing enough room for consensus in order to preserve and promote motivation and commitment, and avoiding endless debates that could jeopardise growth, causing organisational paralysis. Leadership processes in these organisations therefore involve two crucial steps: first, securing at least a modicum of consensus on a strategic initiative from key actors; and, second, motivating the right people to seize that initiative and make it their own, ensuring successful execution across the organisation. In other words, any strategic pursuit needs to be legitimated by key constituencies, while power is used to overcome resistance and to procure critical resources.

A comprehensive framework for deans' leadership tasks

When leadership processes are viewed as including a political perspective, with its two intrinsic actions – issue legitimation and power mobilisation – firmly supported by leaders' reputation, commitment and integrity, it is possible to use power and influence adequately.

---

[12] Interview with Professor Marcelo Paladino, current IAE Business School dean.

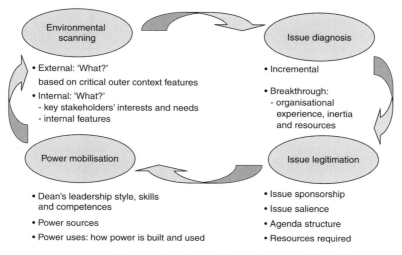

FIGURE 5.3 A comprehensive and dynamic approach to SLPs

After reviewing SLPs in three top business schools over a fifteen-year period, a clear conclusion can easily be drawn: leadership processes should encompass both a contextual and a political perspective in order to build a seamless continuum that reinforces leaders' effectiveness and drives organisational advancement. Figure 5.3 integrates both perspectives into a single framework that provides a comprehensive and dynamic approach to leadership.

Our case studies on LBS, INSEAD and IMD have focused on a set of issues associated with their international expansion and standing. Some of these issues can be categorised as 'breakthrough' initiatives, as they reshaped, recreated or changed each school's strategy, future direction and culture, consequently affecting its values, its resources and its people's academic careers. Others, instead, may be viewed as 'incremental' initiatives, as they accounted for evolutionary steps following the schools' predetermined path and furthering their status quo. Table 5.1 pinpoints the strategic initiatives designed by each school in that period of time to enhance and consolidate its international positioning, characterising them as breakthrough or incremental for easier follow-up in our analysis. This cross-case

Table 5.1 *Breakthrough and incremental strategic initiatives devised at IMD, INSEAD and LBS, 1990–2004*

School		IMD			INSEAD				LBS		
Strategic goal		Consolidating international standing									
Period		1990–1991	1992–1993	1993–2004	1990–1995	1995–1999	1999–2003	2004	1990–1997	1998–2001	2002–2004
Initiative: Set of decisions and actions to reach goal		Making the IMI and IMEDE merge successful	Restoring the school's financial health	IMD's consolidation and success in world-class management education	Enhancing the school's research strategy and profile	Launching a second campus	Making the Singapore campus work	Launching a third campus – in the United States	Turning LBS into a top international school	Deepening LBS transformation to further expand its international brand development	Consolidating LBS as a 'pre-eminent global business school' through greater visibility
Type of initiative	Breakthrough	■		■		■		■	■		
	Incremental		■		■		■			■	■

analysis, therefore, encompasses both types of strategic initiatives deployed at all three schools in the 1990–2004 period, and emphasises breakthrough endeavours, highlighting their genesis, evolution and outcomes, as these truly account for leadership challenges.

5.4 THE USE OF POWER AT WORK

Now that the breakthrough strategic initiatives deployed by LBS, INSEAD and IMD over the 1990–2004 period have been identified, it is useful to examine some common issue legitimation and power mobilisation patterns found across the schools for both successful and unsuccessful breakthrough initiatives – that is, those that were eventually executed and those that failed to materialise. Tables 5.2 and 5.3 summarise these findings in each set of practices. A detailed analysis of these patterns reveals what a strategic initiative – especially if it involves a breakthrough – requires for minimum consensus in order to become an effective decision and to be successfully executed.

As can be inferred from Table 5.2, issue legitimation patterns at all three schools indicate that successful breakthrough initiatives were promoted by deans as leading sponsors who resorted to coalition-building practices to broaden issue sponsorship in their organisations. Deans also engaged in proactive and intense issue-selling activities involving the schools' faculties, boards and key staff members in order to articulate and communicate their organisations' vision with their own initiatives. To align key actors' MGIs with their strategic pursuits, deans reviewed the demands and requirements of outer contexts and major constituencies alike.

For example, as noted in the previous chapter, immediately after joining the school as president, IMD's Lorange requested input in writing from all faculty members so as to collect their impressions and overriding concerns. Quite openly, he asked each and every professor, 'If you were in my shoes, which are the three positive things you would do, if you had my job? And which other three things would you advise me not to do? Please, help me. Send me a little note. [...]

Table 5.2 *Common issue legitimation patterns for breakthrough initiatives shared by all three schools*

			Successful breakthrough initiatives	**Unsuccessful breakthrough initiatives**
Issue sponsorship			■	■
Issue selling			■	
Alignment of key actors' MGI prioritisation			■	
Agenda structure			■	■
Features legitimating initiatives	*Outer context*	Corporate client demands	■	
		Alumni		
		Donors and benefactors	■	■
		Government		
		Competition	■	■
		Location		
		Economic environment		■
	Inner context	Climate		
		Culture		
		Structure		
		Systems		
		Performance	■	
Features de-legitimating initiatives	*Inner context*	Climate		■
		Culture		
		Structure		■
		Systems		■
		Performance		

I think it's critical that we look towards the environment, and that we become more customer-oriented. I'm reading that from you.'[13] Borges made his case to revamp INSEAD's research output by portraying it as the logical next step for a school that was already ranked as the top

[13] Interview with Peter Lorange, IMD president.

European management teaching institution. Having outperformed its competitors in Europe, INSEAD aimed to strengthen its research record to compete with leading US business schools. Before joining LBS as dean, Bain spent six months visiting top American schools to learn about competition and the characteristics of every constituency in a business school. He talked extensively with faculty members – a habit he maintained after becoming dean. Bain had come to understand people's perspectives on the school's situation and their expectations for its future direction, saying: 'I'm a pretty good listener and I took on board everybody's points.'[14] His 'Bias towards a strategy' document was welcomed at LBS because it articulated the school's vision of becoming a top-league player in international management education with input from everyone.

Schools' strategic agendas are shaped by breakthrough initiatives that are intended to help these organisations to move forward in their pre-established paths to success. External context features, such as changing corporate customers' demands, increasing competition and expectations from donors and benefactors, usually trigger the need for business schools to change their strategic agendas by launching breakthrough initiatives that require strong issue legitimation efforts. In turn, weak performance on the part of schools – an internal context feature – also fuels the need for change, as was the case with IMD in 1993, when financial distress threatened its viability. By 1990 LBS's domestic scope had proved insufficient to lead the higher education market in Europe, as painfully revealed by academic rankings, which hailed INSEAD as the number one school in Europe. As Bain explained, 'The school had assumed from its inception that it was the best business school in Europe and was not short of arrogance – a feature in academic institutions, of course. And they had worked on this assumption – I think – since they were founded. There has to be some kind of external shock... It's certainly very helpful. This external shock washed out the whole self-perception of LBS being the best.'

[14] Interview with George Bain, former LBS dean.

Nonetheless, when an organisation is not facing a crisis and its performance is sound, the introduction of bold initiatives becomes a test for leaders' reputations and their track record on delivering results. For example, when Borges presented his initiative to open INSEAD's second campus in Asia, he already had a successful fund-raising campaign and the school's research overhaul under his belt. 'Some faculty members went to Antonio and said, "When did we make this decision?" He replied, "We talked about it; nobody seemed against it, so I assumed we were all in favour."'[15] When asked about this strategic initiative, Borges candidly acknowledged that running the project and negotiating its approval 'was relatively simple... What was really tough was to get the various constituencies to support the project.'[16]

However, unsuccessful strategic initiatives were besieged by poor issue legitimation efforts, with insufficient actions taken to broaden initiative sponsorship or to sell the idea to school con-stituencies. As a result, it was difficult for these strategic pursuits to compete with other initiatives prioritised by other key actors for a pre-eminent spot in the schools' agendas. Despite the fact that sev-eral outer context features, including corporate customers' demands, competition and economic conditions, seemed to support and legit-imate the need for these endeavours, prevailing inner context factors such as organisational climate, structure and systems played a cru-cial role in thwarting their acceptance and effective execution.

Indeed, issue legitimation is key for strategic leadership proc-esses involving breakthrough initiatives. Inner and outer context features can and should be used to justify the need for strategic change – ultimately, breakthrough initiatives usually involve some sort of shift in tactics or operations – while making that change seem like the natural and necessary next step for the institution. This may be accomplished by relying on organisational core values and

---

[15] Interview with Ludo Van der Heyden, former INSEAD co-dean.
[16] Interview with Antonio Borges, former INSEAD dean.

current market needs or conditions, and it also helps if a bold move can be turned into more of an incremental initiative that keeps the school in its intended strategic path. However, stakeholders' interests and opinions should also be taken into account in this process in order to ensure alignment and endorsement. The more an initiative is presented as responding to everyone's needs, the easier it will be for people to 'own' the project and to commit themselves to it.

As shown in Table 5.3, which maps power mobilisation patterns, the deans at IMD, LBS and INSEAD who undertook successful breakthrough initiatives all displayed a directive leadership style, supported by a comprehensive skill and competence set that enabled them to understand the contexts in which their schools were embedded and to communicate their ideas assertively, influencing others through their own commitment. These leaders drew power mostly from personal sources, taking decisive, specific steps to articulate their vision, to delegate execution and to focus their entire organisations on reaching the desired outcomes.

For instance, once he had become convinced that INSEAD should open a new campus in Asia to exploit its experience in that region and to leverage a unique international position, Borges quickly secured the support of the school's board chairman and several key faculty members, who were already familiar and enthused with Asia, to engage them as initiative champions, multiplying issue-sponsoring efforts. In order to persuade faculty members into actually moving to Asia, he organised several regional tours, and summarily discussed the new campus location at a regular faculty meeting. He also used two of the school's core values – entrepreneurship and its unique international character – to leverage this initiative and to build consensus and rally support for this thoroughly breakthrough initiative. Borges explained that, as opening the Asian campus 'was a market-driven process, it was relatively easy to prove that this was a relatively safe pad, that we had grown so much that this was more a method of continuity, and that we were taking advantage of a position of market leadership compared to our competitors; nobody

Table 5.3 *Common power mobilisation patterns for breakthrough initiatives shared by all three schools*

		Successful breakthrough initiatives	Unsuccessful breakthrough initiatives
Sponsors' leadership style	Directive	▇	
	Participative		▇
Deans' skills and competences	Vision	▇	▇
	Communication	▇	
	Ability to deliver results	▇	
	Political skills	▇	
	Entrepreneurship	▇	▇
	Commitment	▇	▇
	Consistency		
	Integration	▇	
Power sources	Position	▇	▇
	Rewards	▇	
	Resource acquisition and allocation	▇	
	Expertise	▇	
	Reputation	▇	
	Referent	▇	
Power uses	Articulation	▇	
	Coalition building	▇	
	Rationality	▇	
	Assertiveness	▇	
	Decisiveness	▇	
	Execution	▇	
	Delegation	▇	
	Listening and scanning		
	Consensus building		▇

was in Asia then. We were very visible and so we should take advantage. So we defined that advantage relative to our competitors before they decided to do it. And so then, although people were sceptical, it was very easy to go ahead. [...] The board of directors also pushed by saying "You have to be bold, you have to do this".[17]

Nevertheless, several power mobilisation weaknesses seemed to come together to render some breakthrough initiatives unsuccessful. At LBS, INSEAD and IMD, defeated strategic initiatives were largely promoted by sponsors with a participative leadership style. Though skilful, visionary and entrepreneurial, these leaders lacked strong power mobilisation abilities and found it difficult to use their power to garner enough support and consensus around their initiatives. Moreover, in some cases, despite an extremely strong reputation for commitment and delivering outstanding results, a remarkable dean such as Gabriel Hawawini seemed not to have adequately scanned INSEAD's internal context at the time he introduced his initiative to open a third campus in the United States. When Hawawini presented his idea to the newly-appointed chairman of INSEAD's board, Cees van Lede was quoted as saying: 'It's just too soon for a third campus.' Apparently not fully aware of the toll the Singapore campus was still taking on most school constituencies, Hawawini underestimated their resistance and, thus, the need for significant issue-selling efforts to build consensus by compellingly reconciling this new bold initiative with INSEAD's long-term vision. In retrospect, Hawawini's expertise had been built on his ability to overcome difficulties in the execution of bold initiatives that were already under way. However, on this occasion, he was playing a different role: he was introducing a new initiative. While he probably viewed this third campus initiative as incremental – and it may indeed have been so, as it would have furthered INSEAD's progress towards a multi-campus learning network – his school's stakeholders perceived it as a breakthrough next step because of the efforts

[17] Interview with Antonio Borges, former INSEAD dean.

and resources that it would require. In the end, his outstanding track record and personal effectiveness did not go unrewarded: more than half the faculty voted for him to have a new term in office.

Common issue legitimation and power mobilisation practices, such as coalition building, issue selling and sponsorship, are sometimes portrayed as the *dark side of leadership*, almost implying that they are used by cunning leaders who beguile their followers with some distorted variant of leadership. This negative approach seems to overlook an inherent feature of human interaction: politics. Though present in management studies, power and influence are mostly excluded as central components in leadership process analyses. This study incorporates the political perspective as a key aspect of power utilisation and, thus, of strategic leadership processes. If leadership is construed as a 'social influence process', a political approach, devoid of any negative connotation, should be accepted as a fact of human interaction. Power can be used to manipulate people, but it can also be used to influence others while respecting their freedom, needs and opinions. It seems that a failure to recognise the need to build and use power effectively fairly often leads to inadequate power utilisation, and even to inadvertent abuse.

5.5   THE ROLE OF THE DEAN IN STRATEGIC LEADERSHIP PROCESSES

The process of studying how IMD, INSEAD and LBS navigated SLPs in the 1990–2004 period so as to compete successfully in the international arena of business education provided a unique opportunity to meet more than 100 remarkable faculty members, a dozen outstanding deans and former deans and a number of committed school board members. It became clear that the role of the dean in schools' agenda-building and execution processes was considered a central issue. The lengthy period covered by the study also allowed for an observation of meaningful interplays between actors and contextual features over time, enriching the study's findings with this significant time horizon.

For example, the suggestion of one experienced faculty member that a dean should act as 'a bridge' between the school's goals and faculty's own intellectual interests and motivation drivers (as there is not much any dean can do about academics) is enlightening, but rather vague and simplistic. However, it does highlight the problems and challenges of leading business schools and PSFs, and it provides a starting point as well as a glimpse at a central aspect in a deanship. Another academic veteran framed the dean's leadership role in four key dimensions: school visibility, fund-raising, intellectual guidance and operations management. More grounded and comprehensive, this approach can help deans to allocate appropriate amounts of time and effort to each of these critical tasks, although it should be noted that very few, if any, people are likely to deal with all four activities effectively; *deans constantly juggle a series of organisational dilemmas and roles* (Davies and Thomas, 2009; Harris, 2006). However, the mere awareness of these challenges should be viewed as an advantage in itself. Bain's notion that the purpose of leadership is 'to produce more leaders, not more followers' became a cornerstone of his strategic initiatives, as he believed that 'for an organisation to be successful, there has to be leadership at several different levels. It is no such great hero at the top of the organisation. It's got to be at several different levels.'[18]

Clearly, deans' overriding responsibility is to lead their schools' strategic agenda – not an easy task considering, in particular, business schools' collegial nature and, as a result, their characteristically diffuse power schemes, with authority stemming from intellectual knowledge, expertise and prestige. Former LBS dean John Quelch admitted, 'I knew what I wanted. If I asked too many questions and I had too much discussion, I knew that there would be – as is always the case in academia – 100 reasons not to do something. So my attitude was "Just do it". [...] From a political management point of view, you launch your first initiative and there are some people who are

---

[18] Interview with George Bain, former LBS dean.

against it. But, before they can organise, you launch another initiative that splits that group because some people who opposed your first initiative are going to be in favour of the second. And so you basically keep splitting through initiative after initiative. You fragment the opposition.'[19]

To make matters even more complicated, the deanship is a temporary job, and faculties often elect their schools' deans, or, at least, are involved in dean election processes. These organisational traits become ever more relevant as business schools face their current challenge to realign some internal and structural systems that are deeply embedded in their culture, while also reformulating both their teaching and research value propositions in order to come closer to real-world businesses and practitioners and their needs. Some leading business schools have responded to this demand and challenge by recruiting experienced management consultants as deans. However, while this is one of the central challenges of deanship, as organisational characteristics remain unchanged, this new breed of 'practitioner deans' needs an even greater understanding of what is different in these environments and dissimilar from the context of a professional service firm populated by professionals not academics.

5.6   LEADING A BUSINESS SCHOOL

Because leadership is all about people and influence, it is important for leaders to develop a thorough understanding of the actors involved and their circumstances. More specifically, strategic leadership should be viewed as a social process in which people interact and interplay from different roles in order to pursue a number of goals based on their organisations' purposes and challenges. Therefore, interpreting interplay and social interaction is critical in formulating strategic direction. In addition, leaders in general – and deans in particular – are required to decipher their organisations' external environment, identifying the threats to them and

---

[19] Interview with John Quelch, former LBS dean.

their opportunities. Outer contexts include local, regional and global issues, trends and developments. Domestic and international
economic cycles and conditions, global corporate clients' needs and
concerns, world-class competitors' offerings and scope, as well as
the expectations of donors and benefactors, are all factors that deans
should be constantly looking at in building their schools' strategic
agendas for sustainable success. Equally important for deans is having a full understanding of and developing their knowledge about
their schools' inner context, and devoting time to getting to know
all school stakeholders, with their respective interests, needs and
skill sets.

For instance, Bain spent six months talking to everyone with
some influence on the school's strategic agenda before he actually
assumed the LBS deanship. This dedicated effort translated into a
significant asset when he set out to define and raise support around
LBS's strategic guidelines. Based on his experience, he confidently
stated that leadership 'is more about having good ears than having a
good mouth'. Indeed, in order to introduce strategic initiatives into
their schools' agendas, deans need to understand not just faculty
and board members' interests but also their priorities. Inspiring and
mobilising a large number of these actors to support – and even to
sponsor – those initiatives would otherwise be impossible.

Clear examples of deans' success and failure in this regard
were found and documented in all three sample schools. Especially
revealing were Borges' breakthrough initiatives at INSEAD: his drive
to turn the school into a research-oriented institution – when most
of the faculty had a different background – and his bold initiative
to open a new campus in Singapore in order to globalise the school.
In fact, this latter – and later – move could easily have come into
conflict with his earlier initiative, distracting the school's efforts to
build its incipient research capabilities to compete with leading US
business schools. However, Borges' ability to sell his initiatives to
key faculty and board members, effectively engaging them as initiative sponsors, made it possible for INSEAD to overcome a multitude

of obstacles and difficulties in both pursuits; as his successor, Hawawini, who successfully opened the Singapore campus and made it work, recalled, 'Everything that could have gone wrong went wrong.'[20]

As 'first among equals', deans are also expected to act as 'integrators' who reconcile short-term financial needs and long-run academic goals, while keeping in sight corporate and private customers' requirements as well as the school's relevant offerings to meet their needs. To do so, deans need to be able to build consensus and to share their vision on school strategy, but, at the same time, they cannot overlook their responsibility to secure the necessary resources to attract the best possible faculty members, finding adequate compensation schemes and facilitating their research agendas. In this setting, deans have little power to drive changes or to introduce bold strategic initiatives that may challenge their school's status quo. In fact, as several interviewees from all constituencies pointed out throughout this research study, the role of the dean usually involves straddling often conflicting forces: the school's board and its faculty, the world of business and academia, and professors' individual academic agendas and institutions' goals, as well as long-term teaching and research excellence versus short-term financial resources and needs. In dealing with these dichotomies, the most crucial abilities required for a deanship include all the skills associated with listening, integrating, communicating and building consensus. These capabilities all hinge on personal credibility, which, in turn, is built on consistent behaviour and the ability to deliver results.

In a nutshell, it is safe to say that leading academic institutions is a difficult task with limited power, great exposure to tough criticism, and little recognition. As LBS's former dean Laura Tyson put it, 'The main thing that I think a dean is trying to do is to represent the institution to the different groups that don't quite see the institution in the same way. So [a dean stands] for the collective interests and

---

[20] Interview with Gabriel Hawawini, former INSEAD dean.

the future of the institution, which the rest of the university depend upon and the faculty depends upon... I don't think having a shared governance is really a bad thing – it's just a complicated thing. I think that the faculty do need to be listened to and be responded to and understand what the [board] says. [A dean] is in the middle, trying to continue to build this bridge. But I actually think this is probably not a bad model for a business school.' Though extreme, this perspective on the dean's role provides a well-rounded picture of the challenges faced by deans in exercising power and introducing changes in their schools' strategic course to overcome market threats or to seize the opportunities.

5.7   DEANS AS CEOS

Deans may also be viewed as CEOs, in charge of setting schools' strategic direction. This notion does not overlook the organisational traits, such as collegiality and shared power, that characterise academic institutions, but it restrains their negative side effects, which can lead to evolutionary paralysis or, at least, to a failure to undertake a breakthrough initiative when necessary. Our study provided clear examples that illustrate this approach to deanship. As former LBS dean Bain put it, 'I think the faculty were very happy; even if they weren't happy with the details, they were happy that now there was a *captain* on the ship who was saying "This is where we should go". If they didn't like it, at least they could argue, but they knew where they were going.' At INSEAD, Borges' thrust to develop the school's research capabilities as a trademark to complement its widely recognised teaching excellence made it possible for INSEAD to compete with leading US business schools. His CEO-like leadership also showed in his ability to promote and execute the initiative to open a second campus in Asia. Over his fifteen-year tenure as IMD's president, Lorange forged an organisational transformation that could only be brought about with unequivocal decision-making power. Moreover, Lorange believed that deans are not only meant to determine a school's strategic focus but that they should also decide which pathways are more effective in order to pursue that goal.

Both Borges and Lorange realised the need for faculty and board members to discuss strategic initiatives so as to enhance and legitimate them before supporting their execution. A similar approach to the dean's role may be attributed to Bain when he set about changing LBS's strategic direction. However, some special circumstances add a certain distinctiveness to his experience. Bain took over as LBS dean amidst a clear consensus that the school needed to focus on the international business school market. The fact that he was not an LBS faculty member could have weakened his position to legitimate his vision, but his successful track record as chairman of Warwick Business School, coupled with his directive yet perceptive leadership style and the six months he devoted to understanding the concerns of all school constituencies, enabled him to build a strong support platform for launching his initiatives.

Like any corporate CEO, a dean is expected to lead his or her school's strategic leadership processes, regardless of the differences found in organisational settings. As our study revealed, deans' MGIs include securing and optimising school performance, rallying support from the school's board and faculty and leading its strategic agenda. A failure to focus on and perform these three central tasks simultaneously and effectively greatly impairs any dean's chances for success. Active, ongoing external and internal environmental scanning provides useful input to detect outer context opportunities, threats and demands as well as inner developments, including key actors' desires, motivations and frustrations. Deans can therefore adjust strategic plans to respond to stakeholders' needs as they evolve over time. This ability to monitor the pulse of the organisation's inner and outer setting is not enough, though, if it does not rest firmly on an outstanding record for delivering results, which affords deans the necessary credibility and stature to undertake bold initiatives. Indeed, performance is both a prerequisite and a crucial source of power for deans to legitimate themselves in order to succeed in their jobs.

However, performance and sound delivery in difficult times and challenging tasks does not always suffice, as illustrated by Hawawini's experience at INSEAD. His remarkable track record was not enough for him to secure the support of a decisive majority of the faculty for his initiative to open a third campus, which he set as a precondition for staying on as dean. Although his accomplishments and leadership style were largely praised by most constituencies, he did not get the support he expected for his initiative. Hawawini recognised that he had underestimated the influence of some inner context features at the time, such as the strain brought onto the school by the Singapore campus. INSEAD's faculty was just not ready to take on a similar challenge so soon after this previous effort.

As Lorange points out in his book, deans also play an internal role in their schools' value creation processes, serving as *catalysts* to encourage 'creative synergy among faculty members' and to drive academic teams' search for excellence. On the external front, deans 'must communicate the school's vision' and lead the school's dissemination of innovative business practices (Lorange, 2002). Combining both roles, deans have to engage in a true balancing act by paying attention to both outer stakeholders' demands and inner constituencies' needs while prioritising the school's ultimate goal of sustainable growth. In *Thought Leadership Meets Business*, the former IMD president argues that a dean must be 'a social entrepreneur' who 'might be able to play a truly significant and proactive role in society so that academic values can be more forward-oriented and in line with society's present and future needs' (Lorange, 2008: 185). In addition, he explains that deans should find a balance between top-down, classic leadership practices based on their inner drive as well as a constant sensitivity for and compatibility with 'the bottom-up issues stemming from the members of the business school community'.

Thus, deans are responsible for setting their schools' direction. Indeed, their mission, central to SLPs, is to shape the school's strategy and to make it work in a way that bold breakthrough initiatives, when needed, can be pursued and effectively executed. This type of organisational setting requires not only inspiration, vision and decision-making capabilities but also an extraordinary 'social and contextual intelligence' – the ability to articulate and communicate a vision by understanding both the organisation's inner and outer contexts. By scanning both environments, deans are able to spot opportunities on both sides: what business practitioners need to overcome current and future challenges and what academics can explore and contribute. The key to playing this manifold role lies in engaging the school's major external and internal constituencies – business leaders, leading competitors, board, faculty and staff – in the process, actively heeding their respective needs and interests to build an effective and well-rounded strategic agenda. The best illustration of this notion may perhaps have been when the former IMD board chairman, Vito Baumgartner, referred to IMD's future challenges as 'maintaining the relationships with partner companies and business associates, and making sure that the system provides value to both and that these partnerships can be perpetuated. I think that it is absolutely critical to continually recognise that it is the people of IMD that makes the difference. And you have to work on your ability to continue to be able to attract the base talent to achieve those goals and successes, to perpetuate the successes of the past.'[21]

5.8   A ROAD MAP FOR DEANS: FOUR KEY TASKS

To provide more practical, down-to-earth guidelines, the role of the dean may be narrowed down to the four key activities identified in the comprehensive and dynamic approach to SLPs presented in Figure 5.3: environmental scanning, issue diagnosis, issue legitimation and power mobilisation. Considering these tasks may help current and future deans in their day-to-day challenges.

---

[21] Interview with Vito Baumgartner, former chairman of the IMD Foundation board.

Environmental scanning

Understanding the school's internal and external context is crucial for identifying opportunities and for finding ways to match them with current faculty aspirations, interests and priorities as well as with board members' concerns and objectives. Indeed, deans need to stay abreast of new trends in schools' marketplaces, changes in customer needs and factual and subjective data on management practices in order to keep tabs on their external context. At the same time, they need to monitor and listen to their internal constituencies closely to detect any changes in inner environmental conditions that may or may not respond to external shifts. As a result, deans will be able to orchestrate a strategy to start a number of initiatives not by imposing them but by wisely articulating and communicating them as means to accomplish a common goal. In this process, potential supporters play a central role, and opposition can be expressed and actually exploited so as to further enhance those initiatives rather than blocking them.

Issue diagnosis

Deans should not just assess initiatives as regular business proposals but should also weigh the effort required to 'legitimate' a strategic issue within their organisations – particularly to ensure faculty and board support. This issue diagnosis task requires the ability to determine whether an initiative involves a major shift or breakthrough in the school's current strategy or whether it accounts for a natural next step towards its existing goals. An incremental initiative of this latter kind will normally proceed unhindered if adequately presented and communicated with sufficient grounds to make its case at that point in time. It will encounter obstacles only when the dean's power and reputation are weak or when there is a mismatch between the dean's priorities and those of the faculty or board – as was the case at IMD during its merger period.

A true challenge comes with initiatives involving a radical change that, for example, rattles the status quo for key constituencies or stretches the school's financial resources. In the case of these breakthrough initiatives, the school's board plays a key role in driving the decision to move forward. As described in the previous chapter, at all three schools in our sample, the support of the board was decisive when breakthrough initiatives were proposed in LBS, IMD and INSEAD's strategic agendas, as these strategic pursuits required significant financial resources. Faculty support and commitment, as also shown by our sample cases, called for the two tasks that will be discussed next.

Issue legitimation

Breakthrough initiatives usually demand extensive legitimation efforts. Deans are sometimes excessively earnest in their attempts to pursue their vision and ideas, and it is often hard to resist the temptation to sell an initiative, pushing it forward, rather than devoting time and thought to understanding how the initiative can be made appealing for other stakeholders. This process may lead to initiative enhancement so as to make it more compelling for others. While a directive leadership style is generally necessary for driving breakthrough initiatives, it needs to be combined with an effort to allow for discussion and contributions from key constituencies. This does not mean engaging in endless, stagnating debates, but the more consensual and legitimated an initiative is, the less it will wear down the dean's power and authority. More legitimated issues also garner greater commitment from all stakeholders, who develop a sense of ownership around an initiative they support wholeheartedly.

At higher education and professional service organisations in general, where there is rarely a hierarchy system in place, issue legitimation becomes crucial. To overcome resistance and to ensure the successful execution of strategic initiatives, a clear understanding and assessment of inner and outer features must precede the careful formulation of a sound strategy to make the case for the initiative at hand in order to sell it, to secure critical sponsorship and to gain enough organisational support. A key step in this process involves considering how a specific breakthrough initiative relates to the organisation's mission and values – for instance, INSEAD's bold initiatives reflected its entrepreneurial roots – as well as whether its current culture and behaviours are part of what needs to be changed – such as the need to open up LBS's originally British mindset to the world. An effective initiative communication should articulate how it will contribute to the organisation's long-term strategy and goals. A breakthrough initiative may therefore be viewed as a natural step forward – though bold and even risky – to accomplish the school's mission. The more an initiative is perceived as 'incremental', the less resistance it will produce and the less it will impair the dean's authority.

Power mobilisation

Finally, deans need to exercise their ability to mobilise power. Leadership is a social influence process intended to help others understand and desire what the leader views as the best choice for the organisation. Once an issue is legitimated, power must be used to complete the leadership process by effectively rallying support and commitment for the successful execution of an initiative. However, it appears from our study that professional service firms in general, and business schools in particular, are reluctant to submit to any kind of hierarchy or managerial authority. Power in these types of organisations is based on personal sources, such as expertise, professional reputation, public prestige, the ability to deliver results, integrity, commitment, interpersonal skills and other traits. This does not mean that deans have no impact or influence but, rather, that positional power is just a starting point – not a 'blank cheque'. To strengthen the power that comes from being elected dean, a sound track record in resource generation for school operations, long-term investments and research activities becomes a key tool in building a dean's reputation and in bolstering his/her power sources. Indeed, deans need to legitimate themselves, proving their worth, courage and effectiveness, before they can legitimate their initiatives.

To summarise, this holistic and systemic approach to strategic leadership should be viewed as a continuum, with these four tasks continually overlapping and demanding – oddly enough – undivided attention from deans. Without such attention, they are unlikely to succeed in building and executing their school's strategic agendas.

We build and reflect on the roles and tasks of deanship in the next chapter by presenting insights and conclusions drawn from our experiences respectively as deans. Fernando Fragueiro served as dean at IAE in Argentina from 1995 to 2007 and Howard Thomas as dean of Warwick Business School in the United Kingdom from 2000 to 2010.

6   Learning from the trenches: personal reflections on deanship

6.1   INTRODUCTION

In this chapter, we hope to offer a much more personal contribution based on our experiences as deans of two very different business schools: Warwick Business School, where Howard Thomas was dean from 2000 to 2010, and IAE Business School, where Fernando Fragueiro was dean from 1995 to 2008. These institutions differ greatly not only because the former is located near the city of Coventry, in the heart of England, and the latter is situated in a Buenos Aires suburb, at Latin America's southernmost tip, but also as a result of their dramatically different outer environments – the United Kingdom and Argentina – and surrounding cultures. Furthermore, their individual inception processes were very dissimilar. While WBS was founded in the 1960s as part of a university embedded in a system characterised by state support and academic oversight, IAE was created in 1978 as a stand-alone institution with neither financial aid nor supervision from the public sector. Eventually IAE's independent status changed, as it became part of a newly created private university – Universidad Austral – in 1991, although it remained autonomous until 2000, when Universidad Austral was formally installed as IAE's parent institution. Incorporating IAE into Universidad Austral's governance structure was not an easy process, but it was successfully driven by both institutions' determination to complement and benefit each other.

Another critical difference between IAE and WBS – as well as many other business schools – involves the dean's decision-making authority. IAE's dean is 'primus inter pares' within a five-member management board, whose decisions are ruled by a collegial govern-ance scheme (unlike the multiple levels of a conventional university governance system). Although a collegial scheme has its advantages and disadvantages, like any other governance system, it clearly influences the culture of an organisation. On the downside, collegial decision-making is more complex and time-consuming, as manage-ment board members need to build consensus around their strategic initiatives. However, collegiality does prevent the natural biases of individual views and choices at an organisation's helm. Openness to other perspectives, self-criticism and the ability to fully endorse and support a board's decision as one's own accounts for a signifi-cant challenge for board members. A potential benefit conferred by a collegial system is the possibility to rotate dean and board members' positions, minimising governance gaps and enhancing strategic consistency.

In our exploration of strategic leadership processes in IAE and WBS we have followed the basic guiding framework of the SLP model in Chapter 4. We have also been influenced by models of the career life cycle – studies of CEOs rather than deans (Davies and Thomas, 2009; Hambrick and Fukotomi, 1991; Miller and Shamsie, 2001) – and tracking strategies and strategy processes (Mintzberg, 2007). For example, studies of CEO leadership and career paths suggest that a dean's tenure, typically involving a period of no more than a dec-ade, would be characterised by initial exploration, enthusiasm and learning (with perhaps a few missteps), followed by planning and clear agenda setting, improved performance over the medium term but declining performance towards the end of the dean's term, aris-ing from strategic inertia or lack of motivation. Mintzberg (2007: 12), in a series of exemplar studies of patterns in strategy formation and strategic decision-making, also offers a set of useful questions, which guided us as we thought through and critically examined the strategic processes longitudinally at our two schools.

(1) What were the patterns of strategic change over time (e.g. life cycles)?
(2) What were the relationships between deliberate and emergent strategies?

(3) What was the interplay between the forces of leadership, organisation and environment in the strategy formation process?

In the following sections, we reflect on deanship and describe, often in first-person narrative form, first Fernando's perspectives as dean at IAE and then Howard's perspectives as dean at WBS.

6.2 LOOKING BACK AT THE IAE SITUATION: FERNANDO FRAGUEIRO'S PERSPECTIVES

Although my deanship at IAE ran from 1995 to 2008, I had served as associate dean for eight years before that, so the insights I share span twenty-two of IAE's thirty-one years of existence. Three key milestones stand out from the 1987–2008 period in the school's strategic leadership path, as fully outlined in Figure 6.1, which shows the key features in the school's history.

First, in 1991, IAE was hailed as Argentina's 'number one' business school by *Apertura* magazine's management education ranking, the first one of its kind ever published domestically. Over the years IAE Business School has been able to consolidate its leadership in the Argentine management education market. Second, IAE moved to its new, world-class campus in Pilar, a classy Buenos Aires suburb, in 1998. Its 240-acre campus, with four modern, fully equipped buildings, gave IAE unprecedented visibility not only locally but in Latin America as a whole. As a result of its successful fund-raising efforts, the school was simultaneously able to embark on a faculty enhancement programme, hiring a large number of research-oriented professors with Ph.D. degrees from leading universities around the world, including Harvard, Columbia, Texas Austin, Purdue, Cornell, IESE, LBS, UCLA, INSEAD and Warwick. Third, since 2000 IAE has consistently ranked among the world's top thirty business schools in *The Financial Times'* executive education ranking, year after year, and it has climbed steadily into the shortlist for the top twenty in custom and open enrolment programmes for executives.

From an SLP contextual perspective, these three landmarks in the history of IAE amounted to major turning points, anticipating

1978 IAE Business School founded

First dean: José Luis Gómez López Egea

Initiation of Top Management Program (PAD)

1979 Creation of the Alumni Association

1981 Initiation of Executive M.B.A. (E.M.B.A.)

1982 Initiation of Program for Management Development (PDD)

1984 Initiation of Small & Medium Companies Management Program

1987 Creation of the Academic Advisory Board: Harvard–IESE–IAE

1991 Ranked by *Apertura* magazine as Argentina's 'number one' business school in terms of management education.

Creation of Universidad Austral as IAE's parent institution

1995 Second dean: Fernando Fragueiro

Initiation of Joint International Executive Program, Harvard–IESE–IAE

1997 Initiation of Global immersion Program E.M.B.A.

1998 Opening of new campus

Initiation of one-year full-time M.B.A. Program

1999 Ranked by *Financial Times* as one of world's top thirty business schools

Creation of the Enterpreneurship Center

AMBA accreditation

2005 AACSB International and EQUIS (EFMD) accreditations

2008 Thirtieth anniversary

50	full-time faculty
400	M.B.A. and E.M.B.A. students per year
2,500	executive education participants per year
10,000	alumni – forty-three nationalities

Third dean: Marcelo Paladino

FIGURE 6.1 IAE Business School milestones, 1978–2008

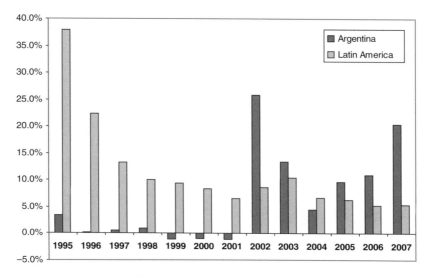

FIGURE 6.2 Inflation rates in Argentina and Latin America, 1995–2007

and responding to significant pressures from the school's external and internal environments alike. IAE's outer and inner contexts changed over time, with remarkable shifts during the twenty-one years that I served on its management board. External developments constantly reshaped the school's competitive landscape, driving adjustments in the list of benchmark institutions chosen to compare programme content and delivery quality as well as overall academic standards. As IAE's visibility grew both domestically and internationally, more sophisticated competition and corporate customer demands called for full-time, highly qualified faculty growth. Thus, the need to find donors and benefactors who would provide funding for long-term school investments became increasingly urgent.

IAE's homeland and primary market, Argentina, posed several unique challenges for a business school – and any other venture, for that matter – on account of its ongoing institutional and financial instability. Argentina's economy features ever shorter cycles, alternating periods of high inflation – or even hyperinflation – and recession with spells of booming growth every five to ten years. Amid

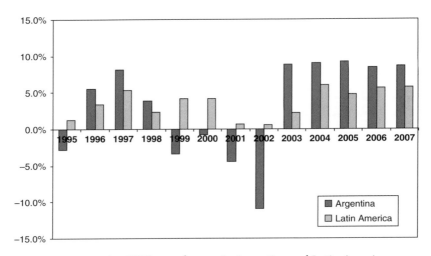

FIGURE 6.3 GDP growth rates in Argentina and Latin America, 1995–2007

such volatile conditions, financial viability can never be taken for granted (see Figures 6.2 and 6.3).

Most Latin American countries are also plagued by a long-standing shortage of student loans and meagre scholarship offerings, which make innovation a must for higher education institutions. State support is also very scarce – if it exists at all – and gifts or donations for these institutions are rare, as philanthropists tend to respond to the dire state of large shares of these nations' populations. As a result, business schools in this region are largely left to their own devices, securing their resources from tuition revenues, with a 5 to 10 per cent surplus target as a safety net. In developing regions, fund-raising requires unusually keen efforts, perseverance and luck. However, if a school manages eventually to build a strong alumni network, it can turn to it for some financial support. Smart pricing policies and creative fund-raising practices are instrumental in promoting relevant academic research and development as well as in fuelling growth through long-term investments.

The changes experienced by IAE's inner context over time across these three milestones were even more striking. As the school expanded its programme portfolio, premises (1998), faculty and staff, catering to an increasing number of students, alumni and corporate clients, its organisational processes and systems grew more complex and required constant upgrading. The internal transformations needed to accommodate these developments were far from smooth and called for entrepreneurial drive and an open mindset from all IAE members. Communication channels evolved from informal daily talks to planned meetings, team-building activities and state-of-the-art information-sharing means. The school also strove to meet international standards, and was certified by three leading higher education accreditation agencies: the United States' AACSB (2005), the European Union's EQUIS (2005) and the United Kingdom's AMBA (1999).

Recruited for their more sophisticated backgrounds and up-to-date skills, faculty and staff newcomers had to be integrated with older IAE organisation members – a task that presented a new challenge for the school's leadership. In fact, building a single, enriched culture and avoiding the danger of grouping 'old' and 'new' faculty members in separate constituencies demanded purposeful efforts at tackling division and criticism – in contrast, for example, to the two camps of 'hunters' and 'farmers' in the case of IMD (Chapter 4). As is usually the case in organisations that embark on substantial recruitment efforts, some old-timers claimed that IAE's original values were being threatened, while new recruits tended to view incumbents as reluctant to innovate in the school's responses to updated academic requirements. The need for the entire organisation to move forward in a cohesive fashion, addressing research and teaching demands as well as developing revenue streams to support its own growth, clearly turned into a distinctive, forceful goal for both myself as dean and IAE's management board. As IAE's academic areas grew in size – the number of faculty members in each department – and research endeavours, there was a need to check a new phenomenon involving the emergence of 'silos'. In this setting, professors and researchers tended to approach specific academic issues with a sense of ownership that could compromise cross-discipline fertilisation.

This behaviour would create barriers across the school, hindering knowledge advancement and impairing the innovation potential for programme content and research development.

A final challenge in this period lay in incorporating IAE into Universidad Austral as its business school in 2000. This merger of sorts bore fundamental implications for the school's autonomy and governance, and it would not have been possible – let alone successful – without common values and an overriding purpose that resulted in remarkable fair play, trust and patience from both sides. Difficulties arose from a number of issues, particularly the fact that, in 2000, the parent institution, Universidad Austral, was a nine-year-old organisation, while IAE had already built a successful twenty-year track record. In addition, perched at the interface between the corporate and academic worlds, business schools differ in nature from most of the other higher education institutions, which for the most part remain closer to academia and academic traditions. Faculty members' salary requirements and career paths, facilities, service quality and programme delivery are different in business schools as a result of enhanced student and stakeholder profiles and expectations. While universities often regard business schools as a potential source of funding to offset financial constraints suffered by other schools under their purview, a business school also stands to benefit from its association with a prestigious university, taking advantage of its strong academic reputation and its large scholar population to conduct joint research in a number of fields, such as sociology, economics, biotechnology, engineering, IT, etc.

Summing up, the years between 1987 and 2008 marked a period of incommensurable growth and remarkable success for IAE Business School. It went from being a small, rather obscure school serving Argentina's domestic market to consolidating its local leadership and ranking among the world's leading twenty executive education providers. It expanded its faculty from barely a dozen professors to an internationally qualified pool of fifty full-time faculty members. It moved from limited, inadequate premises to an exclusive greenfield site with state-of-the-art facilities. Its initially rudimentary outfit evolved into a professionalised organisation, with dedicated, trained staff to manage its non-academic operations. Finally, it became part of a renowned – albeit new in comparison – local university. What is more, all these accomplishments were made against significant odds in a country perenially besieged by political and economic instability.

It should be noted that IAE Business School's long-standing commitment to international academic standards has been both innovative and challenging in a regional setting in which, in the 1970s and 1980s, business schools were very rare and a full-time faculty was even more so. It was only in the 1990s, when Latin America experienced robust growth and opened up to the developed world, that its management education industry started to show signs of greater development, albeit still limited by financial constraints and an overall culture that did not promote higher education. Other developing regions, such as India or south-east Asia, have embraced the search for academic excellence in a more consistent, committed fashion. In fact, since the start of the twenty-first century, higher education institutions in Latin America in general and Argentina in particular seem to have become rather stagnant under the influence of a generalised ideology that shuns development to focus primarily on the region's urgent and widespread poverty issues. Although IAE has incorporated regional and domestic concerns into its management research and teaching pursuits, there is still a long way to go, as Latin America's social pyramid remains very small at the top and enormous at the bottom. Without doubt, local business schools and business communities must strive to contribute ideology-free, creative solutions to the region's crippling poverty problem.

Upon closer inspection

I have often pondered the lessons I learned from this unique experience, especially over the five concentrated years (2003 to 2007 inclusive) that I worked on this research study on strategic leadership processes at business schools. This endeavour afforded me an opportunity to learn from the literature on this field and from the actual experiences undergone by three world-class business schools, INSEAD, IMD and LBS. I was able to reflect on the nature of my job as dean from an enlightened, unique perspective that tapped into the knowledge drawn from these three case studies, observation of the WBS environment during my Ph.D. studies and my own tasks at IAE. I have come to realise that, when all is said and done, the role of a dean is to exercise leadership in an organisational setting in which, sometimes, the exercise of performing managerial tasks and responsibilities effectively is not always viewed as entirely relevant and important to the institution's academics and their focal goals and purposes. However, a school's organisational and financial performance is crucial for its survival, requiring its dean and board to constantly monitor the 'bottom line' so as to ensure its viability.

In my experience as a layman at the helm of an educational institution, I soon learned that it is very difficult to lead academics without an academic background – or, at least, a solid intellectual reputation (see also, for example, Goodall, 2009). Outsiders to academia have a hard time at first; it is like heading a law firm if you are not a lawyer: tricky at best. All the same, academics expect deans to deliver results, to formulate a clear strategy and to secure enough financial resources to support research and innovative teaching. Moreover, like other professionals, faculty members want to be part of a reputable institution with a sound positioning in management education and practice in order to further their own careers. Deans in general – and those coming from other walks of life in particular – need to understand the distinctive idiosyncrasy of the academic world, incorporating faculties' interests and goals into their schools' agendas, in order to succeed at their jobs and, ultimately, to ensure institutional success as well.

Another essential lesson to be learned by a dean involves an acute awareness of how a school's key stakeholders – its faculty and its board – hope to influence major decisions based on their main generic interests as prioritised according to contextual circumstances, personal background and demographics. It helps to keep in mind that, sometimes, opposition is not sparked by an initiative in itself but by the fact that an initiative neglects stakeholders' concerns or objectives. Perceiving and responding to faculty and board members' MGIs is a necessary step to articulating them as part of strategic initiatives that require significant consensus and support. This initiative adjustment process, designed to address directly the range of constituencies' needs, not only enhances strategic choices but also strengthens a dean's issue legitimation and power mobilisation abilities, improving his/her leadership effectiveness.

With this contextual and processual approach to strategic agenda building and executing, the political dimension emerges as a natural aftermath. In fact, before I set out to study SLPs at top business schools, and as stated earlier, I felt that a political perspective tainted leadership processes with the innuendo of 'dark', manipulative practices. I viewed power and influence as unfair, shady tactics and not as necessary tools that I would actually use to do my job effectively. This tour around the SLP literature and three of the most distinguished business schools in the world taught me that a political approach is intrinsic to every social interaction. Problems arise when this core feature of human relationships is deemed as anything other than a value-free dimension of leadership. We often use power without a clear understanding of its nature, and we tend to ignore the proposition that the use of power is not just legitimate but necessary in order to exercise leadership with fairness and effectiveness.

Indeed, power is the energy that makes things happen, and it should be used to influence people's desires and actions. Of course, it can be used to manipulate or to inspire and motivate others to make their own choices freely. As discussed in the previous chapter, issue legitimation accounts for a critical step in avoiding the unfair use – or abuse – of power, for it compels leaders to take into account other people's beliefs and values, incorporating them into their organisations' missions, visions and strategies. When leaders overlook or disregard issue legitimation as part of their SLP activities, they tend to overuse power to set their organisations' strategic direction, endangering the confidence and trust bestowed on them. This study has forcefully revealed that strategic leadership requires a political approach that combines issue legitimation and power mobilisation activities if it is to be successful in building and executing an organisation's mission-oriented agenda with a sound, clear strategy shared by the majority of the faculty and board members.

Issue legitimation is especially critical in organisational settings in which power is shared – more so at a business school such as IAE, where the dean, as first among peers, operates in a collegial governance system with the school's management board. In fact, I soon discovered that issue legitimation practices actually reinforce a dean's power, as stakeholders recognise her/his willingness to include and respect their perspectives and interests. Power mobilisation is the other side of the same coin. Power comes from several sources, and, in these types of organisations, these sources are mostly personal in nature. As George Bain, Peter Lorange, John Quelch, Antonio Borges and Gabriel Hawawini have all asserted, power is a consequence of personal behaviour and accomplishments over time. The recipe for building power takes many ingredients: the ability to deliver results, and to articulate and communicate goals clearly and consistently with the school's overall mission and strategy; expertise and intellectual reputation; commitment, fair play and the disposition to listen to others; the capability to build consensus and to gain support for bold initiatives, when necessary; the skills to act as a catalyst for faculty energy and corporate needs; and the presence of mind and the courage to set clear strategies and broad, ambitious expectations for the school.

A word to the wise

On a more personal note, I would like to share a couple of more specific insights drawn from my own experience as dean. First, a business school located in a developing region such as Latin America – or, to put it more bluntly, in a marginal market for international investors and top decision-makers – needs to formulate a distinctive vision and strategy. It is both tempting and dangerous to be drawn to the common aspiration to become a leading, global business school that tries to offer everything to everyone. Equally alluring is the more subtle and insidious notion that a business school located in a developing region afflicted by severe poverty should keep its distance from the developed world, giving up on any expectations to reach leading academic standards. Higher education institutions in India and, more recently, China have proved that it is possible to avert both risks, while most of their Latin American counterparts still find it hard to solve this strategic puzzle.

Based on my experience, the most sensible path for a business school in a developing region is to aim for the topmost academic excellence while focusing on the local setting and idiosyncrasy. A Latin American business school should deepen its expertise in building business ventures for its regional market. It faces the same dilemma that currently bewilders global companies: how to succeed in a region with social, economic and cultural features that differ greatly from those of developed nations. Clearly, the answer is neither to replicate practices that have proved their effectiveness in the world's richest markets nor to sink into greater isolation. Rather, a small school in an emerging market should focus on differentiation, using its limited resources and unique location to attract the best talent for faculty and the student population alike. It is my belief that, in a mature market such as the management education industry, differentiation is key: imitating top business schools in central markets from a peripheral location and with financial constraints does not provide sufficient international visibility to ensure sustained feasibility. My recommendation is to devise and consistently pursue a 'niche strategy' to become the best school in a specific field of expertise, with a unique value proposition for an individual market segment. This credible and achievable strategy will provide the school with the necessary clout to attract top faculty talent, students from around the world and international companies seeking that particular body of knowledge.

In more general terms, it is necessary for deans to learn how to balance their dual focus on both the inner and outer contexts of their schools. On the internal front, deans should keep their ears open to the faculty and their eyes open to organisational developments, periodically surveying the school's structure, systems and processes, as well as monitoring its key financial indicators on a regular basis. Another area that calls for deans' attention revolves around the overall academic performance of the school – namely the rigour of its research, the relevance of its programme contents, its faculty's output and the quality perceived by students and course attendants. Of course, a dean's relationship with the school's board or its parent university is crucial for the fate of the institution and the dean alike. As seen in all three cases studied, as well as IAE, the support from a school's board and faculty can make or break any strategic initiative – and dean.

Looking beyond, to the world lying outside the school's walls, deans should at least devote 50 per cent of their time to building ties between their institutions and large companies – its current and prospective clients. Their role as bridges to the business community serves a twofold purpose: making their school known to domestic and international firms; and learning as much as possible about their knowledge needs in order to relay that information to the school's faculty and board for strategic fine-tuning. In any school with a proud history, another rich, time-deserving constituency is the alumni community, and deans would be well advised to take time to nurture their relationship with former students – who could, of course, turn into donors, supporting the school's future growth in return for continued knowledge advancement efforts. Staying in touch with these external stakeholders will help deans to collect the information they need to set their schools' direction and to build their strategic agendas while bringing the voice of the outside world into the school.

In closing and reflecting more deeply on my experiences as dean at IAE, I would also like to point to the need to adjust the role of the dean to our changing times, especially in this period of dramatic institutional turmoil. Having served as dean of a business school in a developing nation, where volatility and uncertainty seem to be the only unchanging features, I learned that periodically reassessing one's own agenda in light of new developments can be a healthy way to promote both institutional and personal growth. Indeed, over my deanship years, I developed the habit of revisiting my goals as dean at the end of my yearly vacation, before returning to my hectic schedule. Fully rested, I would ask myself, 'What new issues do I need to introduce into my agenda?' Clearly, in order to make room for new pursuits, I would also need to determine which of the issues prioritised the year beforehand could now be delegated to others. This, in turn, would require analysing who should be assigned to follow up on those issues that I would now devote less time to. As we all know, spontaneous behaviour tends to focus our attention on familiar issues that we feel we know and have mastered. Though they may still be relevant, these pursuits should, and can, be safely passed on to others within the organisation, so as to allow deans to venture into new ground while other leadership team members develop the necessary skills to see former initiatives through. This simple exercise forced me, year after year, to rethink IAE's strategic objectives and to find new adventures for both the school and myself.

We turn now to an examination of the deanship role at WBS, which involved challenges, contexts and different processes from those at IAE.

6.3   LOOKING BACK AT THE WBS SITUATION: HOWARD THOMAS'S PERSPECTIVES

This narrative explores insights and personal reflections from my period of almost a decade (2000 to 2010) as the first appointed dean (previously the post had been held by a series of elected chairpersons) of Warwick Business School. Prior to my appointment at WBS I had had extensive administrative and academic experience in business schools in Australia, Canada, Europe and the United States, and I had previously been dean, for the decade of the 1990s, of the College of Commerce and Business Administration (now the College of Business) at the University of Illnois at Urbana–Champaign, in the United States. Therefore, my two major, and most recent, deanship experiences have involved the leadership of university-based, publicly funded business schools, rather than the 'stand-alone' essentially private schools typified by IMD, INSEAD, LBS and IAE. In such university-based and embedded environments, issues of governance, internal and external context and organisational structure differ markedly from those present in 'stand-alone' schools. To quote Bain (2003), universities have the following contexts and characteristics.

(1) Pluralistic institutions with multiple, ambiguous and conflicting goals.
(2) Professional institutions that are primarily run by the profession (i.e. the academics), often in its own interests rather than those of clients.
(3) Collegial institutions in which the vice chancellor (president) is less a CEO who can manage by diktat and decree and more a managing partner in a professional firm who has to manage by negotiation and persuasion.
(4) Change is extremely difficult to bring about in an institution with these characteristics. ...[A] prerequisite for change is some pressure – often a threat from outside the institution – which convinces its members that change is necessary.

In essence, WBS is a research-led department of the University of Warwick (which has characteristics similar to those noted above) and operates within its regulatory framework. It was created in 1967 as the School of Industrial and Business Studies (SIBS), not taking its present name until 1987.

Background on Warwick University

I begin with a brief historical overview of the founding and evolution of both Warwick University and WBS. This evolution is also explored in detail by Clark (1998) in a chapter entitled 'The Warwick way' in his innovative book on Europe's entrepreneurial universities.

Warwick University was founded in 1965 as one of seven new 'greenfield' universities – the so-called 'seven sisters' (Sussex,

York, Lancaster, Essex, East Anglia, Kent and Warwick) – established by the United Kingdom's University Grants Committee (UGC) (Thompson, 1970: 166). The vision of the UGC for the 'seven sisters' was of universities with strong teaching and undergraduate programmes but with a relatively low priority on research and postgraduate teaching. However, Jack Butterworth, the entrepreneurial and risk-taking founding vice chancellor of Warwick, who served from 1965 to 1985, had a clear and alternative vision for Warwick embodying both strong academic excellence – i.e. discipline-centred, research led departments – and a 'relevant university' perspective (Shattock, 1994a). Butterworth was influenced in the pursuit of relevance by local industry, union and public sector leaders who served on his planning board (Larson, 2003). He was also very close to Lord Rootes (then chair of the Rootes car company in Coventry), who was a strong advocate of the development of Warwick University and particularly for a management institute located in Coventry, the heartland of British manufacturing and engineering strength. This, in turn, led Butterworth to add a business school and an engineering science school to the initial set of new academic units and chairs to be established at Warwick.

Warwick's closeness to industry did not sit at all well with some of its early academics and a cadre of more militant students. A series of major demonstrations and verbal attacks followed, with the administration and vice chancellor accused of being captured by industry and selling out to capitalism. This was a time (1969) when Warwick was described as 'Warwick University Ltd' and widely seen as a 'business university' (Thompson, 1970).

Although the vice chancellor was almost hounded out of office in this period he managed to survive, and proceeded to embark with renewed focus on his entrepreneurial and externally driven vision of academic excellence and relevance. He built new facilities and staff (academic staff grew from sixty in 1965 to over 500 in 1980) and new units in the humanities, physical sciences, social sciences and arts. He presided over the growth of the business school (founded in 1967) and Kumar Bhattacharya's Warwick Manufacturing Group (founded in 1980) – a centre of manufacturing and product engineering excellence – so that both developed strong international reputations as sources of best practice in business and engineering R&D. Equally importantly, they contributed very strongly to the growth of Warwick University's 'earned income policy' (Clark, 1998: 17), in which they – together with other externally focused departments and units – had the ability not only to pay for themselves in terms of income generation but also, through their creation of positive annual surpluses, to provide income to cross-subsidise the growth of the entire university. This 'earned income policy' had its genesis in the draconian budget cuts for universities (Warwick's cut was 10 per cent) mandated by the incoming Conservative government of Margaret Thatcher in 1979. Mike Shattock, the highly successful registrar of Warwick at that time, noted that 'we had to find ways to generate funding from other sources, we did not see why people or companies would simply give us money so we decided to earn it' (Shattock, cited in Clark, 1998). As Clark notes, the actions of the 'Earned Income Group', formally established in 1984/5 (at the end of Butterworth's reign as vice chancellor), provided the vehicle and firm foundation for subsequent income generation and entrepreneurial funding for the growth of Warwick University. Indeed, by 2010 Warwick University has clearly proved itself to be the most successful new university (out of the seven sisters) and is firmly in the top ten of British universities, which are normally headed by Oxford, Cambridge and three London colleges – Imperial, London School of Economics and University College – in recent media ratings in the United Kingdom.

6.4   THE PARALLEL EVOLUTION OF WBS, 1967–2000[1]

Warwick Business School was initially founded in 1967 as the School of Industrial and Business Studies, and became WBS in 1987. At the outset SIBS ran separately but somewhat in parallel with the

---

[1] I am indebted to Robert Dyson, a former chair of the school and a recently retired professor of WBS, for many of the insights and material reported here.

Economics Department, which was developed by able economists such as Dick Sarjeant, Graham Pyatt and Keith Cowling. However, the first chairman of SIBS in 1967, Professor Brian Houlden – a former head of the Operational Research Group at the National Coal Board – was keen to ensure that SIBS had a separate identity. He established the B.Sc. in management sciences to reflect the broad disciplinary base of quantitative analysis, economics and behavioural sciences underpinning business studies. From a slow start initially in 1969/70, this degree gained numbers and credibility in the marketplace during the 1970s and reinforced SIBS' positioning of independence from the Economics Department but as a constituent department of the Faculty of Social Studies.

Butterworth's role in the growth of SIBS was important. His university philosophy of hiring interesting, creative professors and 'turn[ing] them loose in their specialities' (Clark, 1998: 13) created a sense of urgency, creative tension, risk-taking and entrepreneurialism. Hence, the founding professional chair appointments at SIBS reflected both academic excellence and relevance as measured by industrial experience. Houlden, appointed as professor of operational research (OR), was a successful senior OR executive; Derek Waterworth, appointed as professor of marketing, was a former senior lecturer at London Business School but with business experience as director of marketing at Mars; Bob Tricker was appointed as professor of finance and information systems, reflecting his combination of academic and business experience, while Hugh Clegg, appointed as professor of industrial relations, was a very highly respected academic from Oxford. All these four chairs were sponsored by outside agencies, such as the Institute of Directors and Barclays Bank.

These initial appointments were critical – alongside younger faculty such as Robert Dyson in operational research and Keith Sissons and Richard Hyman in industrial relations – in building key strengths in the industrial relations and OR fields. The school's development reflected both pragmatism and academic excellence in the development of business studies as a discipline. Houlden was the ultimate pragmatist and a consummate and strong politician. He secured SIBS' independence from the Economics Department when some thought that business studies should be subservient to that discipline. He also fought the UGC, which had a clear graduate school vision for business studies following the publication of the Franks Report in 1965, which established London Business School and Manchester Business School as elite graduate management schools. He saw the importance of undergraduate study, and promoted the idea of an undergraduate business degree with a strong disciplinary and academic focus as a different and distinctive degree from the then existing menu of practically and functionally oriented undergraduate degrees in business.

Clegg, on the other hand, with his strong academic background, quickly established himself as the academic and research leader of the school. He not only founded SIBS' strong industrial relations research tradition but also kept research firmly on the school's agenda and growth path. He was a research role model for the school through his leadership first of the Centre for Industrial Economics and Business Research and then its successor, the Industrial Relations Research Unit – subsequently led by Professor George Bain, who also joined the school in the 1970s from Oxford.

SIBS grew in faculty strength and programmes (for example, Andrew Pettigrew, a leading organisational behaviour scholar from London Business School, was hired as a professor) in the 1970s and early 1980s. It also generated a series of department chairs – Houlden (1967–73), Fawthrop (a finance professor) (1973–6), Waterworth (1976–8), Dyson (1978–81) and Watson (an organisational behaviour professor) (1981–3) – who were elected by the faculty for a three-year term and could be re-elected for one further three-year term.

However, in 1982 a critical event convinced the university administration that strategic change might be necessary in SIBS. The main pressure for change was a report from the UGC that commented unfavourably on the performance of SIBS. Watson stepped down as chair in 1983 (to take over as chair of the Faculty of Social

Studies) and Bain was elected as the new chairman of SIBS, a post he held until 1989. Bain, an excellent scholar and charismatic personality, is widely credited as the architect of the Warwick Business School; indeed it was he who promoted the name change from SIBS to WBS in 1987. Bain was a man of ideas who captured the imagination of the newer, younger, more recently hired academic faculty who had stronger academic qualifications than the predominantly professionally oriented cadre of founding professors. He also recognised from reports published by the Foundation for Management Education that business schools needed to grow in size. Bain set a specific vision for Warwick Business School, which was to be 'best in class' – that is, the best business school that was an integral part of a university and that taught both undergraduates and postgraduates (i.e. excluding London and Manchester). He realised that this was a 'stretch target' but built a strong platform for achieving it with a series of 'quick wins': hiring two distinguished professors of marketing from LBS (Peter Doyle and Robin Wensley); reinforcing research programmes; enhancing the full-time M.B.A. programme and dedicating its own teaching centre; launching the distance-learning version of the M.B.A. in 1985 (initially in partnership with Wolsey Hall in Oxford); and changing the name of the school to Warwick Business School in 1987. He also stressed the importance of a strong academic teaching and research culture and encouraged the growth of executive, post-experience education.

Bain's period (1983–9) as chair was, therefore, one in which the reputational strength and image of WBS was built. He successfully engaged the older and younger faculty alike in the change process and carefully navigated the pathways for future growth. His success led to his appointment in 1989 as principal of London Business School, whose faculty sought a leader who could improve both their financial performance and reputational stature.

At Warwick, Bain was succeeded as chair by Wensley, who served in that position from 1989 to 1994 and very much followed and incrementally improved Bain's platform for growth. Robert

Galliers, a professor of information systems, was then elected as chair of the school in 1994, and he served until 1998, when Dyson again took over as chair and acting dean until 2000, when I was appointed as dean. Indeed, Clark (1998: 17–18) notes that, by the mid-1990s, WBS had achieved high academic standing, through the presence of Peter Doyle, Robin Wensley, David Storey and Andrew Pettigrew as leading professors, and with top ratings in UK research assessments and a reputation as one of the best UK business schools, with 130 academic and research staff, over 3,000 students (undergraduate, postgraduate and post-experience), 400 M.B.A. graduates per year and around 160 current doctoral students. At the same time, though, Clark (1998: 24) points out that there were signs of questioning in the university as to the ability of the structure of centralised decision-making to cope with a larger and more complex university. Pettigrew and Ewan Ferlie, two business school professors, in a report commissioned in late 1995 by the vice chancellor and his senior management team, pointed out the danger of Warwick becoming too centralised and bureaucratic with unclear decision-making lines (Pettigrew and Ferlie, 1996; cited in Clark, 1998). They argued that greater decentralisation was needed and advocated large-scale operational devolution to departments to achieve crispness of responsibility together with a greater strategic thrust and intent from the centre.

Galliers' period as chair coincided with these external political debates about the appropriateness of the university's governance structure. There was also heightened debate within WBS about its future direction, which some faculty and professors characterised as a period of strategic drift at the school. This culminated with a meeting in the academic year 1997/8 between the then vice chancellor, Brian Follett, and a group of senior WBS professors who wanted to voice their concerns about the school. They were particularly worried about the future strategic direction of WBS. At around the same time, Shattock, the energetic and entrepreneurial registrar, advocated a significant change in the system of electing university department chairs, and pushed for a system of appointed heads in both the mathematics and engineering departments of the university. The university's senior administration then instructed WBS to advertise the job of chair of the school – which they retitled dean of Warwick Business School – with the appointment decision to be made by the vice chancellor and registrar and not through an internal election process. Professor Dyson, a senior and well-respected OR scholar, was then asked to step in as chair and acting dean until an appointment to the permanent deanship was made.

6.5 2000–2010, THE DEANSHIP OF HOWARD THOMAS

I was dean of the College of Commerce and Business Administration at the University of Illinois at Urbana–Champaign when, as a member of the Peer Review Accreditation team from AACSB (the US-based accreditation agency), I visited WBS in January/February 1999 to assess the school's suitability for initial accreditation. Subsequently I was nominated for the dean's post at WBS, and was offered, and accepted, the job in July 1999, at almost the start of the Illinois academic year. As a consequence I was unable to take over the WBS post until the summer of 2000, a year later, but I negotiated an arrangement with the chancellor and provost at Illinois to visit WBS periodically during the intervening period.

At the outset, from a personal viewpoint, it is important to recognise that I saw this transition period from 1999 to 2000 as an unrivalled opportunity to learn about WBS and interview a wide range of faculty and staff about their perceptions and goals for the school. It enabled me to work with, get to know and gain the respect of Robert Dyson, the acting dean, who had successfully piloted WBS through the hurdles of gaining both AACSB and EQUIS (the European accreditation agency of EFMD) accreditation. Together with AMBA accreditation (achieved in the 1990s), WBS became the first UK business school to achieve the 'triple crown' of accreditation by all three agencies, and, thus, clear reputational status as a leading international business school.

Working with Dyson sensitised me to the professionalism of WBS's management and to their continuity in collective leadership of, and commitment to, the school over time. For example, Dyson had served twice as chair, Robin Wensley had served two terms as chair and Jenny Hocking had served as a senior administrator since Bain's tenure as chair of the school. Key academic personalities, such as Peter Doyle, Paul Edwards, Andrew Pettigrew and David Storey, had also contributed significantly to the school's growth in discipline areas such as marketing, industrial relations, organisational strategy and entrepreneurship and the overall programme management of the school.

Meeting with a wide-range of people in that transition year enabled me to ask them their opinions and viewpoints, identify the key issues in the school and formulate strategies for the school's development. I was also helped in this endeavour by a number of professors who I had previously worked with in my career. I had maintained contact with Professors Peter Doyle (marketing), John McGee (strategy), Andrew Pettigrew (organisational behaviour) and Robin Wensley (marketing), who had been academic colleagues of mine in the 1970s at London Business School. I viewed them as important and trustworthy 'sounding boards' for advice and constructive criticism.

Therefore, when I actually arrived at WBS in 2000 I had already joined the AACSB board for the period from 2000 to 2004, which gave the school a greater international profile. I was also ready to 'hit the ground running', with a clear strategic plan already formed in my mind. I had concluded that a strong and respected transition senior management team was needed and I persuaded several key professors and administrators, who represented continued collective school leadership, to join this team. They included Dyson and Wensley as deputy deans, Hocking as associate dean for administration and Edwards as associate dean for research.

The vision in the initial plan was to reinforce WBS's positioning as 'best in class' (the leading UK university-based business school) and to develop its international footprint as a leading European and international business school given the presence of the accreditation 'triple crown'. To achieve this vision and to enhance the morale of the school, a clear set of strategies and consistent, stable leadership were essential. The main strategic elements were the following.

(1) Devolution of the school's financial arrangements.

> My international experience of business schools and my deanship at Illinois, a very strong US-based top ten business school, had convinced me that most successful business schools have some form of devolved budget structure and model. This conviction was confirmed following discussions with WBS colleagues, who pointed out that the time spent negotiating the myriad of different contracts and 'deals' with university committees for over twenty WBS programmes was too bureaucratic. They regarded the existing process as inefficient and ineffective. Further, little strategic freedom and decision-making responsibility was delegated to the dean/chair of WBS.

(2) The criticality of research excellence: WBS is a research-led school.

> The strength and importance of WBS's performance in previous UK research exercises and the school's historical tradition in key research areas such as industrial relations, organisational behaviour, operations research, entrepreneurship and public management indicated that research excellence was a key value, and that a strong submission to the upcoming 2001 research assessment exercise was essential. The importance of high-quality research ratings was clear for the competitive profile and research strategy of the school.

(3) The importance of high-quality business school facilities and investment in them.

> As illustrated in Chapter 2, competition in the business school arena required that a leading business school such as WBS

should provide integrated and top-quality facilities for its students and executive clients. As a consequence, plans initially proposed by Galliers in his term as chair were revised and reshaped so as to provide the necessary set of competitive school facilities.

(4) Upgrading the school's alumni, fund-raising and external advisory board profile.

The school's activities in this area were weak and did not match the profile of peer schools. For example, the advisory board was not used strategically, while the alumni board did not exist, leaving a strong network of alumni essentially untapped. Alumni e-mail contacts and addresses were also sparse and often outdated. Further, the rapid growth of league table rankings of business schools in the 1990s clearly required WBS to raise its international profile through an enhanced rankings position. Therefore, it had to participate and compete effectively in, for example, the *Financial Times* global rankings by leveraging the feedback from school's alumni effectively. Hence, growth was critical in this area to improve league table rankings and the school's international profile; to build a strong alumni relations programme to grow the role of advisory boards; and to begin to raise discretionary external funds for the school.

(5) Programme changes, particularly with regard to the undergraduate programme, the M.B.A. and executive education.

It was clear that the WBS undergraduate programme was highly rated and the 'jewel in the crown' of the school's programme portfolio. My experience at Illinois also suggested that growth in the undergraduate programme, particularly with regard to overseas students, would provide both a strong international presence for the school, with very high-quality overseas students, and also significant income generation potential through the ability to charge premium fees for overseas students. Similarly, the full-time M.B.A. programme needed an enhanced profile. It was relatively small and needed to be repositioned as an internationally competitive M.B.A. programme. I, therefore, proposed a flexible 'one M.B.A.' concept through leveraging and marketing the joint strengths of each of the existing M.B.A. variants: distance-learning, executive and full-time.

Executive education was also considered to be a growth area, for two reasons. First, while WBS had a solid base of executive education, primarily in the customised corporate programme arena, it had not pushed for growth despite clear indications of strong corporate demand. Second, prior personal experience indicated that executive education provides a strong linkage to business and government. It can also increase faculty's awareness of corporate problems and issues, improve teaching quality and generate potential funding for applied management research – a stimulus for rigorous and relevant research.

The evolution of this plan is indicated in Table 6.1, which shows the key players and events in the school's development and its performance over the period 2000 to 2010.

There were probably four critical periods in the duration of my deanship at WBS, with the 1999–2000 visits representing the transition – the 'hitting the ground running' period. The four periods were 2000–2, distinguished by agenda building and planning, and building the commitment to the strategic vision; 2002–6, characterised by settling on a paradigm and marked by successful school faculty, student and programme growth; 2006–8, when I was developing a new paradigm for the 'Vision 2015' for WBS and the university; and 2008–10, when the school was at a strategic crossroads, against the background of the financial crisis, centralised financial control, funding cuts and the search for a new dean (the transition process).

Table 6.1 *Key players and events in the development of WBS, 2000–10*

	2000	2001	2002	2003	2004
Turnover (£ million)	13.2	14.6	18.7	23.5	27.9
Growth per annum (%)	—	10.8	27.3	26.0	18.6
Programmes	M.P.A. (Master of Public Administration) launched	Undergraduate size expansion approved	Undergraduate programme expanded	Exec education expanded New associate dean (Colin Carnell)	
Groups					
Accreditation	First UK triple accredited business school: AACSB AMBA EQUIS				
Facilities		Phase 1 opens	Phase 2 opens		
Vice chancellor and registrar	Brian Follett (V/C)	David VandeLinde			
	Mike Shattock (reg.)	Jonathan Nicholls			Jon Baldwin

2005	2006	2007	2008	2009	2010
30.6	34.2	36.3	39.5	43.8	47.0 (projected)
9.5	12.1	6.0	8.7	11.1	7.5 (projected)
Specialist master's programmes grow: M.Sc. Finance, M.Sc. ISM and M.Sc. Marketing and Strategy	M.Sc. Management	Ph.D. in Finance	Master in Business Analytics and Consultancy	Global Energy M.B.A. (the first specialist M.B.A.)	
15 new professors and 17 sub-professorial staff appointed in the last 18 months					
				Successful AMBA reaccreditation	
		Phase 3a opens		Phase 3b postponed	
	Nigel Thrift				

Table 6.1 (*cont.*)

	2000	2001	2002	2003	2004
Key strategic events		Restructuring			
		RAE result: top 3 in UK (LBS, Warwick, Lancaster)	Development of advisory board and alumni board Financial devolution model for WBS agreed	5-year strategic plan introduced	
Miscellaneous	Rapid growth of EU and Asian business schools				
	2,000th D.L.M.B.A. graduate	1,000th M.A.I.R. graduate			
Howard Thomas	First appointed dean of WBS Elected to board of AACSB, 2000–4				

Notes: BAM = British Academy of Management, D.L.M.B.A. = Distance-Learning Master of Business Administration, GFME = Global Foundation for Management Education, M.A.I.R. = Master of Arts in Industrial Relations, SDR = Strategic Departmental Review, SMS = Strategic Management Society.

2005	2006	2007	2008	2009	2010
Strategic hiring of faculty (e.g. Colin Crouch – public management)		Founders' Association (fund-raising board) Corporate Relations Board introduced	Very good RAE result: top 5 in UK. Financial crisis: tight financial controls	SDR report completed	
		WBS 40 years old	'Vision 2015' – Warwick's vision	Wide criticism of business schools and their role in society	
Inaugural fellow of SMS Vice-president for business schools – EFMD		D.Sc. (Edinburgh) higher honorary degree ISI Highly Cited Scholar Honorary life member of EFMD Elected chair of the GFME Made Companion of ABS Member of board of BAM	Honorary Fellow of the University of Swansea	Chair of AACSB Chair of ABS Named Fellow of Academy of Social Sciences Named dean of fellows SMS Trustee of Strategy Research Foundation	Dean of Singapore Management University

Each of these periods is reviewed briefly in the following subsections.[2]

The 2000–2 period: agenda building and planning

In this period there were a number of clear strategic successes and sources of celebration for the school. First, the goal of a devolved budget model was achieved and implemented in readiness for the 2002/3 academic year. Second, WBS was rated in the top three business schools in the 2001 Research Assessment Exercise, alongside London Business School and Lancaster, which was very important for reinforcing the school's image as a research-led business school. Third, the school assembly, after considerable periods of debate and discussion, approved plans for expanding the size of the undergraduate programme with effect from the 2002/3 academic year. Fourth, phases 1 and 2 of the school's four-phase facilities investment were completed, in 2001 and 2002, respectively. They provided significantly enhanced facilities for some staff and students and created a sense of physical identity for the school. These were clearly important 'quick wins' for WBS, and reinforced the platform for the school's future planned growth.

Perhaps the most critical success – together with the school's high RAE research rating – was the approval of its strategic management devolution model. This involved detailed discussions and significant periods of negotiation between the dean, the school's senior management team and, at the university level, the director of finance (James Hunt) and two vice chancellors (Sir Brian Follett, 2000–1, and David VandeLinde, 2000–2). VandeLinde, in particular, was sympathetic to these ideas, having operated with devolved departmental arrangements in previous institutions. In practice, the school's devolved model involved the production of an annual strategic plan, with a five-year horizon and an associated five-year

---

[2] This analysis draws heavily on school plans, other internal documents and discussions with Jenny Hocking, who wrote most of the plans.

financial plan, which was presented for the first cycle in March/June 2002 and then approved by the vice chancellor and his university steering committee. This plan included priorities for each main area of school activity (research, teaching, programmes and fund-raising) and bids for additional academic and administrative staff and other resources. The approval of the plan meant that the school was then free to hire the agreed staff profile and to acquire those additional resources without further intervention.

The 2002–6 period: settling on a paradigm

It is clear that the devolved model for WBS allowed for significant school and programme growth over the period. This period saw a significant increase in student numbers, turnover and academic staff. Significant strategic accomplishments during the period included the following. First, there was the strong growth of executive education following the hiring of Professor Colin Carnall, from Henley Management School, as associate dean of executive education. Second, well over a dozen new professors were hired, and an equivalent number of younger faculty, to reinforce and grow key strategic research areas such as finance, accounting, public management, information systems, strategy and marketing. Third, the 'one M.B.A.' concept was adopted, thus creating a new common identity across the M.B.A. curriculum and its programme variants while simultaneously affording flexibility to students and corporate clients. It also promoted the development of international alliances and programmes such as the European M.B.A. with Mannheim in Germany and relationships with partners from the Programme of International Management. Fourth, the development of new teaching and interest groups in the school in such areas as public management, operations management, information systems management and entrepreneurship led to new specialist master's programmes in marketing and strategy and information systems. A further new master's programme in finance was also introduced, to cope with increased demand for finance training. Fifth, the school's development and alumni affairs field grew rapidly over the period with the hiring of a director of development and alumni affairs. The school's advisory board was refreshed with high-quality senior members under the leadership of Val Gooding, then CEO of BUPA, and the alumni board was created with a new governance structure and an updated database of alumni e-mail addresses and locations. Plans were set in place for fund-raising (the Founders' Association) and corporate relations boards to assist the dean and development staff in fund-raising activities. A school director of marketing was also hired to reinforce WBS's external profile and image and to enhance the school's online presence. Overall, therefore, this period was one of considerable success and growth, with the school achieving strong ratings in undergraduate, M.B.A. and executive education league tables. In addition, during 2005/6, WBS was successfully and strongly reaccredited by AMBA, AACSB and EQUIS – a further sign of its increased profile and positioning in the global marketplace.

2005/6 was a transition year, in which the vice chancellor, VandeLinde, retired and I undertook a successful performance appraisal of my first five years as dean by a senior university committee, resulting in my reappointment to the summer of 2010 (subject to the approval of the new vice chancellor). In addition, I became an inaugural fellow of the Strategic Management Society and the vice-president for business schools of EFMD, which strongly signalled my credentials as a scholar and reinforced my leadership of WBS as a research-led school.

In summary, the period 2002/3 to 2005/6 worked extremely well for the school. It was able to operate a streamlined business and financial planning process, which encouraged WBS to achieve a sensible degree of strategic and operational autonomy. This longer-term strategic management viewpoint, together with a university-level agreement on a planning and budgeting envelope, enabled the school's senior management and the dean to adapt quickly to changing circumstances. It framed and endorsed a strategy for WBS, closely aligned with that of the university, which identified the resources to deliver that strategy, and which secured those resources.

2006–8: new paradigm development for 'Vision 2015'

A new vice chancellor, Nigel Thrift, a highly cited academic scholar in the field of geography from the University of Oxford, was appointed in the summer of 2006. He regarded Warwick as an excellent university, but one that he perceived to have somewhat lost its entrepreneurial risk-taking character and tradition. He rapidly established a strategic planning agenda and engaged many groups and departments across the university to create his 'Vision 2015', which was launched in 2007. In parallel, and with the encouragement and support of Thrift, the school developed, using a series of focus groups drawn from across the school, its own extended plan and vision for 2015 that framed and shaped the annual devolved planning discussions with the university. A summary of the University of Warwick's and WBS's vision for 2008–15 is shown in Figure 6.4.

The devolution arrangements continued during this period, although there was an ever-lengthening and protracted approval cycle for the adoption of the plan, which included many more detailed discussions with senior university personnel, such as the finance director, registrar and deputy vice chancellor. This longer approval process did not materially hinder strategic developments, and the school moved forward steadily and profitably over the period. Significant developments included the following. First, the fortieth anniversary of the WBS's founding in 1967 was celebrated with the opening of phase 3a of the school's facilities development, known as the Scarman Building, which had the capability to house 75 per cent of the faculty and staff. Second, new specialist master's programmes in management and business analytics and consultancy were successfully launched and a separate Ph.D. progamme in finance was introduced. The school, according to Higher Education Statistics Agency data, continued to rank in the top three of all UK business schools in terms of external grants raised for research.

Ambitions	
University of Warwick	'To take Warwick into the top 50 world universities – as measured by the quality of research output and strength of student demand – by the University's 50th birthday in 2015.'
Warwick Business School	'To be in the top echelon of European business schools by 2015, through strong innovation and a positive step change in investment, encompassing academic and professional expertise, new teaching programmes, physical and IT infrastructure and international profile-raising.'

Strategic objectives, 2008–15						
University of Warwick	Research and scholarship	Teaching and learning	International profile	A Warwick gateway	Income generation	Supporting strategies
Warwick Business School	Fostering research excellence	Fostering excellence in teaching and learning	International profile	Service and practitioner relevance	Securing the long-term future	WBS community

FIGURE 6.4 Alignment of university and WBS visions for 2008–15

Third, the school's international profile was enhanced through additional alliances, such as with the Indian Institute of Management – Ahmedabad, in public management (the M.P.A., or Master of Public Administration). Fourth, as dean I continued to contribute, along with other distinguished colleagues, to an enhanced scholarly and external profile for WBS. For example, I was awarded a D.Sc. by Edinburgh University for published work, joined the Highly Cited Scholar list of ISI Web of Knowledge and became chair of the Global Foundation for Management Education. In 2008 I was awarded an honorary degree by Swansea University, became vice chairman/chairman elect of AACSB and was made both an inaugural companion, and chair, of the ABS.

In summary, although the school grew successfully in this period, increased financial pressures impacted upon the university's budgeting process, leading to the expectation of enhanced and escalating financial targets for WBS. It became clear that such targets could not be achieved for ever by programme expansion – e.g. the significant specialist master's portfolio growth – without adversely affecting other areas of WBS's strategic positioning, particularly the output of research-led scholarship by academic staff, which is critically important to a school that specialises in research.

2008–10: strategic crossroads

While the school's financial performance was strong over this period (with gross surpluses continually exceeding 30 per cent of turnover), the financial crisis and the university's serious financial situation adversely affected the streamlined planning and resource approval mechanism envisaged in the devolution model of 2002. Indeed, the university introduced financial control measures almost as onerous as those that had preceded devolution in 2002, which eroded materially our ability to align staff and infrastructures resourcing with our strategic plans. Further, our projected building plans (phase 3b) to complete our facilities investment were understandably, but disappointingly, postponed by the university administration.

Nevertheless, WBS enjoyed strong programmatic growth during the period as it tried to fulfil the university's increased financial targets and expectations for the school. This included the successful launch of the first subject-specific M.B.A., the Global Energy M.B.A., in 2009 and insightful rebranding of specialist master's programmes in organisational analysis and human resource management. However, although the results of the 2008 Research Assessment Exercise placed the school fifth in the rankings of UK business schools (of which there are around 120 overall), it was not the outstanding result that had been hoped for, or even anticipated. While the school was excellent in the categories of research esteem and environment, its output of highest-quality, world-class publications was well below its aspirations, perhaps because of a combination of increased business school competition and faculty complacency. The result was a shock to the school, and a very serious reverse from the university administration's viewpoint. It has led to a strong refocusing of the school's unyielding commitment to research excellence and research income growth and stimulated the creation of detailed plans to achieve the top ranking in the RAE of 2013.

At the same time, as noted in Chapter 2 and elsewhere, during this period business schools, in general, were the subject of extensive external criticism for their roles in helping to create the financial crisis, through their unabated production of M.B.A.s considered to be unethical and financially motivated – so-called managerial 'masters of the universe'. The legitimacy of the business school as an academic discipline, therefore, has been seriously called into question.

Clearly, these events have placed WBS at a strategic crossroads. This was also highlighted by the advisory comments of a very positive expert Strategic Departmental Review of the school in 2009, commissioned by the university. As a result, the RAE 2008 result and the financial crisis required a renewed and refreshed strategic analysis of the school's strategic positioning and direction. Answers to the question 'What kind of business school does WBS want to be in a comprehensive, high-quality research university?' need to be determined. Is it one that prioritises high-quality research spinning off into excellent teaching, or one that views it as a 'cash cow' generating continued 'cash flow' for the university from an ever-widening programme portfolio (rather like continually 'running up a down escalator') and increasing managerial complexity – with an inevitable decline in research profile and positioning?

These are questions that are central to the strategic analysis of the new dean of the school, Professor Mark Taylor, appointed in March 2010. I left WBS in January 2010 to take up a position as dean of the Lee Kong Chian School of Business at Singapore Management University. I believe that I have fulfilled my promise to vice chancellor Sir Brian Follett and registrar Mike Shattock in 1999/2000, that I would serve a term of ten years to ensure stable and consistent strategic leadership and a renewed strategic vision and direction for WBS. Over my tenure the school's turnover tripled, and it generated gross surpluses equivalent to around 30 per cent of turnover for each year of the entire period. Impressive new facilities were built. The school's alumni, corporate and international profiles were significantly enhanced and its image and reputation were raised substantially in league table rankings across the school's entire research and programme portfolio. WBS was also one of the top 500 'Business superbrands' in a survey published by *The Daily Telegraph* in 2008/9.

6.6   FINAL REFLECTIONS FROM MY DEANSHIP EXPERIENCE AT WBS

It was a privilege to lead such a wonderful, collegial business school. In my view, WBS is 'best in class' as a university-based business school with a strong research-led and social science focus. In the five phases of my deanship, namely transition, agenda building and planning, settling on a paradigm, developing a new paradigm and arriving at a strategic crossroads, I covered the whole range of human emotions and activities. I started with learning about the school, relishing the challenge of change, negotiating, cajoling and leading a new strategic agenda, successfully achieving goals and targets and refreshing the vision with the advent of Nigel Thrift as an eager, enthusiastic and challenging vice chancellor. My period ended with the financial crisis and the frustrations and tensions of managing in a much more centralised, financially oriented and constrained environment. At all stages I enjoyed the task, building many lasting friendships across WBS and the university and learning how to legitimate issues and mobilise power, as with the adoption of the devolved budget model, so as to achieve the school's goals.

As I look back on my time at WBS I sincerely believe that a dean has to listen carefully and be straightforward, approachable, honest, direct and diplomatic. Humour and negotiating skills are also important in achieving appropriate goals and strategies. In university-based business schools such as WBS, a dean is 'the meat in the sandwich' between the central administration and the school staff, students and faculty. A dean can promote and implement an agreed agenda, he/she can cut out activities that are not sustainable and he/she can expand the programmes when there are product champions – e.g. the Global Energy M.B.A. However, he/she cannot necessarily mandate the conditions and arrangements that the university specifies to regulate the activities of the school.

As a governance mechanism during my tenure, devolution was extremely valuable and gave me the confidence to commit myself to a challenging ambition, devise a strategic plan to achieve that ambition and achieve control over the resources needed to deliver it. It will be interesting to discover, once the financial crisis has subsided, whether the policy of devolution as a governance arrangement will continue in Warwick University, or whether the anticipated environment of continued government spending cuts will lead to greater centralisation, enhanced bureaucracy and tighter and more strategic financial control. Alternatively, it may produce the managerial creativity that underlay the development of the Earned Income Group in the 1980s by Shattock, exemplified by his well-quoted statement in response to the Thatcher government cuts of the 1980s (Clark, 1998: 16): 'the save half, make half policy' – i.e. make savings to eliminate half the shortfall and generate new income to cover the other half. Time will tell which strategy and outcome will prevail!

References

AACSB (2002) *Management Education at Risk: Report of the Management Education Task Force to the AACSB International Board of Directors*. Tampa, FL: AACSB International.

—(2007) *Final Report of the AACSB International Impact of Research Task Force*. Tampa, FL: AACSB International.

ABS (2003) *Pillars of the Economy: How UK Business Schools Are Meeting the Global Competitive Challenge*. London: ABS.

Adenekan, S. (2009) 'Ethics arrive in business schools', BBC News, 3 April, http://news.bbc.co.uk/1/hi/education/7978928.stm (last accessed 20 April 2010).

Aharoni, Y. (1997) 'Management consulting', in Y. Aharoni (ed.) *Changing Role of State Intervention in Services in an Era of Open International Markets*: 152–77. New York: State University of New York Press.

Albert, S., and D. A. Whetten (1985) 'Organizational identity', *Research in Organizational Behavior*, 7: 263–95.

Allison, G., and P. Zelikow (1999) *Essence of Decision: Explaining the Cuban Missile Crisis*. London: Longman.

Alsop, R. J. (2002) *The Wall Street Journal Guide to the Top Business Schools 2003*. New York: Simon & Schuster.

Alvesson, M. (1995) *Management of Knowledge-Intensive Companies*. Berlin: Walter de Gruyter.

—(2004) *Knowledge Work and Knowledge-Intensive Firms*. Oxford University Press.

Amdam, R. P. (1997) 'The business school in European perspective', *Business History*, 39(4): 183–4.

Antunes, D., and H. Thomas (2007) 'The competitive (dis)advantages of European business schools', *Long Range Planning* 40(3): 382–404.

Baden-Fuller, C., and S. H. Ang (2001) 'Building reputations: the role of alliances in the European business school scene', *Long Range Planning*, 34(6): 741–55.

Baden-Fuller, C., F. Ravazzolo and T. Schweizer (2000) 'Making and measuring reputations: the research ranking of European business schools', *Long Range Planning*, 33(5): 621–50.

Bain, G. (2003) Annual lecture to Association of University Administrators, Belfast, 27 November. Available at www.aua.ac.uk.

Barnes, W. (1989) *Managerial Catalyst: The Story of London Business School 1964–1989*. London: Paul Chapman.

Barsoux, J.-L. (2000) *INSEAD: From Intuition to Institution*. New York: Palgrave.

Bartol, K. M. (1979) 'Professionalism as a predictor of organizational commitment, role stress, and turnovers: a multidimensional approach', *Academy of Management Journal*, **22**(4): 815–21.

Benjamin, B. A., and J. M. Podolny (1999) 'Status, quality and social order in the California wine industry', *Administrative Science Quarterly*, **44**(3): 563–89.

Bennis, W. G., and J. O'Toole (2005) 'How business schools lost their way', *Harvard Business Review*, **83**(5): 96–104.

Berger, P. L., and T. Luckmann (1966) *The Social Construction of Reality: A Treatise in the Sociology of Knowledge*. New York: Doubleday.

Bisoux, T. (2009) 'A return to reality', *BizEd*, **8**(3): 16–22.

Blackler, F. (1995) 'Knowledge, knowledge work and organizations: an overview and interpretation', *Organization Studies*, **16**(6): 1021–46.

Bloom, P. N. (1984) 'Effective marketing for professional services', *Harvard Business Review*, **62**(5): 102–10.

Boal, K. B., and R. Hooijberg (2001) 'Strategic leadership research: moving on', *Leadership Quarterly*, **11**(4): 515–49.

Bourdieu, P. (1996) *The State Nobility: Elite Schools in the Field of Power*. Cambridge: Polity Press.

Boyatzis, R. E., S. S. Cowen and D. A. Kolb (1994) *Innovation in Professional Education: Steps on a Journey from Teaching to Learning*. San Francisco: Jossey-Bass.

Boyatzis, R. E., E. C. Stubbs and S. N. Taylor (2002) 'Learning cognitive and emotional intelligence competencies through graduate management education', *Academy of Management Learning and Education*, **1**(2): 150–62.

Bradshaw, D. (2009a) 'Perhaps schools are partly to blame?', *Financial Times*, 26 January.

(2009b) 'A familiar face with a promise of fresh ideas', *Financial Times*, 23 March.

Bryman, A. (1992) *Charisma and Leadership in Organizations*. London: Sage.

(1996) 'Leadership in organizations', in S. Clegg, C. Hardy and W. R. Nord (eds.) *Handbook of Organization Studies*: 276–92. London: Sage.

(2007) 'Effective leadership in higher education: a literature review', *Studies in Higher Education*, **32**(6): 693–710.

Bucher, R., and J. Sterling (1969) 'Characteristics of professional organizations', *Journal of Health and Social Behavior*, **10**(1): 3–15.

Burgelman, R. A. (2002) *Strategy Is Destiny: How Strategy-Making Shapes a Company's Future*. New York: Free Press.

Cabrera, A. (2003) 'Diversity is strength – personal view', *Financial Times*, 8 September.

Capelli, P., and P. D. Scherer (1991) 'The missing role of context in OB: the need for a meso-level approach', *Research in Organizational Behavior*, **13**: 55–110.

Castells, M. (2000) *The Rise of the Network Society, vol. 1, The Information Age: Economy, Society and Culture*, 2nd edn. Oxford: Blackwell.

Cheit, E. F. (1985) 'Business schools and their critics', *California Management Review*, **27**(3): 43–61.

Clark, B. R. (1998) *Creating Entrepreneurial Universities: Organizational Pathways of Transformation*. Oxford: Pergamon Press.
   (2008) *On Higher Education: Selected Writings, 1956–2006*. Baltimore: Johns Hopkins University Press.

Cohen, M. D., J. G. March and J. P. Olsen (1972) 'A garbage can model of organizational choice', *Administrative Science Quarterly*, **17**(1): 1–25.

Collins, J. C. (2001) *Good to Great: Why Some Companies Make the Leap ... and Others Don't*. New York: HarperCollins.

Collins, J. C., and J. I. Porras (1994) *Built to Last: Successful Habits of Visionary Companies*. New York: HarperCollins.

Cooley, T. (2007) 'The business of business education', *Stern Business*, Fall/Winter: 23–5.

Cooper, D. J., B. Hinings, R. Greenwood and J. Brown (1996) 'Sedimentation and transformation in organizational change: the case of Canadian law firms', *Organization Studies*, **17**(4): 623–47.

D'Aveni, R. A. (1996) 'A multiple-constituency, status-based approach to inter-organizational mobility of faculty and input-output competition among top business schools', *Organization Science*, **7**(2): 166–90.

Davies, J., and H. Thomas (2009) 'What do business school deans do? Insights from a UK study', *Management Decision*, **47**(9): 1396–419.

Denis, J. L., A. Langley and L. Cazale (1996) 'Leadership and strategic change under ambiguity', *Organization Studies*, **17**(4): 673–99.

Denison, D. R., J. Dutton, J. A. Kahn and S. L. Hart (1996) 'Organizational context and the interpretation of strategic issues: a note on CEOs' interpretations of foreign investment', *Journal of Management Studies*, **33**(4): 453–74.

Devinney, T., G. R. Dowling and N. Perm-Ajchariyawong (2006) 'The *Financial Times* business schools ranking: what quality is this signal of quality?', *European Management Review*, 5(4): 195–209.

DfES (2002) *Government Response to the Report of the Council for Excellence in Management and Leadership*. Nottingham: DfES Publications.

DiMaggio, P., and W. W. Powell (1983) 'The iron cage revisited: institutional isomorphism and collective rationality in organizational fields', *American Sociological Review* 48(2): 147–60.

(1991) *The New Institutionalism in Organizational Analysis*. University of Chicago Press.

Durand, T., and S. Dameron (eds.) (2008) *The Future of Business Schools: Sceanarios and Strategies for 2020*. New York: Palgrave Macmillan.

Dutton, J. (1986) 'The processing of crisis and non-crisis strategic issues', *Journal of Management Studies*, 23(5): 501–17.

Dutton, J., and R. B. Duncan (1987) 'The creation of momentum for change through the process of strategic issue diagnosis', *Strategic Management Journal*, 8(3): 279–95.

Economist, The (2005) 'The brains business', 10 September.

Eden, D. (1988) 'Pygmalion, goal setting and expectancy: compatible ways to raise productivity', *Academy of Management Review*, 13(4): 639–52.

Eisenhardt, K. M. (1989) 'Building theories from case-study research', *Academy of Management Review*, 14(4): 532–50.

Empson, L. (2000) 'The triumph of commercialism: mergers between accounting firms and the transformation of the professional archetype', paper presented at Academy of Management annual conference, Toronto, 6 August.

Engwall, L. (2000) 'Foreign role models and standardisation in Nordic business education', *Scandinavian Journal of Management*, 16(1): 1–24.

Engwall, L., and V. Zamagni (eds.) (1998) *Management Education in Historical Perspective*. Manchester University Press.

Fagin, C. M. (1997) 'The leadership role of a dean', *New Directions for Higher Education*, 98: 95–9.

Ferlie, E., G. McGivern and A. Moraes (2008) 'Developing a public interest school of management', Working Paper no. SoMWP-0804, School of Management, Royal Holloway University of London. Available at http://eprints.rhul. ac.uk/748/1/EF-GM-AM_WP_0804.pdf (last accessed 20 April 2010).

Fiegenbaum, A., S. S. Hart and D. Schendel (1996) 'Strategic reference point theory', *Strategic Management Journal*, 17(3): 219–35.

Finkelstein, S., and D. C. Hambrick (1996) *Strategic Leadership: Top Executives and Their Effects on Organizations*. St. Paul, MN: West.

Fortune International (1988) 'Europes's best business schools', 23 May.

Franks, O. (1966) *Report of Commission of Inquiry.* Oxford: Clarendon Press.

Freidson, E., and B. Rhea (1965) 'Knowledge and judgment in professional evaluations', *Administrative Science Quarterly*, **10**(1): 107–24.

Gay, E. F. (1927) 'The founding of Harvard Business School', *Harvard Business Review*, **4**(4): 397–400.

Ghemawat, P. (2007) 'The globalization of business education: through the lens of semiglobalization', *Journal of Management Development* **27**(4): 391–414.

Ghoshal, S. (2005) 'Bad management theories are destroying good management', *Academy of Management Learning and Education*, **4**(1): 75–91.

Gioia, D. A., and K. G. Corley (2002) 'Being good versus looking good: Business school rankings and the Circean transformation from substance to image', *Academy of Management Learning and Education*, **1**(1): 107–20.

GMAC (2005) *The Future of Graduate Management Education in the Context of the Bologna Accord.* Reston, VA: GMAC.

Gmelch, W. H. (2004) 'The department chair's balancing acts', *New Directions for Higher Education*, **126**: 69–84.

Goodall, A. H. (2007) 'Does it take an expert to lead experts? The case of universities', Ph.D. thesis, Warwick Business School.

(2009) *Socrates in the Boardroom: Why Research Universities Should Be Led by Top Scholars.* Princeton University Press.

Goode, W. (1960) 'A theory of role strain', *American Sociological Review*, **25**(4): 483–96.

Gordon, R., and J. Howell (1959) *Higher Education for Business.* New York: Columbia University Press.

Gosling, J., and H. Mintzberg (2004) 'The education of practicing managers', *MIT Sloan Management Review*, **45**(4): 19–22.

Greenwood, R., C. R. Hinings and J. Brown (1990) 'The P2-form of strategic management: corporate practices in professional partnerships', *Academy of Management Journal*, **33**(4): 725–55.

(1994) 'Merging professional service firms', *Organization Science*, **5**(2): 239–57.

Grey, C. (2002) 'What are business schools for? On silence and voice in management education', *Journal of Management Education*, **26**(5): 496–511.

(2005) *A Very Short, Fairly Interesting and Relatively Cheap Book about Studying Organisations.* London: Sage.

(2007) 'Re-imagining relevance: a response to Starkey and Madan', *British Journal of Management*, **12**(Special issue 1): S27–S32.

Grint, K. (2000) *The Arts of Leadership.* Oxford University Press.

Hagen, A. F., M. T. Hassan and S. G. Amin (1998) 'Critical strategic leadership components: an empirical investigation', *SAM Advanced Management Journal*, **63**(3): 39–44.

Hall, R. (1968) 'Professionalization and bureaucratization', *American Sociological Review*, **33**(1): 92–104.

Hambrick, D. C. (1981) 'Specialization of environmental scanning activities among upper-level executives', *Journal of Management Studies*, **18**(3): 299–320.

(1989) 'Guest editor's introduction: putting top managers back in the strategy picture', *Strategic Management Journal*, **10**(Special issue): 5–15.

Hambrick, D. C., and G. D. S. Fukotomi (1991) 'The seasons of a CEO's tenure', *Academy of Management Review*, **16**(4): 719–42.

Harney, S. (2009) 'Experience is not enough', *Times Higher Education Supplement*, 30 July: 70–7.

Harris, S. E. (2006) 'Transitions: dilemmas of leadership', *New Directions for Higher Education*, **134**(Summer): 79–86.

Hawawini, G. (2005) 'The future of business schools', *Journal of Management Development*, **24**(1): 770–83.

Hay, M. (2008) 'Business schools: a new sense of purpose', *Journal of Management Development*, **27**(4): 371–8.

Hayes, R. H., and W. J. Abernathy (1980) 'Managing our way to economic decline', *Harvard Business Review*, **58**(4): 67–77.

Hedmo, T., K. Sahlin-Andersson and L. Wedlin (2006) 'The emergence of a European regulatory field of management education: standardizing through accreditation, ranking and guidelines', in M.-L. Djelic and K. Sahlin-Andersson (eds.) *Transnational Governance: Institutional Dynamics of Regulation*: 308–28. Cambridge University Press.

Hill, C. J., and W. H. Motes (1995) 'Professional versus generic retail service: new insights', *Journal of Services Marketing*, **9**(2): 22–35.

Hill, C. J., and S. E. Neeley (1988) 'Differences in the consumer decision process for professional vs. generic services', *Journal of Services Marketing*, **2**(1): 17–23.

Hinings, C. R., J. Brown and R. Greenwood (1991) 'Change in an autonomous professional organization', *Journal of Management Studies*, **28**(4): 375–93.

Hodgkinson, G. P., and G. Johnson (1994) 'Exploring the mental models of competitive strategists: the case for a processual approach', *Journal of Management Studies*, **31**(4): 525–51.

House, R. J., and R. N. Aditya (1997) 'The social scientific study of leadership: quo vadis?', *Journal of Management*, **23**(3): 409–73.

Howard, J. H. (1991) 'Leadership, management and change in the professional service firm', *Business Quarterly*, **55**(4): 111–18.

Hrebiniak, L. G., and J. A. Alutto (1972) 'Personal and role related factors in the development of organizational commitment', *Administrative Science Quarterly*, **17**(4): 555–72.

Hunt, J. G. (1991) *Leadership: A New Synthesis*. Newbury Park, CA: Sage.

Ivory, C., P. Miskell, H. Shipton, A. White, K. Moeslein and A. Neely (2006) *UK Business Schools: Historical Contexts and Future Scenarios*. London: Advanced Institute of Management.

Kerr, S. (1995) 'An academy classic: on the folly of rewarding A, while hoping for B', *Academy of Management Executive*, **9**(1): 7–14.

Kerr, S., M. A. Von Glinow and J. Schriesheim (1977) 'Issues in the study of professionals in organizations: the case of scientists and engineers', *Organizational Behavior and Human Performance*, **18**(2): 329–45.

Khurana, R. (2007) *From Higher Aims to Hired Hands: The Social Transformation of American Business Schools and the Unfulfilled Promise of Management as a Profession*. Princeton University Press.

Khurana, R., and N. Nohria (2008) 'It's time to make management a true profession', *Harvard Business Review*, **86**(10): 70–7.

Kipping, M., and O. Bjarnar (1998) *The Americanization of European Business: The Marshall Plan and the Transfer of US Management Models*. London: Routledge.

Kotter, J. P. (1990) *A Force for Change: How Leadership Differs from Management*. New York: Free Press.

Larson, M. J. (2003) 'Practically academic: forming British business schools in the 1960s', paper presented at the annual meeting of the Business History Conference, Lowell, MA, 27 June. Available at www.h-net.org/~business/bhcweb/publications/BEHonline/2003/Larson.pdf.

Larson, M. S. (1977) *The Rise of Professionalism: A Sociological Analysis*. Berkeley: University of California Press.

Liedtka, J. M., M. E. Haskins, J. W. Rosenblum and J. Weber (1997) 'The generative cycle: linking knowledge and relationships', *Sloan Management Review*, **39**(1): 47–58.

Lippman, S. A., and R. P. Rumelt (1982) 'Uncertain imitability: an analysis of interfirm differences in efficiency under competition', *Bell Journal of Economics*, **13**(2): 418–53.

Lorange, P. (2002) *New Vision for Management Education: Leadership Challenges*. Oxford: Pergamon Press.

(2005) 'Strategy means choice: also for today's business school', *Journal of Management Development*, **24**(9): 783–91.

(2008) *Thought Leadership Meets Business: How Business Schools Can Become More Successful*. Cambridge University Press.

Lorsch, J. W., and T. J. Tierney (2002) *Aligning the Stars: How to Succeed When Professionals Drive Results*. Boston: Harvard Business School Press.

Løwendahl, B. R. (1997) *Strategic Management of Professional Service Firms*. Copenhagen: Handelshøjskolens.

— (2000) *Strategic Management of Professional Service Firms*, 2nd edn. Copenhagen Business School Press.

Maister, D. H. (1993) *Managing the Professional Service Firm*. New York: Free Press.

Manz, C. C., and H. P. Sims (1981) 'Vicarious learning: the influence of modeling on organizational behavior', *Academy of Management Review*, 6(1): 105–13.

Mayo, A., and N. Nohria (2005) *In Their Time: The Greatest Business Leaders of the Twentieth Century*. Cambridge, MA: Harvard Business School Press.

McGee, J., H. Thomas and D. C. Wilson (2005) *Strategy: Analysis and Practice*. Maidenhead: McGraw-Hill.

Middlehurst, R. (1993) *Leading Academics*. Milton Keynes: Open University Press.

Miller, D., and J. Shamsie (2001) 'Learning across the life cycle: experimentation among the Hollywood studio heads', *Strategic Management Journal*, 22(8): 725–45.

Mills, P. K., J. L. Hall, J. K. Leidecker and H. Margulies (1983) 'Flexiform: a model for professional service organizations', *Academy of Management Review*, 8(1): 118–31.

Mintzberg, H. (1979) *The Structuring of Organizations: A Synthesis of the Research*. London: Prentice Hall.

— (1983) *Structure in Fives: Designing Effective Organizations*. Englewood Cliffs, NJ: Prentice Hall.

— (1989) *Mintzberg on Management: Inside Our Strange World of Organizations*. New York: Free Press.

— (1998) 'Covert leadership: notes on managing professionals', *Harvard Business Review*, 76(6): 140–7.

— (2004) *Managers Not MBAs: A Hard Look at the Soft Practice of Managing and Management Development*. London: Pearson Education.

— (2007) *Tracking Strategies: Toward a General Theory*. Oxford University Press.

Mintzberg, H., and J. Gosling (2002) 'Educating managers beyond borders', *Academy of Management Learning and Education*, 1(1): 64–76.

Montagna, P. D. (1968) 'Professionalization and bureaucratization in large professional organizations', *American Journal of Sociology*, 74(2): 138–45.

Morgan, G. (1986) *Images of Organization*. London: Sage.

Morgan, G. (1997) *Images of Organization*, 2nd edn. London: Sage.

Morris, T. (1992) 'New forms of partnership', paper presented at the conference 'Knowledge workers in contemporary organizations', Lancaster, 19 September.

Morris, T., and L. Empson (1998) 'Organization and expertise: an exploration of knowledge bases and the management of accounting and consulting firms', *Accounting, Organizations and Society*, **23**(5): 609–24.

Nachum, L. (1999) *The Origins of International Competitiveness of Firms: The Impact of Location and Ownership in Professional Service Industries*. Cheltenham: Edward Elgar.

Nahapiet, J., and S. Ghoshal (1998) 'Social capital, intellectual capital and the organizational advantage', *Academy of Management Review*, **23**(2): 242–66.

Narayanan, V. K., and L. Fahey (1982) 'The micro-politics of strategy formulation', *Academy of Management Review*, **7**(1): 25–34.

Northouse, P. (2001) *Leadership: Theory and Practice*, 3rd edn. London: Sage.

Nye, J. S. (2008) *The Powers to Lead*. Oxford University Press.

Parham, J. B. (1994) 'The effects of the leadership process on organizational performance: an empirical analysis', Ph.D. thesis, University of Michigan, Ann Arbor.

Paulin, M. (2000) 'Business effectiveness and professional service personnel: relational or transactional managers?', *European Journal of Marketing*, **34**(3/4): 453–72.

Pettigrew, A. M. (1973) *The Politics of Organizational Decision-Making: Organizations, People, Society*. London: Tavistock.

—— (1979) 'On studying organizational cultures', *Administrative Science Quarterly*, **24**(2): 570–81.

—— (1992) 'On studying managerial elites', *Strategic Management Journal*, **13**(Special issue): 163–82.

—— (1997a) 'What is processual analysis?', *Scandinavian Journal of Management*, **13**(4): 337–48.

—— (1997b) 'The double hurdles for management research', in T. Clark (ed.) *Advancement in Organizational Behaviour: Essays in Honour of Derek S. Pugh*: 277–96. Aldershot: Ashgate.

Pettigrew, A. M., and E. Fenton (2000) 'Becoming integrated global networks: transforming four professional service organizations', paper presented to the Academy of Management annual conference, Toronto, 5 August.

Pettigrew, A. M., and E. Ferlie (1996) 'Some research challenges facing Warwick', paper for discussion, University of Warwick.

Pfeffer, J., and C. T. Fong (2002) 'The end of business schools? Less success than meets the eye', *Academy of Management Learning and Education*, **1**(1): 78–95.

(2004) 'The business school business: some lessons from the US experience', *Journal of Management Studies*, **41**(8): 1501–20.

Pierson, F. C. (1959) *The Education of American Businessmen: A Study of University-College Programs in Business Administration*. New York: McGraw-Hill.

Podolny, J. M. (1993) 'A status-based model of market competition', *American Journal of Sociology*, **98**(4): 829–72.

(2009) 'The buck stops (and starts) at business school', *Harvard Business Review*, **87**(6): 62–7.

Porac, J. F., and H. Thomas (2002) 'Managing cognition and strategy: issues, trends and future directions', in A. M. Pettigrew, H. Thomas and R. Whittington (eds.) *Handbook of Strategy and Management*: 165–81. London: Sage.

Porac, J. F., H. Thomas and C. Baden-Fuller (1989) 'Competitive groups as cognitive communities: the case of Scottish knitwear manufacturers', *Journal of Management Studies*, **26**(4): 397–416.

Porac, J. F., H. Thomas, F. Wilson, D. Paton and A. Kanfer (1995) 'Rivalry and the industry model of Scottish knitwear producers', *Administrative Science Quarterly*, **40**(2): 203–27.

Porter, M. E. (1980) *Competitive Strategy: Techniques for Analyzing Industries and Competitors*. New York: Free Press.

Raelin, J. A. (1991) *The Clash of Cultures: Managers Managing Professionals*. Boston: Harvard Business School Press.

(1995) 'How to manage your local professor', *Academy of Management Proceedings*, 207–14.

Raimond, P., and C. Halliburton (1995) 'Business school strategies for the single European market', *Management Learning*, **26**(2): 231–47.

Richards, D., and S. Engle (1986) 'After the vision: suggestions to corporate visionaries and vision champions', in J. D. Adams (ed.) *Transforming Leadership: 199–214*. Alexandria, VA: Miles River Press.

Rosser, V. J., L. K. Johnsrud and R. H. Heck (2003) 'Academic deans and directors: assessing their effectiveness from individual and institutional perspectives', *Journal of Higher Education*, **74**(1): 1–25.

Schein, E. H. (1992) *Organizational Culture and Leadership*, 2nd edn. San Francisco: Jossey-Bass.

Schoemaker, P. J. H. (2008) 'The future challenges of business: rethinking management education', *California Management Review*, **50**(3): 119–39.

Scott, W. A., and R. Scott (1965) *Values and Organizations: A Study of Fraternities and Sororities*. Chicago: Rand McNally.

Scott, W. R. (1965) 'Reactions to supervision in a heteronomous professional organization', *Administrative Science Quarterly*, **10**(1): 65–81.

Selznick, P. (1957) *Leadership in Administration: A Sociological Interpretation.* Berkeley: University of California Press.

Sharma, A. (1997) 'Professional as agent: knowledge asymmetry in agency exchange', *Academy of Management Review,* **22**(3): 758–98.

Shattock, M. (1994a) *The UGC and the Management of British Universities.* Milton Keynes: Open University Press.

(1994b) 'Optimising university resources', paper delivered to the Conference of European Rectors, Warwick, 12 April.

Simon, H. A. (1967) 'The business school: a problem in organizational design', *Journal of Management Studies,* **4**(1): 1–16.

Smith, A. C. T., and F. Graetz (2006) 'Complexity theory and organizing form dualities', *Management Decision,* **44**(7): 851–70.

Spender, J.-C. (1989) *Industry Recipes: An Enquiry into the Nature and Sources of Managerial Judgement.* Oxford: Blackwell.

(2007) 'Management as a regulated profession: an essay, *Journal of Management Inquiry,* **16**(1): 32–42.

Starkey, K. (2008) 'Business schools – look at history to broaden your intellectual horizons', *Financial Times,* 20 October.

(2009) 'Demolishing the fortress: Foucault, design and the business school', paper presented at the European Academy of Management conference 'Renaissance and renewal in management studies', Liverpool, 13 May.

Starkey, K., A. Hatchuel and S. Tempest (2004) 'Rethinking the business school', *Journal of Management Studies,* **41**(8): 1521–30.

Starkey, K., and P. Madan (2001) 'Bridging the relevance gap: aligning stakeholders in the future of management research', *British Journal of Management,* **12**(Special issue 1): S3–S26.

Starkey, K., and N. Tiratsoo (2007) *The Business School and the Bottom Line.* Cambridge University Press.

Symonds, M. (2009) 'B-school deans in the hot seat', 13 May, www.forbes.com/2009/05/13/business-school-deans-leadership-careers-education.html (last accessed 20 April 2010).

Teece, D. J. (2003) 'Expert talent and the design of (professional services) firms', *Industrial and Corporate Change,* **12**(4): 895–916.

Thakor, M. V. (2000) 'What is a professional service?', *Journal of Services Marketing,* **14**(1): 63–82.

Thomas, H. (2007a) 'The competitive (dis)advantages of European business schools,' *Long Range Planning,* **40**: 382–404.

(2007b) 'An analysis of the environment and competitive dynamics of management education', *Journal of Management Development,* **26**(1): 9–21.

(2009) 'To the ends of the earth', *Biz/ed*, **8**(5): 50–5.

Thompson, E. P. (1970) *Warwick University, Ltd: Industry, Management and the Universities*. Harmondsworth: Penguin Books.

Tolbert, P., and R. Stern (1991) 'Organizations of professionals: governance structures in large law firms', in P. Tolbert and S. Bacharach (eds.) *Research in the Sociology of Organizations: Sociology and the Professions*: 97–117. Greenwich, CT: JAI Press.

Tucker, A., and R. A. Bryan (1991) *The Academic Dean: Dove, Dragon, and Diplomat*, 2nd edn. New York: Macmillan.

Van Baalen, P. J., and L. T. Moratis (2001) *Management Education in the Network Economy*. Boston: Kluwer.

Van de Ven, A. H. (1992) 'Suggestions for studying strategy process: a research note', *Strategic Management Journal*, **13**(Special issue): 169–88.

Van Roon, I. (2003) 'Steer clear of B-school spin', *European Business Forum*, **15**(September): 39–40.

Wankel, C., and B. DeFillippi (2004) *The Cutting Edge of International Management Education*. Greenwich, CT: Information Age.

Weick, K. E. (1995) *Sensemaking in Organizations*. Newbury Park, CA: Sage.

Weisman, R. (2003) 'Harvard Business broadening its world', *Boston Globe*, 9 September.

White, H. C. (1981) 'Where do markets come from?', *American Journal of Sociology*, **87**(3): 517–47.

(1992) *Identity and Control: A Structural Theory of Social Action*. Princeton University Press.

Winch, G., and E. Schneider (1993) 'Managing the knowledge-based organization: the case of architectural practice', *Journal of Management Studies*, **30**(6): 923–37.

Yin, R. K. (1994) *Case Study Research: Design and Methods*, 2nd edn. London: Sage.

Yukl, G. A. (1998) *Leadership in Organizations*, 4th edn. London: Prentice Hall.

Zell, D. (2005) 'Pressure for relevancy at top-tier business schools', *Journal of Management Inquiry*, **14**(3): 271–4.

Zimmerman, J. L. (2001) 'Can American business schools survive?', Working Paper no. FR 01–16, Simon School of Business, University of Rochester, NY.

Zucker, L. G. (1987) 'Institutional theories of organization', *Annual Review of Sociology*, **13**: 443–64.

Index